African American Statewide Candidates in the New South

African American Statewide Candidates in the New South

CHARLES S. BULLOCK, III,
SUSAN A. MACMANUS, JEREMY D. MAYER,
AND MARK J. ROZELL

OXFORD
UNIVERSITY PRESS

OXFORD
UNIVERSITY PRESS

Oxford University Press is a department of the University of Oxford. It furthers
the University's objective of excellence in research, scholarship, and education
by publishing worldwide. Oxford is a registered trade mark of Oxford University
Press in the UK and certain other countries.

Published in the United States of America by Oxford University Press
198 Madison Avenue, New York, NY 10016, United States of America.

© Oxford University Press 2022

Library of Congress Cataloging-in-Publication Data
Names: Bullock, Charles S., 1942– author. | MacManus, Susan A., author. |
Mayer, Jeremy D., author. | Rozell, Mark J., author.
Title: African American statewide candidates in the new South /
Charles S. Bullock, III, Susan A. MacManus, Jeremy D. Mayer, Mark J. Rozell.
Description: New York, NY : Oxford University Press, 2022. |
Includes bibliographical references and index.
Identifiers: LCCN 2021035241 (print) | LCCN 2021035242 (ebook) |
ISBN 9780197607428 (hardback) | ISBN 9780197607435 (paperback) |
ISBN 9780197607442 | ISBN 9780197607466 | ISBN 9780197607459 (epub)
Subjects: LCSH: African American political candidates—Southern
States—History—21st century. | Elections—Southern States—
History—21st century. | Political campaigns—Southern States—
History—21st century. | Governors—Southern States—Election. |
United States. Congress. Senate—Elections. | Southern States—
Politics and government—1951–
Classification: LCC F216.2 .B849 2022 (print) |
LCC F216.2 (ebook) | DDC 324.97509/05—dc23/eng/20211027
LC record available at https://lccn.loc.gov/2021035241
LC ebook record available at https://lccn.loc.gov/2021035242

DOI: 10.1093/oso/9780197607428.001.0001

1 3 5 7 9 8 6 4 2

Paperback printed by LSC Communications, United States of America
Hardback printed by Bridgeport National Bindery, Inc., United States of America

Contents

Preface

This volume is a sequel to our previous book, *The South and the Transformation of U.S. Politics* (Oxford University Press, 2019). That book examined the fundamental changes in southern politics over a half century that had substantially altered the national political landscape. We focused on the shifting demographics, partisan competition, race relations, and role of religion in explaining the shifting politics of the South.

These changes portended a vastly different future political landscape for minority candidates in statewide political campaigns in the region, particularly African Americans. Indeed, as we were finishing the previous book, there were two gubernatorial campaigns in the Deep South—in Georgia and Florida—featuring highly competitive Black nominees, both of whom came up barely short in their bids, but in so doing confirmed that in some of the southern states, rapid political change was happening.

This book takes up the same themes as our earlier study, applying our findings there to a description and analysis of what factors lead to competitive races in the South for Black statewide candidates. Our focus is on the growth states of the South[1]—those that are experiencing significant economic, demographic, cultural, and political change. These are the states of the South in which black statewide candidates now are competitive. Our analysis draws from detailed studies of several recent nationally prominent campaigns specifically in Florida, Georgia, South Carolina, and southern transformation leader Virginia.

Similar to our previous book, each of us took the lead on individual chapters and we then collaborated and agreed on all of the contents in the volume. The studies in this volume cover through the 2021 runoff election for U.S. Senate in Georgia. Bullock took the lead on the introduction and the chapters on the 2018 and 2020–2021 statewide campaigns in Georgia; MacManus on the chapter on the 2018 Florida gubernatorial campaign; Rozell on African American statewide candidates in Virginia, the 2020 US Senate campaign in South Carolina, and the conclusion; and Mayer on African American national candidates in the southern states. Anthony Cilluffo co-wrote the South Carolina chapter.

Each of the four book authors presented our initial findings on Black statewide candidates in the South at the April 2019 annual conference of the British Association of American Studies in Brighton, England. The focus at that time was on the Black statewide candidacies coming up short of victory in 2018, with Virginia looking like the leading indicator of southern political change.

The US Senate race in South Carolina in 2020 provided an additional disappointing outcome for a Black statewide candidate, as did the US Senate race in Georgia that year that ended with neither major party candidate securing a majority, thus requiring a runoff election in January 2021 under the state's elections law. Yet most importantly, the 2020 election cycle produced major breakthroughs. The historic victory of a Black US Senator from Georgia in the 2021 runoff election, the vital role that Black voters in South Carolina played in securing Joe Biden's nomination, as well as the unprecedented addition of a Black woman to his general election ticket, showed the ongoing importance of the South and the southern Black electorate in US politics. Our analysis suggests that the future will present many more electoral victory opportunities for African American statewide candidates in these and in other southern states—and for other minority candidates too.

1

Introduction

Black Statewide Candidacies in the South

Blacks can definitely win statewide nominations. . . . However, the
general election is always likely to be hard.

—Raphael Sonenshein

For most of its history the South thwarted African American political
ambitions. Following a brief flurry of success during Reconstruction, for
the first two-thirds of the twentieth century the participation of Black citizens was largely eliminated and the election of Blacks to public office ceased
(Kousser 1974). Not until implementation of the historic 1965 Voting Rights
Act did Black registration rates come close to equaling those of Whites in the
region. Estimates place the number of Black office holders in the region at
that time at one hundred or less and many of these served in tiny all-Black
towns. As African Americans became increasingly politically active, the
ranks of those eager to hold public office increased. By 2002 when the Joint
Center for Political and Economic Studies did its last census of Black office
holders, the eleven-state South had 5,400, with almost 1,000 in Mississippi
alone. While no comprehensive count has been conducted recently, many
more African Americans have won office, in part by attracting greater support from new generations of White voters. As of 2020, twenty-three African
Americans represented southern states in the US House of Representatives
and more than three hundred served in the region's legislative chambers.

As Black office holding has expanded from rare to commonplace,
southern African Americans have achieved numerous firsts. The region's first
Black state legislator in decades, Leroy Johnson, joined the Georgia Senate in
1963. Six years later, Howard Lee became the first Black mayor of a majority-
White southern city when elected to lead Chapel Hill, North Carolina. The
first southern African Americans sent to Congress in the twentieth century

African American Statewide Candidates in the New South. Charles S. Bullock, III, Susan A. MacManus,
Jeremy D. Mayer, and Mark J. Rozell, Oxford University Press. © Oxford University Press 2022.
DOI: 10.1093/oso/9780197607428.003.0001

arrived on Capitol Hill in 1973, when Atlanta's Andy Young and Houston's Barbara Jordan took the oath. The first Black mayor of a major southern city, Maynard Jackson, won the first of three terms as Atlanta's chief executive in 1973. Virginia's Douglas Wilder was the first African American elected governor of a state (1989), four years after he reached office as the South's first Black lieutenant governor since Reconstruction. In 2014 Tim Scott (R-SC) became the first popularly elected African American senator from the South, having initially been appointed to fill a vacancy a year earlier. At the local level thousands of communities have witnessed the election of the first Black member of the city council, school board, or county commission in modern times. A number of communities which had not had an African American elected official for decades now see minorities holding most of the seats on their local collegial bodies.

For many years after the Voting Rights Act knocked down literacy tests and other obstacles to Black political participation, African Americans who won public office succeeded in predominantly Black jurisdictions. The same White resistance that had denied the ballot to Blacks fueled a reluctance to vote for Black candidates regardless of their qualifications. The rejection of Black candidates by most White voters led to the rewrite of Section 2 of the Voting Rights Act in 1982. Under this new provision, plaintiffs no longer had to prove that the portion of the election code that they challenged had been adopted or maintained with the intention of discriminating against minorities. Section 2 enabled plaintiffs to succeed by showing that Black voters had less opportunity to elect their candidates of choice than did White voters.

Unwillingness to vote for Blacks was so widespread among Whites that in the early 1980s several federal judges and Department of Justice officials operated on the belief that the population of a jurisdiction needed to be at least 65 percent Black for an African American candidate to have a realistic chance of success (Strickland and Whicker 1992; Bullock 2018b).[1] This assumption rested on expectations about the rates at which Whites and Blacks registered and turned out as well as recognition that the Black population in most communities is younger than the White population. Over the years, the threshold at which the election of African American candidates has become feasible has declined. In 1986 when the Supreme Court provided guidance on the implementation of Section 2 of the Voting Rights Act as amended in 1982, it held that a jurisdiction had no obligation to create a minority district unless the plaintiffs could show that the minority population was sufficiently large and compact to constitute a *majority* in a proposed district (*Thornburg v. Gingles*, 478 U.S. 30, 1986). In time the standard was defined to require that the minority group be a majority of the voting-age, citizen population. The redistricting that came after the 1990 census frequently saw African Americans working to maximize the number of districts with concentrations of Blacks judged sufficient to elect a Black (Bullock and Gaddie 2009). Congressional plans were often prepared in order to secure the approval of the Justice Department that, pursuant to Section 5 of the Voting Rights Act, was necessary across the South except for Arkansas and Tennessee. To the extent that a belief that Black candidates needed a constituency of 65 or 50 percent African American in order to be elected was correct, there was little reason to expect African Americans to win statewide offices.

Over time greater numbers of Whites have become willing to support Black candidates. With less need to rely exclusively on Black voters to elect Black candidates, civil rights activists in parts of the South, especially in urban areas, now call for districts in which Blacks constitute less than half the population. Also encouraging those efforts has been the increased diversity of the population in many urban areas where growing numbers of Hispanics and Asian Americans are locating. Recent litigation has succeeded in having districts redrawn in Virginia and North Carolina to *reduce* the Black concentrations in existing districts with the prospect that removing some of the Black population would create adjacent districts in which Black candidates might compete successfully. This is a dramatic change from the efforts of civil rights activists and attorneys in the 1990s when drawing districts in which the Black population was slightly below half was seen as a racial gerrymander designed to thwart Black political ambitions. Lowering Black concentrations had the intended effect in Virginia where the Third Congressional District, which had had a Black majority since 1992 and was 57.2 percent Black as drawn following the 2010 census, had its population reduced to 45.5 percent Black. In the next election, held in 2016, the neighboring Fourth District, which had swapped Whites for Blacks from the Third District and had a 40.9 percent Black population, replaced its White Republican member of Congress with Donald McEachin, the second African American in the state's congressional delegation. The Third District reelected Bobby Scott, the state's first African American member of Congress in the twentieth century to his thirteenth term.

The improved prospects for African Americans winning with smaller concentrations of Blacks in the electorate has meant that Black candidates can now hope to win statewide offices in some states. As described in this volume, a Black candidate won the office of lieutenant governor in Virginia in 2017. Other African Americans have won statewide positions in southern states. In Georgia Thurbert Baker served as attorney general from 1997 to 2011. During most of Baker's tenure he was joined by another African American, Labor Commissioner Mike Thurmond, from 1999 to 2011. In North Carolina, Ralph Campbell served as auditor from 1993 to 2005. In 2021, as described later in this volume, Georgia sent Raphael Warnock to the Senate. Blacks who have been elected statewide have usually been able to hold off challengers, although Campbell lost in 2004 by 29,000 votes.

The judicial branch has seen African Americans elected to statewide appellate courts in several states. Many of the jurists originally came to the bench via a gubernatorial appointment but subsequently won reelection. In 1976, Florida's Joseph Hatchett became the first African American elected to a southern Supreme Court and the first African American in the South to win a statewide office in the twentieth century (MacManus 2017). Racial diversification began in Georgia when Robert Benham joined the Court of Appeals in 1984 and advanced to the state Supreme Court in 1989, a body on which he served until 2020, ultimately becoming chief justice. Since 1984, six African Americans have served on Georgia's Court of Appeals and three on the Supreme Court. Georgia's Leah Sears became the first and only Black, female chief justice of a state Supreme Court in 2005 (Davis 2017). African Americans have also won statewide judicial contests in Alabama, North Carolina, and Texas although not all of these currently have Black jurists.[2] In North Carolina, a total of five Blacks have sat on the Court of Appeals and the same number, beginning with Henry Frye in 1984, have served on North Carolina's highest tribunal (Bitzer 2019).

With the exception of Senator Scott and North Carolina Lieutenant Governor Mark Robinson, Blacks who have held statewide posts in the South have been Democrats or in the case of some jurists they have held non-partisan posts. The vast bulk of Black state legislators are also Democrats as are all the region's 2019 members of the US House except for Will Hurd (R-TX), although two other African American Republicans have served from the South in recent years.[3]

The region's realignment to the GOP made the South less hospitable to Black statewide candidates. But today the challenge confronted by most Black candidates has about as much to do with their race as with their partisan designation as Democrats. In 2019, Arkansas, Georgia, Mississippi, South Carolina, Tennessee, and Texas had no Democrats in statewide offices.

Alabama and Florida have a single Democrat. At the other extreme, only in Virginia did Democrats hold all the statewide offices.

As part of partisan realignment in the South, African Americans have been overwhelmingly Democrats since the 1964 presidential election that pitted Lyndon Johnson, who had just secured passage of that year's Civil Rights Act, against Barry Goldwater who opposed that landmark legislation. Whites have now gradually but largely forsaken the Democratic Party. High-profile Democrats have frequently struggled to attract a third of the White vote, and many have received less.

As a result of the shifting partisan preferences of southerners, Black and White, the electorate in Democratic primaries has become increasingly Black and in some states majority Black. In Georgia, most primary voters have been Black since 2010 and in 2014 peaked at 65.6 percent. In South Carolina, 62.2 percent of the voters in the 2018 Democratic primary were non-White.[4] Non-Whites have dominated Democratic primaries in the Palmetto State beginning with 2002. As larger shares of the Democratic primary vote have come from African Americans, more Blacks have secured Democratic nominations statewide. In 2014, for example, Georgia Democrats, almost two-thirds of whom were Black, nominated five African American women for statewide offices. None of these women won, but it was not due to their race since no Whites won statewide on the Democratic ticket that year. In 2018 three African Americans won Democratic nominations for statewide offices.

Black statewide victories in partisan contests have all but disappeared with the dominance of the GOP in most of the South—Virginia and Georgia excluded. However, African American candidates continue to have a degree of success in districts that are not majority Black. The most recent significant wins came in 2018 as Lucy McBath (D-GA) unseated Karen Handel in a 12.7 percent Black district in suburban Atlanta (61.8 percent White). In Texas, Colin Allred (D) retired eleven-term incumbent Pete Sessions (R) in the Thirty-Second District, which is 12 percent Black and 50.4 percent White non-Hispanic. In 2016, in Orlando, Florida, voters, only 27.2 percent of whom were Black, sent former police chief Val Demings (D) to Congress.

African Americans' ability to win congressional districts in the urban South despite Blacks not constituting a majority of the population extends back to the first victories in 1972. Young's Atlanta district was 44 percent Black and he did not have the sizable Hispanic population that helped Jordan win a Texas district that was 42 percent Black but also had a 19 percent

Hispanic population. From 1972 to 2006, fifteen of the thirty-three congressional victories registered by African Americans in Georgia came in districts less than majority Black (Bullock and Gaddie 2006–2007: 26).

The South's Growth States of Florida, Georgia, North Carolina, South Carolina, Texas, and Virginia are attracting an increasingly diverse electorate (Bullock et al. 2019). Instead of the Black-White dichotomy that traditionally characterized the South, the Growth States as a group now have more Hispanics than African Americans and some communities see growing concentrations of Asian Americans. While these new ethnic groups are not as unified in their support for Democratic candidates as African Americans are, their partisan choices often look more like those of African Americans than non-Hispanic Whites. As these new ethnics become politically mobilized, they pose serious threats to the Republican hegemony that has characterized the region for years. As long as Republican candidates rely almost exclusively on White votes, the Growth States' demographic trends point to a Democratic resurgence.

The changing demographics and the willingness of a share of the White electorate to support Black candidates has encouraged a growing number of African Americans to wage campaigns for the top offices in their states. While the success rate for these efforts remains low, it is not out of line with what White Democrats currently experience. These African Americans are competitive even if not elected, when seeking support in overwhelmingly non-Black constituencies.

Aside from Douglas Wilder, who became Virginia's lieutenant governor in 1985 and its chief executive four years later, one of the first fully competitive candidates for a top office was Harold Ford Jr., who attracted 48 percent of the vote in a bid to represent Tennessee in the Senate. Ford had served five terms in the House where he succeeded his father, Harold Ford Sr., who had held the same Memphis district for twenty-two years. In the end, the younger Ford lost to Bob Corker, the former mayor of Chattanooga, in a hard-fought contest. Another contest that seemed promising saw former Dallas mayor Ron Kirk seek a Texas Senate seat as part of the "Dream Team" (Frederick and Jeffries 2009); a Democratic ticket so-named because of its ethnic balance. In addition to Kirk, an African American, the ticket had Hispanic entrepreneur Tony Sanchez running for governor and slated seasoned, Anglo office holder, John Sharp for lieutenant governor. But by 2002 Texas was solidly red and none of the Dream Team members succeeded.

The size of the Black share of the Democratic primary vote saw Mississippi, the state with the highest African American percentage in its population, nominate Blacks for governor in 2011 and 2015, but these candidates were not competitive in the general election, polling 39 and 32 percent of the vote, respectively. The Magnolia State also nominated Black Democrats for the Senate in 2006, 2008, 2018, and 2020. Alabama has also had Black Senate candidates on the Democratic ticket in 2004 and 2008, sacrificial lambs competing against popular incumbent Republicans. The defeats suffered by these African Americans were not out of line with the fate of the Democratic slate overall. Until Senator Doug Jones's special election victory in 2017, Alabama had last elected a Democrat to a statewide position in 2006. Mississippi Democrats have met with similar frustration, as none in that party, save for long-serving Attorney General Jim Hood, has won statewide in more than a decade.

The latter half of the second decade of the twenty-first century has witnessed new, better-funded and more aggressive efforts by southern African American candidates with statewide ambitions. In 2017 Justin Fairfax attracted 49.2 percent of the vote to beat two opponents in the Democratic primary and snare the nomination for lieutenant governor in Virginia. As detailed in Chapter 4, Fairfax won the general election with 53 percent of the vote, just a single point behind Ralph Northam who led the ticket on his way to becoming governor. That Fairfax ran stride for stride with Northam is impressive since Northam, as the sitting lieutenant governor, had already succeeded statewide, while Fairfax's political resume was limited to an unsuccessful bid to become attorney general.

The next year African Americans entered the Democratic primaries for governor in Florida and Georgia. As described later in this volume, both had to hold off credible White competitors on the way to securing the nomination. Ultimately Andrew Gillum in Florida and Stacey Abrams in Georgia came up short, each losing by less than 2 percentage points. Nonetheless, in their losses these individuals demonstrated that at least in the region's Growth States a Black candidate who runs on a mainstream, progressive Democratic platform can push the GOP nominee right to the precipice of defeat. The Abrams and Gillum near misses contrast with the much weaker showings by Black candidates in Alabama and Mississippi, two of the South's Stagnant States where populations are much less diverse and larger shares of the White electorate are committed to the GOP (Bullock et al. 2019).[5]

The 2020 election cycle saw a bonanza of Black, Democratic Senate candidates, two of whose efforts, Warnock in Georgia and Jaime Harrison in South Carolina, are chronicled in this volume. In addition, Mike Espy made a second bid in Mississippi, Marquita Bradshaw represented the Democratic Party in Tennessee, and Adrian Perkins was one of three African Americans challenging the reelection of Bill Cassidy in Louisiana's jungle primary.

While Abrams and Gillum tested the GOP, it maintained power by retaining the loyalty of a sufficient component of the White electorate. Donald Trump's takeover of the GOP has yet to alienate large swaths of southern White voters. The greater support for the GOP from southern compared to northern Whites underlies the anomaly that the region with the heaviest concentration of African Americans is not the base for some of today's high profile Black political figures. In Illinois, California, and a few other northern states with smaller concentrations of Black votes than found in the South, African Americans have been elected statewide.

None of the most visible African Americans who have sought the presidency have come from the South. Early on, the top tier in the massive field of aspirants for the 2020 Democratic nomination featured two competitive Black candidates, Senators Kamala Harris from California and Cory Booker from New Jersey, along with a lesser candidate.[6] President Obama came from Illinois and, like Harris and Booker, had no ties to the South. Jesse Jackson, who sought the presidency in 1984 and 1988, was born in Greenville, South Carolina, and educated in North Carolina, but by the time of his presidential bids had long been a Chicago resident, well established in the electorate that sent his son and namesake to Congress. The two African Americans to become governors post-Wilder—Deval Patrick (MA) and David Patterson (NY)—are also non-southerners. All of the popularly elected Black senators prior to Warnock, other than South Carolina's Scott, have come from the North, beginning with two-term solon Edward Brooke (R-MA) (Sonenshein 1990; Jeffries 1999) and the first Black female senator, Carol Moseley Braun (D) of Illinois.[7]

Conditions for African American Electoral Success

For southern African Americans to achieve statewide successes akin to those in the North, it will be necessary to either win back some of the Whites—or their offspring—who traditionally voted for Democrats or, alternatively, see minority voters turn out at unprecedented levels. Christian Grose's (2011: 33) work on the election of African Americans to the US House suggests the nature of potential winning coalitions. Deep South states, like Georgia (31 percent Black) and South Carolina (27 percent Black), have African American concentrations at what Grose designates as Black-influence venues, that is, the Black population is 25–49 percent of the total. In the absence of a Black majority, it is more likely that Whites will be elected, but Democratic winners will rely on and be responsive to the Black electorate under the right conditions. For African Americans to win in Black-influence districts, Black support is crucial, but a degree of White support is also necessary. In addition, there must be high Black mobilization relative to White mobilization.

Florida and Virginia with Black populations of 16 and 20 percent, respectively, have what Grose considers to be low Black concentrations, and he does not spell out a path by which Blacks win in these situations (33). Grose does explain why he does not specify conditions for Black electoral success in jurisdictions that are less than 25 percent Black: "These Black cells are not detailed as empirically since there are almost no cases that fit in these cells, and thus the possible electoral coalitions and turnout differentials cannot be examined. As of this writing, there are no . . . Black Democrats elected in [congressional] districts with a Black population less than 25 percent" (33). "Even if Black voters are mobilized highly in this sort of district, a Republican has little to worry about if he or she is taking care of the White voters in the district" (34).

In short, assuming that the White electorate is heavily Republican, then all the GOP nominee needs to do is get supporters to the polls. Grose's careful study of congressional elections suggests that the prospects for a Black victory in statewide contests is greater in Georgia than Florida or Virginia. Nonetheless, each of these three states has seen African Americans mount competitive statewide efforts in recent years. The 2016 presidential election sheds light on how the elements Grose focuses on played out. Exit polls in 2016 showed Florida Whites splitting 64–32 percent between Trump and Clinton with Trump winning the state by 113,000 votes. In Virginia, a larger share of Whites has migrated back to the Democratic Party, as shown by Clinton managing 35 percent to Trump's 59 percent. African Americans and Latinos were also more supportive of Clinton in Virginia than Florida, which enabled her to carry the Old Dominion by 212,000 votes. Contributing to Clinton's success in Virginia, and in keeping with Grose's observations, Black turnout more closely approximated White turnout in Virginia than Florida.

According to the Census Bureau estimates, turnout among citizens was 64.9 percent for Virginian African Americans compared with 69.6 percent for non-Hispanic Whites. In Florida, the comparable figures were 50.5 percent for Blacks and 63.8 percent for non-Hispanic Whites. Georgian African Americans approximated White turnout with 59.7 percent of Black citizens and 63.8 percent of Whites going to the polls. But in Georgia, Clinton had much less success in appealing to Whites. The Black electorate for the three states lined up solidly behind the Democratic nominee.

The first step to success when seeking public office usually requires winning the primary. From the perspective of Grose's research, it is surprising that Andrew Gillum won the Democratic nomination for governor and that Justin Fairfax emerged as the Democratic nominee for lieutenant governor in Virginia, since Grose hypothesizes that Whites will likely dominate the Democratic primary when African Americans constitute less than a quarter of the electorate. However, as Whites have forsaken the Democratic Party in the South, it becomes likely that, if African Americans vote cohesively, they will be able to nominate their preference if three or more candidates compete and a plurality suffices. Majorities are not needed for nominations in Florida, North Carolina, Tennessee, and Virginia, nor in some non-southern states with sizable Black populations such as Maryland, Illinois, and Michigan. Florida's secretary of state reports that at the time of the 2018 primary, African Americans constituted 28.4 percent of the Democratic registrants while non-Hispanic Whites were almost a majority at 48.2 percent. Gillum's surprise victory in the primary owed much to the large field of seven candidates and the absence of a majority-vote requirement, which Florida eliminated in 2002. He advanced to the general election with 34.4 percent of the primary vote, beating his top competitor, a White woman, by 3 percentage points. Fairfax also won the nomination with a plurality against two opponents. African Americans cast 60.2 percent of the vote in Georgia's Democratic primary, which facilitated Abrams's landslide nomination victory. In 2020, Jaime Harrison received the Senate nomination without opposition, and Raphael Warnock led a field of twenty contenders in a jungle primary, which assured his presence in the January 5, 2021, runoff.

Abrams and Gillum almost won, but Black candidates competing in earlier statewide elections often fared less well. The path taken by the two near winners and Lieutenant Governor Fairfax was less treacherous since they did not confront incumbents. Competing for an open seat also promoted the viability of Harold Ford's Tennessee Senate bid. African American candidates who have taken on sitting senators have usually not come close to victory. Warnock defeated incumbent Kelly Loeffler but her incumbency resulted from her appointment to fill the vacancy created by Johnny Isakson's (R) resignation, so she did not have the established relationships with the electorate that incumbents usually enjoy.

Incumbency is an equal opportunity conveyor of advantage. The few African Americans who have won statewide in the South and the much greater number who have served in Congress or state legislatures are generally as immune to defeat as Whites. While Black congressional incumbents usually win, they tend to get less White support than White incumbents (Grose 2011: 32). Research has shown that Black candidates generally receive less White support than comparable White candidates (Grofman and Handley 1989; Parker 1990; Reeves 1997; Terkildsen 1993). Bullock and Dunn (1999) estimated that the difference is about 10 percentage points. However there is also evidence that Black candidates can get a reasonable share of White votes (Bullock and Dunn 1999; Highton 2004; Voss and Lublin 2001; also see Bullock 1984 and Grose 2007). Abrams got about the same share of the White vote as did other Democrats at the top of the ticket recently in Georgia including Jason Carter (2014 gubernatorial nominee), Michelle Nunn (2014 Senate nominee), and Hillary Clinton.

Party or Race

Until recently, African Americans had poor prospects for success in the South. During the long tenure of Jim Crow, Whites ruled even in predominantly Black districts. The success of scores of law suits brought using Section 2 of the Voting Rights Act rested in part on documentation that candidates preferred by Black voters could not win consistently in majority-White districts. It therefore is not unreasonable to attribute recent defeats of African Americans competing before primarily White electorates to the discriminatory practices that characterized the region for so long. While African American candidates may still be somewhat disadvantaged compared to White Democrats, the defeats of southern Black candidates today cannot be dismissed as due to nothing more than persistent racism. Recently, across the region, Republicans have dominated statewide positions, congressional delegations, and state legislative chambers. Especially in situations where no or few Democrats have succeeded, it does not appear that the race of the Democratic nominee has been the disqualifying factor in the eyes of the electorate. If Democrats are losing regularly, then it may be more their party label than race or ethnicity of a particular candidate that constitutes the greatest obstacle. An assessment of the defeats of Senate candidate Ron Kirk (TX) and gubernatorial aspirant Carl McCall (NY) reached much the same conclusion. "The important finding, however, remains that neither the survey data nor the election result analysis indicate that race was a dominant factor in either election" (Frederick and Jeffries 2009: 715). Race may have played a role, but other elements contributed to the outcomes.

To explore the relationships between race and electoral success, we built a dataset of statewide contests for the US Senate and constitutional offices in the South. The data come from all of the states of the former Confederacy except Louisiana, which is excluded due to its unique electoral system that combines a jungle primary with a majority-vote requirement. For the other ten states, all contests involving two-party competition, beginning with 1989, are included: that year was selected as the start date as it is the year in which Douglas Wilder won the Virginia governorship. The thirty-year period also allows for the inclusion of years when Democrats dominated as well as the more recent period of GOP hegemony.

Although the time period is the same for each state, the number of contests varies widely. The only positions elected statewide in Tennessee are governor and senator. Virginia also fills relatively few positions statewide: Senator, governor, lieutenant governor, and attorney general. Other states have a range of offices, usually including secretary of state, attorney general, and commissioners of various occupations such as agriculture, insurance, and labor. Some states elect a treasurer, auditor, and state school superintendent; until recently, South Carolina elected an adjutant general. Contests for collegial bodies like public service commission or railroad commission and judicial contests are excluded. Of course, not every office has a contest every election cycle. Some well-entrenched incumbents avoid a challenge. In a few cases the only challenger was from a third party or someone who ran as an independent, and these were excluded. The number of election contests in the data set totals 540.

Black statewide candidacies have been infrequent.[8] A total of seventy-four contests involving African Americans appears in the dataset, and all but five of them ran as Democrats, which amounts to 12.8 percent of Democratic candidates but only 0.9 percent of Republicans. Hispanics are even more scarce, totaling twenty-five, of whom sixteen competed as Democrats. Black Democrats won eleven elections and Republicans won one. Six of

Table 1.1 Success of Candidates Competing for Statewide Office by Race, 1989–2018

A. Democrats

Race of Candidates	Democrat Won (%)	Democrat Lost (%)	N
White	42.6	57.4	455
Black	15.9	84.1	69
Hispanic	25.0	75.0	16
Total	38.7	61.3	540

B. Republicans

Race of Candidates	Republican Won (%)	Republican Lost (%)	N
White	61.4	38.6	526
Black	20.0	80.0	5
Hispanic	77.8	22.2	9
Total	61.3	38.7	540

Note: The number of cases differs between the two parts due to an inability to determine the race of some candidates.

Source: Prepared by the author.

the Democratic successes occurred in Georgia, with three victories each in contests for attorney general and labor commissioner.

Table 1.1 shows the rates of success for candidates by race. The upper half of the table presents results for Democrats. As evidence of the success enjoyed by the GOP in the South during the last three decades, White Democrats won 42.6 percent of the time. The success of Whites is much greater than that of African Americans who won 15.9 percent of their contests and Hispanics who won a quarter of their bids. The lower half of Table 1.1 shows that Republican candidates are overwhelmingly White, 61.4 percent of whom won. Senator Tim Scott (R-SC) and seven of nine Hispanics also won. Due to the paucity of African Americans competing as Republicans, the rest of the analysis will focus on Democrats.

Conditions were more favorable for Democrats during the first half of the period included in this study. Whites won 55.9 percent of their 1989–2002 contests as reported in Table 1.2. Minorities also fared better during this autumn of Democratic dominance, with African Americans winning 40 percent of the contests they entered, while Hispanics did even better. These results suggest that the fate of minority Democrats competing statewide is closely

Table 1.2 Success of Democratic Candidates Competing for Statewide Office by Race, 1989–2002

Race of Candidates	Won (%)	Lost (%)	N
White	55.9	44.1	236
Black	40.0	60.0	20
Hispanic	57.1	42.9	7
Total	54.8	45.2	263

Source: Prepared by the author.

Table 1.3 Success of Democratic Candidates Competing for Statewide Office by Race, 2003–2018

Race of Candidates	Won (%)	Lost (%)	N
White	28.3	71.7	219
Black	6.1	93.9	49
Hispanic	0	100	9
Total	23.5	76.5	277

Source: Prepared by the author.

linked to the general success of the Democratic Party. While many states did not see minorities winning Democratic nominations, when a minority made it on to the November ballot, that individual often succeeded prior to 2003.

Focusing on the second half of the period covered in this analysis, elections after 2002, shows the deteriorating fortunes of the Democratic Party. Table 1.3 shows that White Democrats won just 28.3 percent of the time, but minorities did much worse. African Americans won only 6.1 percent of their contests while none of the nine Hispanic candidates succeeded.

Some popular incumbents can use name recognition and good will developed during years of public service to hold on even against a rising tide of partisan realignment. Table 1.4 presents success rates for recent Democratic non-incumbents. Once incumbents are removed from the data, the win rate for White Democrats since 2003 falls by almost half to 15.7 percent. Minority Democrats have faced even longer odds. The only non-incumbent minority Democrat to win is Virginia Lieutenant Governor Justin Fairfax whose election is analyzed in Chapter 4 of this volume.

Table 1.4 Success of Democratic Non-Incumbents
Competing for Statewide Offices by Race, 2003–2018

Race of Candidates	Won (%)	Lost (%)	N
White	15.7	84.3	172
Black	2.2	97.8	46
Hispanic	0	100	9
Total	12.3	87.7	227

Source: Prepared by the author.

Even as the prospects for minority Democrats have paled during the new century, the ranks of African Americans serving as standard bearers for their party have swelled. From 1989 to 2002, twenty African Americans and seven Hispanics secured Democratic nominations. In the succeeding years, forty-nine African Americans and nine Hispanics represented their party in a general election.[9]

These increases are likely the product of multiple forces. First, members of minority groups have become increasingly active politically. Second, the success of minority-group activists has grown as they have come to constitute a larger share of the Democratic Party primary electorate. Some of the clearest evidence of how African Americans have become more numerous in Democratic primaries comes from Georgia and South Carolina, two of the few states that report the numbers of primary election voters by race and party. Trends in these states confirm our suspicions. In Georgia, the share of the Democratic primary vote coming from African Americans grew from 22.1 percent in 1992 to 65.6 percent in 2014. Blacks have cast the bulk of the Democratic primary ballots since 2010. A similar pattern prevails in South Carolina where in 2018, non-Whites cast 61.5 percent of the Democratic primary votes.[10] The impact of a largely non-White primary electorate has resulted in Georgia nominating numerous African Americans in recent years, the most prominent of whom is Stacey Abrams, whose bid to become governor of Georgia, is analyzed in Chapter 2 of this volume. Over eight election cycles ending with 2018, Georgia Democrats have nominated fourteen Blacks and twenty-one Whites. The pattern is much more muted in South Carolina where four of twenty-nine Democratic nominees during the recent period have been Black. From 1989 to 2002, the Palmetto State saw three African Americans among thirty-six Democratic nominees. Elsewhere in the

Deep South, Black statewide nominations have occurred almost exclusively in the more recent period, with eight in Alabama and twelve in Mississippi.

A third consideration is the quality of the competition. With the White electorate in most of the South now largely Republican and with Republicans dominating the ranks of statewide office holders except in Virginia, politically ambitious Whites today disproportionately compete for the GOP nomination. The logic behind the decision in which party primary to compete is much the same today as it was when quality White candidates disproportionately competed as Democrats. Savvy candidates seek the nomination most likely to yield a general election victory.

Increased nominations of African Americans is more of a Deep South phenomenon.[11] Neither Florida nor Virginia saw a dramatic increase in Black nominees. During the earlier period, two Blacks represented the Democratic Party in each state. Since 2003, Democrats have nominated four African Americans in Florida, while two have been nominated in Virginia, with Lieutenant Governor Fairfax scoring the only success during the latter period. A factor to consider for Virginia is that in the South it is second only to Tennessee in having the fewest statewide offices.

The increased share of the Democratic nominations going to African Americans in Deep South states indicates a weakening in the racial constraints that excluded Blacks from politics for decades prior to the 1965 Voting Rights Act. While African Americans increasingly appear on general election ballots, throughout the period White Democrats have attracted larger shares of the vote than minority Democrats. Table 1.5 shows that for the thirty-year period, White Democrats have averaged slightly less than a majority while both African American and Hispanic Democrats have averaged 5–6 percentage points less. A similar difference existed during the first half of the period, but with candidates of each ethnic group doing better. The mean for Whites was 50.9 percent while for Blacks it was 45.0 percent and Hispanics averaged 48.6 percent. During the recent Republican-dominant period, Democratic performances have suffered. White Democrats have averaged 46 percent of the vote, with Blacks attracting 41 percent and Hispanics 39.3 percent. Even these figures are inflated by incumbency. Among non-incumbent Democrats, Whites again did best, but averaged just 43.2 percent with Blacks averaging 40.1 percent. None of the Hispanics had been incumbents, so their average remains at 39.3 percent.

Note that over time the disparity between Whites and Blacks narrowed slightly. During the first period, Whites got 5.9 percentage points more than

Table 1.5 Average Vote Shares for Democratic Statewide Candidates
Controlling for Race

	Non-Incumbent			
	1989–2018 (%)	1989–2002 (%)	2003–2018 (%)	2003–1018 (%)
Black	42.1	45.0	41.0	40.1
	(7.1)	(7.3)	(6.8)	(6.1)
Hispanic	43.4	48.6	39.3	39.3
	(7.1)	(7.4)	(3.4)	(3.4)
White	48.5	50.9	46.0	43.2
	(9.4)	(9.3)	(8.9)	(6.6)

Note: Standard deviations are presented in parenthesis.
Source: Created by the author.

Blacks. During the latter half, the difference was 5 points. Incumbency provided an advantage enjoyed more often by White than Black candidates,
and once it is removed, the difference in vote shares shrinks to 3.1
points. Interestingly in Georgia, the difference between White and Black
performances was minimal as Stacey Abrams contemplated her run. From
2003 to 2016 the average vote for a non-incumbent White in Georgia was
42.0 percent compared with 40.7 percent for Blacks. This small difference
may have encouraged Abrams to run. Neither Florida nor Virginia has
enough Black non-incumbents to make meaningful comparisons.

To explore the influence of race along with other variables on Black
Democratic candidate success, multivariate models were estimated. These
models include variables for three levels of Democratic and Republican experience. Incumbents usually have an advantage in name recognition, experience, and an ability to raise funds. Incumbents are not immune to defeat,
but they typically begin with a lead over the challenger in the polls. For non-
incumbent Blacks, chances for success, not surprisingly, are much improved
when competing for an open seat (Sonenshein 1990; Strickland and Whicker
1992; Frederick and Jeffries 2009). Among non-incumbents, an individual
who has held a statewide post has a degree of name recognition at the outset
of a campaign that a competitor without that experience has to work hard
to achieve and for which they may need to spend heavily on television advertising. Sonenshein (1990) argues that having held statewide office is especially important for candidates seeking top offices, such as governor or

senator. Even a candidate for statewide office who has held only a local office may be advantaged when seeking higher office compared with the political novice. Any successful campaign demonstrates that the winner mastered some of the finer points of appealing for public support.

Of particular interest is whether the Democratic nominee is an African American. Another variable indicates the presence of a Latino nominee. The normal vote, defined as the share of the two-party vote for the Democratic presidential nominee in the most recent election or in the election coinciding with the statewide contest, is included as a measure of party strength. The percent Black in the state's population is another variable included in the models. The models also control for each state, although coefficients will be presented only if the relationship with a state achieves statistical significance. (The excluded state is Alabama, so coefficients compare a state vis-à-vis Alabama.)

Most of the relationships in Model 1, presented in Table 1.6, are as expected. Democratic incumbents fare 8.5 percentage points better than in races with no incumbent, while the Democratic nominee performs 6 percentage points worse when challenging a GOP incumbent. Having previously held a statewide post increases the showing for a Democrat by 3.7 points while having experience in a non-statewide post boosts the Democratic performance by 1.4 points. Competing against a Republican who had held office but is not the incumbent reduces the Democratic vote share by about 1.5 points with the coefficients significant at the 0.1 level. Democrats do better when the normal vote is more favorable to Democrats. Once all of these variables have been controlled for, an African American vote share is 3.7 percentage points less than that of a comparably situated White Democrat. Neither the performance of Hispanic Democrats nor the percent Black in the state is associated with the vote share. Model 1 also shows that Democrats fare significantly worse in Tennessee and Texas than in Alabama.

The second model in Table 1.6 adds a control for those contests held after 2003; the addition of this variable has little impact on the contribution made by the existing variables. As anticipated, Democrats running since 2003 have performed less well than those who competed earlier, with the difference amounting to 2.1 percentage points. In this new configuration, African Americans get 3.5 percentage points less support than their White peers.

Two states differ significantly from Alabama, the excluded state. The results for the states which figure significantly into the model are not surprising in light of recent election outcomes. No Democrat has won a statewide office in

Table 1.6 Correlates of the Share of the Democratic Vote Won in Statewide Contests, 1989–2018

	Model 1	Model 2
Democratic Incumbent	8.476***	7.947***
	(.91)	(.917)
Dem. Statewide Office	3.715***	3.294***
	(.968)	(.968)
Dem. Other Office	1.431+	1.228
	(.776)	(.772)
GOP Incumbent	−6.05***	−5.727***
	(.84)	(.84)
GOP Statewide Office	−1.658+	−1.455
	(.917)	(.912)
GOP Other Office	−1.393+	−1.249+
	(.761)	(.756)
Black Democrat	−3.695***	−3.499***
	(.924)	(.918)
Hispanic Democrat	.753	.886
	(1.955)	(1.939)
Democratic Normal Vote	.286***	.229**
	(.071)	(.073)
Percent Black	−.035	−.039
	(.025)	(.025)
Tennessee	−7.991***	−7.701***
	(1.872)	(1.858)
Texas	−4.728**	−4.718**
	(1.417)	(1.405)
Post 2002	—	−2.056**
		(.648)
Constant	36.617	40.053
Adjusted R^2	.468	.477
N	533	533

Notes: Standard errors are in parentheses. ***$p<0.001$; **$p<0.01$; *$p<0.05$; $p<0.1$

Texas in about a generation, so it comes as no surprise that the coefficient for that variable invariably has a negative sign. Tennessee elects only three offices statewide—the governor and the two senators—and since 1994 the GOP has dominated these offices, which explains why the variable for this state is always negative.

While attracting more of the vote is essential to political success, the ultimate determinant of anything other than a moral victory is to gain the office being sought. Table 1.7 presents the results of logit models in which a win by the Democrat is coded 1. In the first model, which contains the same variables as the first model in Table 1.6, most of the variables that attained statistical significance when explaining the share of the vote are significant. African American Democrats are less likely to win than Whites. The Democrat does better when already holding the office or having held some other statewide post. Competing against a Republican incumbent or a Republican who has other officeholding experience reduces Democratic prospects. Democratic candidates were more likely to win in states where the normal vote is more favorable to Democrats. Hispanic Democrats do not experience disadvantages comparable to those faced by Blacks. Since African Americans are the core constituency for the Democratic Party the negative relationship with percent Black may come as a surprise. However, this reflects the poorer prospects for successes in heavily Black states like Mississippi and South Carolina that Republicans have dominated.

The second model in Table 1.7 adds a variable for the more recent elections. Most of the predictors that achieved statistical significance in the first model remain significant in the second. Black Democrats continue to be somewhat less likely than Whites to win. As anticipated, the prospects for Democratic victories beginning with 2003 have dimmed. The variables for percent Black and the Democratic normal vote were no longer significant in Model 2.

Model 3 replaces the post-2002 variable with one that codes open seat contests beginning with 2003 with a 1. This variable is also strongly negatively related to the likelihood of Democratic success. Black candidates continue to have somewhat poorer prospects than White Democrats with the coefficient significant at the 0.1 level. Other variables remain much the same. A comparable model was not included in Table 1.6 due to it being so like the second model.

Of greatest interest to this study, while African Americans have had greater success in winning nominations in recent years, they convert those nominations into general election triumphs less often than Whites, and the

Table 1.7 Correlates of Democratic Victories in Statewide Contests, 1989–2018

	Model 1	Model 2	Model 3
Democratic Incumbent	1.942***	1.699***	1.069**
	(.344)	(.36)	(.391)
Dem. Statewide Office	1.397***	1.242***	1.182**
	(.362)	(.37)	(.375)
Dem. Other Office	.531	.431	.368
	(.328)	(.342)	(.344)
GOP Incumbent	−2.13***	−2.033***	−2.086***
	(.374)	(.388)	(.39)
GOP Statewide Office	−985**	−.883*	−.938*
	(.364)	(.374)	(.372)
GOP Other Office	−.585*	−.527+	−.577*
	(.275)	(.285)	(.285)
Black Democrat	−.866*	−.883+	−.875+
	(.425)	(.458)	(.456)
Hispanic Democrat	1.01	1.139	1.206
	(.866)	(.903)	(.872)
Democratic Normal Vote	.063*	.027	.036
	(.028)	(.030)	(.029)
Percent Black	−.269	−.092	−.12
	(.166)	(.179)	(.176)
Tennessee	−4.157*	—	—
	(1.785)		
Texas	−5.221*	—	—
	(2.429)		
Post 2002	—	−1.342***	—
		(.278)	
Post 2000 Open Seats	—	—	−1.603***
			(.323)
Constant	3.719	1.151	1.628
Nagelkerke R^2	.509	.548	.551
N	533	533	533

Standard error in parenthesis. *** $p<0.001$; **$p<0.01$; * $p<0.05$; +$p<0.1$

share of the vote they attract is about 3.5 percentage points less than that of comparably situated White Democrats. The results of the multivariate models in Tables 1.6 and 1.7 confirm expectations that office holding, especially incumbency, strongly impacts political success. Incumbents of both parties attract larger vote shares and have enhanced prospects for retaining their posts. Democrats who have held statewide offices other than the one in the analysis also perform better. Experience in lesser offices is less helpful to Democrats. Democrats opposed by Republicans with any office holding experience, but especially when trying to dislodge an incumbent, perform less well and are less likely to win. Democrats have encountered tougher sledding in recent years.

Our objectives do not include attempting to determine what share of the White vote Black Democrats attract, but the size of the difference in the overall vote share for Black and White Democrats suggests that African American candidates are having greater relative success today. When Bullock and Dunn (1999) analyzed congressional district voting patterns in the 1990s, Black candidates attracted about 10 percentage points less of the White vote than did African American candidates. If Black Democrats poll at least as large a share of the Black vote as do White Democrats, then the disparity in the total vote of about 3.5 percent would largely be the extent to which Whites are less likely to vote for a Black than a White Democratic candidate. Some of the difference seen in the models in Table 1.6 could be attributable to different responses by Latino and Asian voters to Black as opposed to White candidates. Exit polls show that African Americans give more support to a Black than a White Democratic candidate, which would mean that the difference in the White voter response to a Black candidate would exceed 3.5 percentage points but remain well below 10 points.

How do the experiences of the five African American candidates who will be the subjects of the next five chapters fit with the results of the models reported here? In his successful bid to become lieutenant governor of Virginia, Justin Fairfax benefitted from the changing partisan orientation of his state, which is now the most Democratic-leaning state in the region. His biggest challenge was to secure his party's nomination. Once he had accomplished that, the general election was his to lose. He did not confront a Republican incumbent. And while Jill Holtzman Vogel (R) had the advantage of holding a state Senate seat, she, unlike Fairfax, did not have statewide recognition. While lieutenant governor is the first office Fairfax has held, he probably had more widespread name recognition than Vogel since he narrowly lost the Democratic nomination for attorney general in 2013, a contest in which he secured the endorsement of the *Washington Post*, the "hometown" newspaper for northern Virginia. The coefficient for a Black Democrat in Table 1.6 indicates that a White Democrat will run 3.5 points better than a Black peer, ceteris paribus. Fairfax outperformed that estimate, finishing slightly more than 1 percentage point behind Governor Ralph Northam. Part of that difference could be attributable to the boost that service in a statewide office gave Northam as he moved up from lieutenant governor. All other things being equal, having held a statewide post would add 3.7 percentage points more to Northam's vote than a candidate like Fairfax who had not served statewide would receive.

The 2018 Florida and Georgia gubernatorial candidates, Andrew Gillum and Stacey Abrams, had the advantage of seeking open seats. Both had held public office, with Abrams rising to minority leader in the Georgia House, while Gillum served as mayor of Tallahassee. While former Senator Edward Brooke (R-MA) and former Governor Douglas Wilder (D-VA) told Judson Jeffries (1999) that having won the most recent election is critical to a Black statewide candidate's success, Sonenshein (1990) warns that having served as mayor is often not an asset. Offsetting the Democrats' experience, Abrams's opponent, Brian Kemp, had twice won the office of secretary of state and competed unsuccessfully for agriculture commissioner, all of which gave him extensive statewide name recognition. Although she had not previously competed statewide, Abrams's voter mobilization work, as will be discussed in the next chapter, gave her visibility far outside the House district she represented. Coefficients from Table 1.6 indicate that Abrams's service as a state legislator and Kemp's statewide service balance out. Abrams led the ticket so got a larger vote share than any White Democrat on the ticket and may not have suffered the loss of votes that the model predicts when a Black candidate is compared with a White.

Gillum's opponent, Ron DeSantis, had less visibility than Kemp, but had served in Congress from the Daytona Beach area. The coefficients for past service in the kinds of offices DeSantis and Gillum held pretty much cancel one another out. Like Abrams, Gillum ran well compared to White Democrats on the same ticket. Although Gillum trailed incumbent Senator Bill Nelson (D) the difference was minimal. Gillum ran less than a percentage point behind Agriculture Commissioner Nicole Fried, the only successful statewide Florida Democrat in 2018 faring much better than the roughly 3.5 percentage point penalty that the models in Table 1.6 suggest Black candidates pay.

Both Gillum and Abrams did better than White Democrats competing recently for governor in their states. Each of the last three Florida gubernatorial contests have been photo finishes won by the Republican by a percentage point or less; Gillum's 33,000 vote deficit is the narrowest. Abrams's loss by 55,000 votes was less than a third the size of Jason Carter's 2014 loss.

Warnock and Harrison confronted a challenge not posed to the three Black candidates for state office: the two Senate candidates had to dislodge an incumbent. Harrison's opponent, Lindsay Graham, was more rooted, having served three terms, while Kelly Loeffler, Warnock's opponent, had less than a year as an appointed replacement. Table 1.6 suggests that incumbency gave Graham an advantage of more than five points. It is unlikely that Loeffler would reap as much of a reward, having had less time to secure federal funding for the state or otherwise promote name recognition, although Georgia ballots indicate incumbency with an (I) beside a candidate's name. Neither of the Democratic challengers had held office, and Warnock, a preacher, had only tangentially been involved in elections.

While three of the five contests examined in this volume saw the White candidate prevail, the victories of Fairfax in Virginia and Warnock in Georgia may be harbingers of better times to come, not just for African American candidates but for Democrats generally in Florida and Georgia. At a minimum, the strong showings made by Abrams and Gillum demonstrate that the efforts of an experienced African American candidate cannot be dismissed as hopeless or the result of more viable White candidates having taken a pass on the contest. The themes articulated by all five Black candidates suggest further convergence of southern politics with that of the rest of the nation. Democrats running in these southern Growth States embraced progressive programs and national Democratic personalities that Democrats in previous election cycles would have gone out of their way to avoid.

Case studies of Black candidacies for statewide offices offer suggestions for conditions linked to success that cannot be easily put into a model. Nonetheless when evaluating the outcomes of the case studies, the relevance of some of these elements will be discussed. The literature hypothesizes that to succeed the Black candidate needs to be a political insider (Sonenshein 1990; Strickland and Whicker 1992). It will help if the party unites behind the candidate and if the opposition is in disarray (Sonenshein 1990; Strickland and Whicker 1992; Jeffries 1999). Statewide campaigns are expensive so the candidate needs to have a viable effort on that front (Sonenshein 1990;

Frederick and Jeffries 2009). Scholars who have done case studies of Black statewide candidate stress that to win they must seek open seats. In line with Grose's (2011) research, the candidate will need strong support from the African American community but also the backing of a non-trivial share of the White electorate. Increasingly, Black success will also require a share of the vote from Hispanics and Asian Americans. If the Black electorate is more mobilized than the White, that will benefit the Black Democrat nominee. As will become apparent in some of the case studies to follow, mobilization relies heavily on the involvement of Black women. The successes of Warnock and Fairfax and the strong showings of Abrams and Gillum undermine one of the imperatives from the earlier literature, which maintained that the candidate should develop a moderate or even slightly conservative image, run a conciliatory campaign by de-emphasizing issues related to race, but be a forthright supporter of law and order (Sonenshein 1990; Strickland and Whicker 1992; Jeffries 1999; Frederick and Jeffries 2009).

Plan of the Book

The bulk of this volume contains five case studies of African Americans who mounted impressive efforts to win high-profile statewide offices in recent years. While only two attempts resulted in a victory, two of the three defeats came up just a couple of percentage points short.

Chapter 2 reports on the 2018 Georgia gubernatorial contest. Democrats nominated former state legislator Stacey Abrams who hoped to become the nation's first female African American governor. She narrowly lost to Brian Kemp who had competed more than two terms as Georgia's secretary of state. Abrams believed that she could win by expanding the electorate, a goal that took precedence over trying to win back individuals who had voted for Republicans in previous elections. Abrams broke with tradition in Georgia by embracing progressive policies calling for the expansion of healthcare coverage and restricting access to guns. She also welcomed leading liberal Democrats such as former president Barack Obama and Senator Kamala Harris (D-CA), a dramatic change from previous Democrats who avoided national leaders of their party. Criticism of her opponent's performance as secretary of state was a constant theme of the Abrams campaign: she charged Kemp with acting to keep minorities from voting. Kemp, who ran as a politically incorrect conservative when seeking the GOP nomination, moderated his image during the general election. In an election that set records for participation in a mid-term cycle, Kemp narrowly avoided a runoff.

Florida's 2018 gubernatorial contest is the subject of Chapter 3. Andrew Gillum, former mayor of Tallahassee, sought to become the Sunshine State's first Black governor. His opponent, Ron DeSantis, had represented Daytona Beach in Congress. Both nominees won upset victories in their party primaries, casting the general election as the "battle of the underdogs," and calling attention to the state's changing electorate. Polls showed Gillum leading former Republican congressmember DeSantis during much of the fall. The contest went down to the wire. Gillum, with his progressive platform and #BringItHome slogan, lost to the Trump-endorsed, anti-socialism DeSantis by a scant 32,463 votes out of 8.4 million votes cast.

Gillum's campaign based its microtargeting and turnout strategies on the state's increasingly diverse electorate demographics (MacManus and Benner 2020). Gillum himself embodied what minority and younger voters seek in a candidate—someone who can inspire them and talk about their issues, and who reflects diversity. Nonetheless, post-election analyses concluded that the campaign did not focus enough on Democratic-leaning Hispanics, especially Puerto Ricans. Race became an integral part of the general election, following a DeSantis comment deemed racist by Gillum and his supporters.

Chapter 4 examines two successful Virginia Black candidates' very different paths to winning. These campaigns are separated by a three-decade period of vast social and demographic changes in the Commonwealth. The chapter analyzes the factors that explain the successful runs by L. Douglas Wilder and Justin Fairfax.

In the 1980s, Wilder had to counter images of him as a "radical Black," which he did by showing deference to Virginia history and customs and touting his military background and his moderate conservatism. In 2017, Fairfax did not face a hostile environment and campaigned on criminal justice reform, gay and lesbian rights, raising the minimum wage, affordable college education, Medicaid expansion, and pay raises for public school teachers and other state employees. Each candidate crafted a campaign that suited the political environment of Virginia at the time he ran for office.

Because Lindsay Graham, who criticized Donald Trump during the 2016 presidential primary, ultimately became such a Trump sycophant, Democrats were especially eager to defeat him. When polling showed Jaime Harrison might pull off the upset, he attracted stunning amounts of cash. Although he had never held office, Harrison had been around politics throughout his adult life, having worked for Rep. James Clyburn (D-SC), lobbied with the Podesta Group, and chaired the South Carolina Democratic Party. Despite an overflowing treasury and a sizable Black electorate, South Carolina is further from a realignment than the other Growth States, with White voters more attached to the GOP, as detailed in Chapter 5.

Raphael Warnock's defeat of Kelly Loeffler is the subject of Chapter 6. When Loeffler was appointed to fill the vacancy left by Senator Johnny Isakson's resignation, her defeat by another Republican in the jungle primary seemed more likely than a loss to a Democrat. Since the turn of the century, no Republican incumbent had lost a statewide contest and Democrats had not won any open seats. Work done by Stacey Abrams and others registering minorities and young voters set the stage for a possible upset. Donald Trump provided the key to Warnock's victory by inspiring not just minorities but also critical shares of White college graduates to turn out for the runoff. Even as dislike for Trump was mobilizing Democrats, his unfounded claims that chicanery had cost him Georgia's electoral votes planted seeds of doubt about the utility of voting among Republicans. Democrats used the nine-week runoff to recruit new voters, while Trump's actions kept enough Republicans away from the polls that, for the first time, a Democrat won a general election runoff.

Chapter 7 examines the efforts in the South made by African Americans who had their eyes on the presidency. The South has been essential to Black candidates competing for the Democratic presidential nomination. The only successful Black candidate so far, Barack Obama, used his popularity among Black primary voters in the South in 2008 to send a message to voters everywhere: the Clinton machine was beatable. Although in Obama's general elections the South largely stayed loyally Republican, his strength among Southern Blacks won him three states. The greatest victories of the Democratic presidential nomination runs of Jesse Jackson were Southern ones, in both 1984 and 1988. The 2020 Democratic Party nomination process featured an unprecedented four Black candidates (New Jersey Senator Cory Booker, California Senator Kamala Harris, former Massachusetts governor Deval Patrick, and Miramar, Florida, Mayor Wayne Messam). Chapter 7 describes and analyzes how the nomination fight played out in the South, as well as the impact of a Black vice-presidential nominee in the general election in the southern states.

The closing chapter projects the likely future of African American state-wide candidates in the South. The evidence suggests that these recent, featured elections portend a major breakthrough for Black candidates in the near future, with significant implications for the partisan composition and public policies in the southern states as well as nationally.

2

Georgia

Stacey Abrams's Bid to Become America's First Black Woman Governor Comes Up Short

> Abrams's campaign is built on the proposition that a compelling can-
> didate can get elected in the South with a progressive message that
> attracts liberal whites and minorities to the polls in greater num-
> bers.... if she can pull it off, the implications would be profound, not
> just for Georgia but for the whole region and potentially the nation.
>
> —Molly Ball

> Of all the races to watch Tuesday night, the Georgia governor's race
> may be the most important, both for the history it could make...and
> for what the results in the quickly changing state could tell us about
> trends in the rest of the country.
>
> —Patricia Murphy

Since the enactment of the Voting Rights Act in 1965, the ranks of public officials across the South have become far more diverse. At the time of the enactment of that landmark legislation fewer than one hundred African American elected officials served in the region with only three in Georgia. Today all but two of the eleven states have African Americans in their congressional delegations, and in Georgia the five Black legislators achieve proportional representation for the African American population. The region has hundreds of Black legislators and thousands of African Americans have won election at the local level. Virginia's L. Douglas Wilder (D) became the first African American governor elected in the United States and Tim Scott (R-SC) is one of three African American senators. With the changes registered in just over half a century, there are few "firsts" remaining to be achieved. One of these, however, would be to become the nation's first,

African American Statewide Candidates in the New South. Charles S. Bullock, III, Susan
A. MacManus, Jeremy D. Mayer, and Mark J. Rozell, Oxford University Press. © Oxford University Press 2022.
DOI: 10.1093/oso/9780197607428.003.0002

female, African American governor, and it was that glass ceiling that Stacey Abrams (D) set out to shatter in Georgia.

This chapter traces the challenges Abrams faced in her gubernatorial bid. What issues did she have to confront in the Democratic primary and later in the general election? How close did she come to achieving her goal? What accounts for her near miss? These are the topics to be discussed.

Background

Georgia's history does not suggest that it would be an auspicious locale for the statewide candidacy of an African American woman. As elsewhere across the South, Georgia once employed a full array of techniques to minimize African American political participation, beginning with being the first state to levy a poll tax. And while Georgia African Americans mobilized earlier than elsewhere in the region with 130,000 registered for the 1946 gubernatorial primary (Bullock et al. 2015), only after passage of the 1965 Voting Rights Act did Blacks begin to achieve more than miniscule representation in the ranks of public officials.

Georgia has not had an African American governor, but Blacks have won statewide contests, usually after initially being appointed to fill a vacancy. From 1997 to 2011, when he failed in a bid to win the Democratic gubernatorial nomination, Thurbert Baker served as attorney general. During most of his tenure, Baker was joined by Michael Thurmond who won election as labor commissioner in 1998 and served three terms before running for the Senate. One African American has served on the Public Service Commission, and multiple Blacks have won statewide election and reelection as members of the two state appellate courts. While Georgians have elected African Americans to statewide offices, the state did not succumb to Barack Obama's charm or platform. Obama lost the state by 5 percentage points in 2008—the same deficit Hillary Clinton encountered eight years later.

In recent years Georgia voters have provided little evidence of rejecting African American candidates because of their race. Instead Black candidates have struggled not because of their race but because of their party label. Since the three Democrats reelected in 2006 opted not to seek additional terms in 2010, Republicans have filled all of the statewide partisan positions. Democratic office holders managed to retain what they had even as the

Republican tide rose around them but no Democrat has won a statewide open seat since 1998.

Hopes entertained by Abrams and other Democrats who have set their sights on statewide success in recent years have hinged on the state's demographic change. Georgia has always had a sizable African American population. After reaching its apex in 1880 when Blacks composed 47 percent of the population, their share receded, bottoming out at 26 percent in 1970 before rebounding to 32 percent in 2018. With Hispanics accounting for another 10 percent along with 4 percent Asian, the White population is back to about the level of 1880. Since the GOP has made few inroads among minority voters, Democrats expect that ultimately a rainbow coalition that includes a minority of Whites will deliver victory. The question hanging over Georgia in 2018 like mist above Tallulah Gorge was whether enough new and often minority voters could be motivated to elect Abrams. Or would the GOP majority hold for another election?

Abrams's Background

Abrams grew up in a well-educated but often impoverished household. She spent much of her youth in Mississippi before her parents moved to Atlanta to prepare for the Methodist ministry. Abrams remembers times when the utilities were cut off in her childhood home. When she graduated as her high school valedictorian, her family had no car and therefore took a bus and walked to the reception for valedictorians at the governor's mansion. She did her undergraduate work at Spellman and then used a highly competitive Truman Scholarship to earn a master's degree in public affairs at the University of Texas. She completed her education with a law degree from Yale University, Abrams returned to Atlanta where she developed expertise in tax law.

In 2006 Abrams won a seat in the Georgia House representing several of Atlanta's older suburbs. She arrived in the chamber two years after Republicans had ended more than a century of Democratic control. The ranks of the dispirited Democrats continued to shrink and in 2011, with their numbers down to 63 in the 180-member chamber, she became the first woman or African American to lead either party. She served as minority leader until 2017 when she stepped down to concentrate fulltime on her gubernatorial bid.

Abrams quickly developed a reputation for being one of the most intelligent members of the Georgia legislature. Her intelligence, education, and work as a tax attorney enabled her to digest the content and implications of complex legislation, and she shared those insights in a cogent, unbiased fashion. Her reputation expanded beyond the confines of the Democratic Caucus and even Republicans sought her out for explanations of what they were about to vote on. Abrams reports that some Republicans asked her to review their bills before presenting them to the House (Ball 2018).

With Democrats constituting little more than a third of the chamber, Republicans could largely ignore them, although on occasion the majority party suffered defections so that Democratic votes were needed to pass legislation. Abrams shrewdly made the most of these opportunities. When the wildly popular HOPE scholarship that reduces tuition costs at state institutions of higher education for tens of thousands of students ran into funding difficulties, Abrams co-sponsored the legislation that saved the program. The revenue for HOPE comes from the state lottery and, confronted with rising costs and growing numbers of eligible students, the program could no longer pay full tuition for everyone one who graduated from a Georgia high school with a 3.0 GPA and maintained that grade during college. With many students now destined to receive smaller HOPE stipends, Abrams fashioned a low-interest loan to help them continue their studies. She also pointed out that through her efforts HOPE would continue to pay for pre-K education, the demise of which, she warned "would have lost a generation of children who don't get a do-over" (Bluestein 2017). She also worked with Governor Nathan Deal (R) in his extended efforts to recast the state's criminal justice system so as to reduce the number of incarcerated individuals. She single-handedly stopped a bill that would have cut the rate for the state sales tax but increased taxes on cable services. Drawing on her mastery of the tax code, she demonstrated that most Georgians would pay more in taxes with the change, which until then had seemed well on its way toward enactment. Abrams also supported legislation reducing the early voting period from forty-five to twenty in order to reduce the amount counties spend on elections.

By delivering critical votes and working with the Republican leadership, Abrams developed a reputation for pragmatism and bipartisanship now largely absent from Congress. Abrams saw her actions as enabling her to secure the few benefits available for a party outnumbered by almost two to one in the chamber. Her work with Republicans drew criticism from some of her fellow Democrats who wished she had held out against the GOP initiatives, even though such efforts would have been steamrolled by the majority party (Fausset 2018a).

In addition to serving in the legislature and practicing law, the unmarried Abrams found time for other activities. She undertook to increase voter registration, leading her to become a frequent critic of the way in which Georgia's election laws are implemented. In 2013 she created the New Georgia Project and set out to register 800,000 new voters. In the six months leading up to the 2014 election, Abrams claimed that 800 volunteers helped the New Georgia Project sign up 86,000 new voters. She later admitted that more than 10 percent of the applications were incomplete, while Secretary of State Kemp's office judged 6,000 to be invalid, some because they were duplicates and 40,000 because they were already on the voter rolls (Bluestein and Malloy 2015). A Lawyers Committee for Civil Rights suit charging that Kemp was too slow in processing the registration forms was dismissed. Abrams's attempts to bring new minorities into the electorate and charges that Kemp was impeding these efforts echoed throughout the 2018 gubernatorial campaign. She frequently criticized authorities for what she identified as efforts at voter suppression.

Not everything that Abrams did had political overtones. The high-energy lawyer-legislator found the time to pen eight romance novels using the pen-name Selena Montgomery. Under her own name she produced an autobiography, *Minority Leader*.

Despite her success in becoming House minority leader and her universally recognized intelligence, she ruffled feathers in her own party. Critics judged her too ambitious, and a less than diplomatic approach when disagreeing with others alienated some in her caucus. Stacey Evans was not alone among Democrats in viewing what Abrams considers pragmatism as selling out party positions by cooperating with Republicans. Some of this may be due to jealousy.

Abrams's Strategy

Abrams pinned her gubernatorial hopes on a different approach than recent Democratic candidates had pursued. Until 2002 Democrats dominated Georgia politics, except for the congressional delegation that had gone Republican as a result of the affirmative action gerrymander imposed by the Department of Justice following the 1990 census (Bullock 2018; Bullock

2010; see also Chapter 6). Election of the first Republican governor in 130 years saw Democrats lose a large share of the blue-collar vote, especially in the southern half of the state.[1] For the next fourteen years Democrats competing statewide sought to reclaim that vanished vote but with not enough success to win back any of the statewide positions that they had lost, so that after 2010 Republicans held every statewide partisan office in Georgia. Jason Carter and Michelle Nunn, the 2014 Democratic nominees for governor and Senate, respectively, came up short with only 45 percent of the vote. The Democrats' approach showed some success as Governor Nathan Deal's victory margin dropped from 258,000 in 2010 to 200,000. The unsuccessful appeals to blue collar Whites rather than making more efforts to mobilize non-voters in the minority population drew criticism from Abrams and others. (The 2018 exit poll conducted by the combined forces of multiple media outlets did not identify blue collar voters but did show that among White, non-college graduates, Carter managed only 18 percent of the vote.)

Jon Ossoff, who came within 2 percentage points of winning the 2017 special election in the Sixth Congressional District on Atlanta's north side, tried a different approach. Competing in a district where only 13 percent of the population is African American, Ossoff focused on well-educated White women and young voters. In some instances, his teams of canvassers would ask to speak to young voters, ignoring their parents even when the parents answered the door (Bullock and Owen 2021; Bullock and Owen 2018). Mailings also targeted young voters. This approach netted Ossoff a larger share of the vote than any of the Democrats who challenged Tom Price (R) had received but, nonetheless, proved insufficient.

Abrams was among those who thought Nunn and Carter should have worked harder to attract minority voters, especially those who rarely if ever voted. Sure, she welcomed any prodigal blue-collar Whites, but in large part her campaign hinged on the willingness of minority voters to turn out in large numbers. Abrams bet her candidacy on mobilizing individuals who had not registered to vote or who participated in presidential but not midterm elections. Based on the 2014 and 2016 elections, Abrams would need to find at least 200,000 more votes than Democrats at the top of the ticket had attracted in those years. Abrams believed that there were as many as a million "low-propensity" voters who might support her if convinced to go to the polls. This far exceeded the 90,000 individuals the campaign had identified as weak Republicans who might be induced to support Abrams (Barrow 2018). To make voting easy, the households of 1.6 million low propensity voters received pre-paid applications for absentee ballots. Abrams's models that showed her winning pegged the share of the vote from African Americans at a third of all ballots. That would be extraordinary. With Barack Obama on the ballot, African Americans had cast 30 percent of the ballots. In the 2010 and 2014 midterms, the Black vote share declined, but not by much, to between 28 and 29 percent. However with Hillary Clinton atop the ticket, the Black component sagged to 27.6 percent of the turnout.

If Abrams's efforts to mobilize the inactive stimulated a counter mobilization on the Republican side, she would have to inspire even more turnout. A large part of her message charged that the other side was not playing fair—accusing it of raising impediments to make it more difficult for Abrams's supporters to cast votes. The incorporation of these charges into the gubernatorial campaign was the culmination of efforts that Abrams had pursued for years.

Democratic Primary

Abrams's leadership position in the House did not secure her a free pass on the way to nomination. She drew one opponent, another female attorney legislator. White, thirty-eight-year-old Stacey Evans also had a rags-to-riches story. Unlike Abrams who grew up with two college-educated parents, Evans matured in an unsettled household in which books were not that common. She was the child of a single mother who struggled to make ends meet as a truck stop waitress and fell into abusive relationships. In a television ad that pictured one of the sixteen houses she lived in as a child, Evans referred to having called the police to protect her mother from a violent boyfriend. Having excelled in school, Evans went to the University of Georgia where she earned a bachelor's degree in political science and then a law degree. She won a metro Atlanta seat in the state House in 2010.

Evans tried to turn what had been considered a strong point on Abrams's legislative resume against her, charging that in negotiating the new terms for the HOPE scholarship Abrams had not done enough to protect its beneficiaries. With funding for HOPE running low, the legislation that Abrams helped negotiate established a new category, so that about one in ten rather than all HOPE recipients would get full tuition. Only students who graduated high school with a 3.7 GPA and made at least 1200 on the two traditional parts of the SAT would pay no tuition, and only as long as they maintained at least a 3.3 GPA in college. High school graduates with a GPA between 3.0 and 3.69 have a share of their tuition covered, with the amount depending on the receipts from the lottery. In her first television ad, Evans vowed that as governor she would ensure that HOPE was fully funded, restoring its previous pay out of full tuition for all who graduated high school with a 3.0 GPA. She noted that HOPE enabled her to become the first member of her family to attend college (Bluestein 2018d). Countering Evans's attacks Abrams claimed to have saved the scholarship program from even deeper cuts.

The changes in HOPE stood out as one of the few issues on which Abrams and Evans disagreed. They both took progressive stands highlighting the numbers of Georgians lacking healthcare as they called for the expansion of Medicaid. The two also favored expanding gun control and facilitating access to medical marijuana.

Evans raised $3.6 million, more than two million of which came from her payout from a lawsuit that proved the federal government had been cheated out of $324 million by a chain of dialysis clinics (Prabhu 2018a). In addition to investing in her campaign, Evans used her earnings to endow scholarships to the tune of $500,000 at the University of Georgia Law School for first-generation college graduates.

Despite her experience, story, and efforts to portray herself as the defender of HOPE, Evans had little success against Abrams, who won the Democratic primary by a margin of more than three to one. Since 2010, African American voters have dominated Democratic primaries, so if there were rigid racial polarization, Abrams would have won. In 2018, African Americans cast 60.2 percent of the vote in the primary, and Abrams got the vast share of this vote. Statistical estimates put Abrams's share of the White vote at 58 percent. In this two-person heat, Abrams took 76.4 percent of the total vote.

Participation in the Democratic primary showed signs that Abrams's strategy was working. Traditionally, decisions about who would govern Georgia were made in the Democratic primary, and as recently as 1990, 90 percent of the primary ballots were cast on the Democratic side. As Republicans began to win offices, growing numbers of voters opted for the GOP primary in Georgia, which is an open primary state. However even after Republicans took control of the state's top offices and secured majorities in the legislature, most primary voters asked for the Democratic ballot. Not until 2010, when African Americans constituted most of the Democratic primary electorate, did Republicans cast more primary votes than Democrats. The Republican appeal reached its apex in 2012 when 67 percent of the primary ballots came on the GOP side. Republicans continued to out-number Democrats in the 2018 primary but by just 56,000, as Democratic turnout reached its highest point since 2004. While Democratic turnout increased by 165,000 compared to 2016 to 563,000, the 619,000 Republican voters were in line with that party's numbers in the 2014 and 2016 primaries. The surge in Democratic participation was especially surprising, since for the previous quarter century the pattern had been for Democratic primary turnout to be higher in presidential years then decline in midterms. Drawing so many more voters to the Democratic primary suggested that Abrams's efforts to expand the electorate might be bearing fruit.

Securing the Democratic nomination in the May primary allowed Abrams to begin wooing Evans's supporters. This gave Abrams a nine-week head start on party reunification since, as described in the next section, Republicans had to hold a runoff election to decide who would carry their banner into the general election, and it is in runoffs that the most vicious ads appear in a fratricidal fight to the death.

Republican Selection Process

In contrast with the Democrats head-to-head competition between Evans and Abrams, the Republican contest featured five credible candidates. From the outset, the candidate to beat was Casey Cagle who was wrapping up a dozen years as Georgia's first Republican lieutenant governor. Being the number two in the executive branch is invariably seen as a launching pad for the governorship, and nine of the eleven men who have held this post have run for governor, although only four succeeded and none since 1990.[2] Like the two Democratic aspirants, Cagle came from a modest background, growing up in a trailer, the child of a single mother. He went to Georgia Southern but after injuries cut short his football career he dropped out of school and bought a tuxedo rental shop. He prospered and, by the time he was twenty-eight, was a member of the state Senate.

Among those who stepped forward to challenge him was Secretary of State Brian Kemp who had held that post for more than two terms after initially being appointed to fill a vacancy by then governor Sonny Perdue. Four of the last five incumbents in this post have run for governor, although no secretary of state had become governor since 1898. Kemp grew up in a successful Athens family, where he became a developer after graduating from the University of Georgia. Two members of the state Senate also entered the lists, with Hunter Hill being considered the more viable. However, the other senator, Michael Williams, could boast that he was the state's first public official to climb onto the Trump bandwagon. A fifth candidate, who could not be discounted despite being a political novice, business executive Clay Tippins, had demonstrated his toughness and leadership during four years as a Navy SEAL. In light of the election of Donald Trump as president and retired business executive David Perdue as one of Georgia's US senators, Tippins may have judged 2018 as an auspicious time for a successful entrepreneur to transition to public office.

Early polling showed the fifty-two-year-old Cagle comfortably ahead but well short of a majority, with 41 percent of the sample indicating an intention to back him. Well back were Kemp and Hill at about 9 percent, while Tippins and Williams lagged still further behind with about 3 percent each (Bluestein 2018k). It was at this point that Brian Kemp unleashed a television ad that separated him from Hill. The ad, which received national attention, showed the candidate with Jake, a high school student portrayed as interested in dating one of Kemp's three daughters. Jake recites key elements of the Kemp platform while the candidate brandishes a shot gun, much to the dismay of those who favor gun control. The ad concludes that if Jake is to date a Kemp daughter he must show her respect and have "a healthy appreciation for the Second Amendment."

Kemp's second ad also targeted males who would cast the bulk of the Republican votes. Like a country song it had four verses, and each featured an item that a good old boy could identify with. The ad began with an explosion for which the candidate explained, "I am so conservative, I blow up government spending." In the second scene, he vowed that "No one takes my guns." In the next scene he observed that "My chain saw is ready to rip up regulations." The final scene showed him in his pickup as he explained, "I got a big truck just in case I need to round up criminal illegals and take them home myself." Kemp summed up the presentation: "If you want a politically incorrect conservative, that's me." As part of his platform Kemp, promised to secure the nation's most restrictive abortion law and to restrict the size of the state budget. All of this fit into a narrative that frontrunner Cagle was not sufficiently conservative.

Both Kemp and Cagle signed on to efforts to enact a religious freedom statute—a version of which Governor Deal vetoed, and which much of the business community opposed as potentially LGBTQ hostile and perhaps likely to deter investment in the state. Both candidates promised to en-hance Georgia's attractiveness as a site for business expansion, building on Governor Deal's oft-repeated boast that the state was ranked first in the na-tion in terms of a place to move a business. Toward that end, Cagle passed out copies of his recently published book on Georgia education policy and the initiatives he would pursue as governor.[3]

At the outset, Cagle had been almost a prohibitive favorite with the lobbying corps who had worked with him for a quarter of a century, first as a senator and more recently during his dozen years as lieutenant governor. As one long-time observer of Georgia politics explained "The power struc-ture in business and government is lined up behind him. It's not split, it's not splintered, they are all behind him" (Salzer and Bluestein 2018). Lobbyists could give directly to the Cagle campaign, but they could also provide un-limited amounts to the Georgia Conservative Fund or Citizens for Georgia's Future, two PACs that supported the lieutenant governor. As more than one lobbyist told the author, it was essential to contribute generously to Cagle early on since if, as expected, he became the next governor, those who signed on late in the campaign would suffer with poor access. These lobbyists believed that if they miscalculated and one of the other candidates became the GOP nominee, there would be time to make amends. Further advancing the lieutenant governor's fund raising advantage were Cagle's efforts to dis-suade contributors who might try to hedge their bets.

Despite a steady diet of television advertising, launched by the well-funded Cagle team, their candidate had little success in building on his early lead, although he came in first in the GOP primary with 39 percent of the vote. Kemp was a distant second at 25.6 percent. Georgia requires that candidates win a majority in order to advance, so Cagle and Kemp girded for a runoff that would occur nine weeks after the primary.

Almost immediately the wheels began to come off the Cagle bandwagon. A common practice in runoff states, like Georgia, sees candidates who make it to the second round approach individuals eliminated in the primary to so-licit an endorsement. Cagle met privately with Tippins, who had finished fourth with 12.2 percent of the vote, candidly telling him that as lieutenant governor he had helped push through a proposal to provide tax credits for private school tuition even though he considered it a bad idea. Cagle took this step to head off funding that he feared would have gone to the Hill cam-paign, and he feared Hill more than Kemp in a runoff. But, the measure Cagle backed defeated an initiative sponsored by Tippins's uncle, Senator Lindsey

Tippins. Unfortunately for Cagle, Clay Tippins secretly recorded their conversation and released it to the public. Cagle now appeared to be a duplicitous politician who would enact bad public policy in order to advance his career.

Later Tippins released a second recording in which the lieutenant governor spoke disparagingly about GOP primary voters. Taking a swipe at Kemp, Cagle mused, "This primary felt like it was who had the biggest gun, who had the biggest truck, and who could be the craziest" (Bluestein 2018b). This made Cagle appear to be not only an unprincipled seeker of power but to have a low opinion of the electorate.

In the runoff, Kemp's fundraising picked up even as some of Cagle's contributors doubled down. Since the runoff is considered to be a separate election, contributors who maxed out in the primary could give again in the second round.

Despite the bad publicity stemming from the Tippins recordings, Figure 2.1 shows how close the contest was going into the final week, even as many voters took advantage of early voting, which begins twenty days before Election Day. On Monday of the final week of the runoff, Cagle scored what

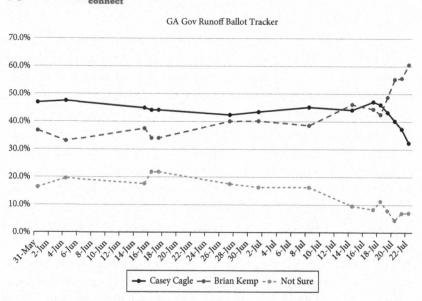

Figure 2.1 Tracking Poll Showing Support for Casey Cagle and Brian Kemp
Source: Provided by the Casey Cagle campaign. Data gathered by Battleground Connect.

his team thought would be a knockout punch when the popular out-going governor Nathan Deal endorsed the lieutenant governor. Until this time, Deal had shown no favoritism, and while he and Cagle were not rivals, neither were the two close.

But then, just two days later, Kemp got the boost that sealed his victory when President Trump unexpectedly announced his support. As often happens, the president conveyed his decision via a tweet: "Brian is tough on crime, strong on the border and illegal immigration. He loves our Military and our Vets and protects our Second Amendment. I give him my full and total endorsement" (Burns 2018). The endorsement came as a surprise. Neither Kemp nor Cagle were early supporters of Trump in 2016, but both had enthusiastically backed his agenda as president—not surprising in a state where 80 percent of Republicans approved of Trump's job performance (Bluestein 2018l). Trump had no connection to Kemp, but the president's leading Georgia supporters, the Perdue cousins, Agriculture Secretary Sonny Perdue and Senator David Perdue who had been one of the president's strongest supporters in the Senate, wanted to enhance their influence in Georgia. As governor, Sonny Perdue had appointed Kemp to the office of Secretary of State. He used his influence with the president to secure the endorsement.

The president backed up his tweeted endorsement with action. On the Sunday before Election Day the president appeared with Kemp at a rally in Macon. The Republican nominee wrapped himself in Trump's cape promising, "We'll work hard with this president to continue to make America great again" (Ellis 2018a). Earlier, Vice President Pence had also joined Kemp at a campaign event.

The Trump endorsement had the desired effect. Immediately voters flocked to Kemp. Following the Deal endorsement, Figure 2.1 shows Cagle had a narrow lead, but the day after Trump's tweet found Kemp ahead by about 5 points. The lead widened so that when the tracking poll ended, two days before the vote, Kemp led by about 30 percentage points.

Figure 2.2 further documents the stunning impact of Trump's tweet, which sucked all the air out of Cagle's balloon while firing Kemp's rocket-like trajectory to the nomination. Prior to the Trump endorsement, both candidates enjoyed about 60 percent approval among likely GOP voters. But once Trump tipped his hand, and although the Trump endorsement said nothing bad about Cagle but only that the president thought Kemp the better candidate, assessments of the lieutenant governor collapsed from above 60 percent

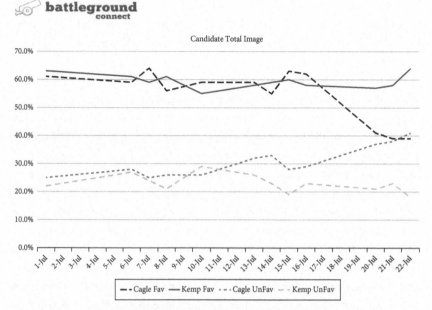

Figure 2.2 Candidate Favorable and Unfavorable Ratings during July in the GOP Runoff

Source: Provided by the Casey Cagle campaign. Data gathered by Battleground Connect.

favorable to less than 40 percent positive. The electorate turned so dramatically against Cagle that, just before Election Day, slightly more Republicans viewed him negatively than positively. Yet another indication of the impact of Trump's endorsement becomes visible when comparing early voting results with those on Election Day. Early voting starts twenty days before an election in Georgia and ends on the Friday before Election Day so that all but the last two days and a few hours of early voting occurred prior to Trump's decisive tweet. Kemp received 57.8 percent of the early vote but 75 percent of the ballots cast on Election Day.

A survey by the University of Georgia's School of Public and International Affairs during the runoff's early voting period had foreshadowed the impact of Trump's endorsement. When a sample of likely Republican voters was asked what would be most important to them in the runoff, 21 percent said it would be which candidate was closer to Trump. Closeness to Trump was cited by more likely voters than considerations of what would be best for Georgia or candidate trustworthiness. At the time of the survey these voters who were trying to decipher which candidate was more loyal to Trump were divided evenly between the two candidates (Bluestein 2018e). Once Trump made his pick, a share of the undecideds, along with some Cagle supporters, took the cue and embraced Kemp.

With the president in his corner, Kemp administered a humiliating thrashing to Cagle taking 69.5 percent of the vote. The defeat was so lop-sided that Cagle lost his home county by 56–44 percent and managed to win in only two of Georgia's 159 counties. Kemp's vote share increased by 43.9 percentage points from 25.6 in the primary—the largest increase be-tween a primary and runoff registered in any statewide, congressional, or state legislative contest in at least 46 years. The scope of Kemp's victory went a long way to dampening fears that supporters of the losing candidate would sit out the general election. Even before the votes were counted the GOP took steps toward reunification by scheduling a unity rally that included the two candidates along with Governor Deal and Senator Perdue.

The General Election Campaign

In late July as Abrams and Kemp suited up for the general election, the Republican Party was widely considered to have the inside lane. Since 2011 Republicans had filled every statewide, partisan position in Georgia. No non-incumbent Democrat had won statewide since 1998.

Despite this recent history, Democrats had high hopes as they looked to November. Trump had carried the state, as had every Republican presidential candidate since Bill Clinton capitalized on the third-party candidacy of Ross Perot to beat George Bush in 1992 by 13,714 votes, the smallest margin in the nation. But Trump secured just 51 percent of the Georgia vote, a narrower margin than in Iowa or Ohio, two toss-up states. Georgia Democrats drew further encouragement from the 2017 special election in the Sixth Congressional District. First-time candidate, thirty-year-old Jon Ossoff got 48 percent of the vote running against three-time, statewide candidate and former secretary of state Karen Handel (R) in a district Mitt Romney had carried by 24 points but Trump had won by just 1.5 points.

Abrams, like Ossoff, demonstrated a magnetism that attracted nation-wide funding. The willingness of well-heeled contributors to back the Abrams campaign indicated the viability of her effort. Abrams had a unique appeal for Democratic contributors since should she win, she would be-come the nation's first, female, African American governor. Her articulate and inspiring speeches fueled her far-flung fund seeking. Abrams's report filed with the Georgia Government Transparency and Campaign Finance Commission at the end of 2018 showed receipts of $27.6 million, while Kemp raised $22.1 million. By the end of June, Abrams had already received contributions from more than 31,000 donors (Bluestein and Salzer 2018). More than $8.3 million given to Abrams came in checks for less than $100 (Bluestein and Hallerman 2019).

Neither campaign relied exclusively on Georgia donors, but Abrams cast a wider net with fundraising forays in New York and California where donors lavished $4.6 million on her campaign (Bluestein and Ho 2018). In addition to prospecting for funds across the nation, Abrams visited all 159 Georgia counties.

Kemp sought to turn Abrams's success with out-of-state contributors into a liability. "My opponent is out there in San Francisco while I'm here [in Leesburg]," Kemp warned. "She's running a national campaign to be governor of Georgia. She's not listening to you. She's listening to socialist billionaires" (Bluestein and Felicien 2018). Since Kemp was not favored to win the GOP nomination, most of his funds came in *after* the runoff. Of his total, $17 million came in after the report filed six days prior to the runoff. Some Cagle supporters keyed off Trump's endorsement and began hedging their bets while others waited until after the runoff to begin making amends with Kemp (Salzer 2018a).

As has become common in high-profile contests in the wake of the *Citizens United* opinion, PACs supporting the candidates received millions of dollars from the wealthy and from politically involved entities. PowerPAC with almost $3.5 million through August and Black PAC with another $1.65 million served as seconds in Abrams's corner (Chira 2018). In addition, as a pro-choice Democratic woman, she received hundreds of thousands of dollars bundled by EMILY's List (Salzer 2018b). The Republican Governor's Association, headed up by Georgian Paul Bennecke, who cut his teeth in the 2002 Sonny Perdue campaign, anted up $2 million for Kemp (Salzer 2018c).

Each candidate attacked the other with carpet bombing thoroughness. Abrams was especially critical of Kemp's performance as secretary of state. She was thoroughly familiar with election law and practices as a result of "on-the-job training" during efforts to sign up tens of thousands of minorities. Some of her critiques highlighted issues of competence, while a second line of attack alleged that Kemp used his position to keep minorities from casting ballots. This was a continuing theme in her gubernatorial campaign, but

Abrams's concerns about Georgia's electoral systems—the difficulties that individuals seeking to register and vote encountered—predated her state-wide bid and have continued after her defeat.

In anticipation of the 2014 elections, Abrams observed that Georgia had at least half a million African American adults who had not registered to vote. Barack Obama lost Georgia to Mitt Romney by 305,000 votes in 2012. If a large share of these unregistered residents could be encouraged to add their names to the voter lists, Georgia's red might fade to purple. Toward that end, Abrams launched the New Georgia Project. Another entity, Voter Access, concentrated on promoting turnout. These efforts, which attracted millions of dollars in funding and from which Abrams drew salaries, dovetailed smoothly with her 2018 strategy. She had charged Kemp, as secretary of state, with failing to process 200,000 of the 2014 registrations forms her group sub-mitted. The secretary of state's office replied that it had received just 87,000 forms but that 5,000 were duplicates, 53 were fraudulent, and thousands more could not be verified (Fausset 2018b; Prabhu 2018b; Niesse 2018a). She continued criticizing Secretary of State Kemp, who was responsible for over-seeing voter registration and the conducting of elections, pointing to mul-tiple actions that she said were motivated by a desire to suppress the minority vote. Abrams labeled her opponent the "architect of voter suppression" (Ellis 2018b).

Kemp recognized the potential in Abrams's mobilization efforts and warned as early as 2014: "Democrats are working hard, and all these stories about them, you know, registering all these minority voters that are out there and others that are sitting on the sidelines, if they can do that, they can win elections in November" (Anderson 2018). Abrams picked up on her opponent's warning: "He said he is concerned that if everyone eligible to vote in Georgia does so, he will lose this election. Let's prove him right" (Goldberg 2018). An Abrams representative believed that efforts to deter minority par-ticipation, if indeed Republicans were engaged in that, would backfire. "For many voters, knowing that Brian Kemp doesn't want them to vote is a moti-vating factor not just to vote themselves but also to encourage others to do the same" (Ellis 2018b).

Not all of Abrams's criticisms came from 2014; she zeroed in on mul-tiple actions in 2018. Gwinnett County, where more than a generation of solid GOP support ended when it narrowly went for Clinton in 2016, be-came embroiled in controversy. The county election board rejected mail-in absentee ballots at four times the rate across the state, and the rejections disproportionately excluded minority votes. The board threw out 2.5 percent of White ballots compared with 4.3 percent of the ballots from Hispanics, 8 percent of Black ballots, and 14.8 percent of Asian ballots (Estep and Coyne 2018). Most of the problems involved failure to provide all of the information associated with the oath required to cast an absentee ballot such as birthdate (some people put down the date on which they submitted the ballot) and a signature. Individuals whose absentee ballots are rejected are notified by mail or email and given the chance to correct the problem or to vote in person on Election Day (Niesse and Estep 2018). Two lawsuits succeeded in getting a number of these ballots that had been rejected for trivial errors, such as omission of the voter's birth date, reinstated.

South Georgia's lightly populated, rural Randolph County drew national attention when a consultant recommended closing seven of nine precincts, one of which had only a dozen voters in a recent election. Opponents of closure charged that eliminating these locations would impose a disproportionate hardship on African Americans who constitute 56 percent of the county's registered voters. The proposed actions in Randolph County—which were never executed—were in line with the closure of more than 200 precincts since 2012 (Hallerman 2019).[4]

Also coming in for criticism was Georgia's exact match law, which flagged 53,000 voters whose names on the registration rolls was not identical to that on their driver's license or Social Security card. Trivial errors such as a hyphen in the name on one document but not the other could cause the registration to be put on hold. Of those affected by this, 80 percent were minorities, and 70 percent were Black (Brater and Ayala 2018; Estep and Coyne 2018). Being in this so-called pending group was not an impediment to voting since these individuals could cast ballots by showing a government-issued photo ID, which is required of all Georgia voters. Another issue was the purging of 1.4 million individuals who had not voted in the three previous elections and had not responded to a mailed notification warning of their imminent removal.

Asserting that Kemp's office was intent on suppressing the vote had the advantage of mobilizing Abrams's supporters who were not regular voters—nothing makes an activity more desirable than having it placed off limits. By charging her opponent with voter suppression, Abrams encouraged some infrequent voters to cast a ballot. Claims of voter suppression had a ring of authenticity in light of historic efforts to block African American participation through use of the White primary, poll tax, literacy test, and the intimidation that surrounded the first surge in Black registration that followed World War II (on suppression tactics in 1946 see Bullock et al. 2015).

In addition to charging Kemp with trying to keep minorities from voting, Abrams repeated Cagle's indictment of the secretary of state as incompetent. Among the problems were the release of voters' Social Security numbers and birthdates and a lack of security for the servers used with the state's voting machines. According to the cybersecurity expert who discovered the problem, not only was the personal data of voters accessible but the election files for all registrants could have been changed (Judd 2018b). On Kemp's watch, the names, addresses, and Social Security numbers of all Georgia voters had been inadvertently released.

Kemp could have avoided most of these attacks had he heeded Democrats' calls to step down rather than continuing as the state's top election official and overseeing a contest in which he was participating. By continuing in office Kemp opened himself up for criticism whenever any problems with the registration of voters or conduct of elections came to light.

As a rejoinder to Abrams's charges, Kemp boasted of the increased number of registrants. At the time of the 2018 general election, 7,006,952 had signed up to vote, almost a million more than in 2014 and 1.2 million more than in 2010, when Kemp took office. He bragged about making it possible to register online as well as at various public sites. He sought to deflect the charges involving Randolph and Gwinnett counties by noting that in these specific instances, as with many other decisions affecting elections, local officials and not the secretary of state are responsible. The defense Kemp used for exact match was that he was simply carrying out state law and that these individuals could nonetheless vote in person.

In response to litigation, federal judges generally sided with critics. One judge chided exact match as overly burdensome. Another ordered election officials to allow 3,000 new citizens to vote so long as they presented evidence of their naturalization when they went to the polls (Tarrant 2018). Local officials were ordered to accept absentee ballots that had only minor errors in their signatures.

The exit poll did not ask questions about Abrams's allegations but did ask respondents whether they believed that the government had done enough to protect the election. The electorate split almost evenly on this, with 47 percent responding positively and 43 percent negatively. Of those critical of government inaction, 78 percent preferred Abrams while 76 percent of those approving of government efforts backed Kemp.

In addition to having a road map to victory that differed from that used by other Democrats in Georgia, Abrams did not back away from appeals that others had judged taboo. She eagerly welcomed Barack Obama, who campaigned for her. She advocated progressive policies long thought to be non-starters in Georgia. Like many Democrats running in 2018, Abrams focused on improving healthcare access. Georgia is one of the states that opted not to expand Medicaid pursuant to the Affordable Care Act. As a consequence of this decision to pass on billions of dollars in federal aid, healthcare provision in rural Georgia has suffered. In the lead up to the 2018 elections, eight rural hospitals had closed their doors. Abrams vowed that as governor she would sign Georgia up for Obamacare, a position favored by more than 70 percent in a recent poll and even by a bare majority among Republicans (Hart 2018). Abrams explained that participating in the program would stabilize financially shaky rural hospitals, create 56,000 jobs, and pump $8 million a day into the state's economy (Jarvie 2018a). Had Abrams won, the promise to implement Obamacare might have been difficult to fulfill since only the legislature and not the governor can decide to participate in the Affordable Care Act. Not surprisingly Abrams got 78 percent of the votes of the third of the electorate that identified healthcare as the most important issue facing the nation.

Abrams also took on the powerful gun lobby with some of her proposals. Recent legislative sessions had expanded the places to which those who have concealed-carry permits can take their weapons, e.g., to portions of college campuses, airports up to the TSA check points, bars, and churches. Constitutional carry, which would eliminate the permit requirement, is popular with some outspoken Georgians. In contrast, Abrams supported universal background checks for firearms' purchasers, including private sales, a ban on assault rifles, and making college campuses gun free (Bluestein 2018m).

Abrams signed on to a key progressive goal to almost triple the state's minimum wage to $15 per hour. Early in the primary she had risked alienating moderate, older Whites when she called for redoing the enormous carving on Stone Mountain in the state park of the same name, a memorial to the Confederacy with images of Robert E. Lee, Stonewall Jackson, and Jefferson Davis. During the general election, talk of removing the carving largely disappeared.

Having secured the GOP nomination, Kemp sought to soften his image. For the general election campaign he locked up the shotgun in his gun case and parked his big pickup truck out behind the barn. In the primary Kemp proudly claimed to be a politically incorrect conservative, and that worked well with the GOP electorate dominated by men. But the general election with its Independents, moderate Republicans, and Democrats would be solidly female:[5] women would cast 55.8 percent of the votes. Some of Kemp's most effective general election ads featured his attractive wife and three daughters and these softened the primary and runoff good old boy image. By putting the spotlight on the women in his life, Kemp hoped to appeal to well-educated, suburban White women whose choices might be decisive. During the nomination slugfest Kemp promised to promote the nation's most restrictive law on abortions. As he took aim at women in the electorate, he did not walk back his primary contest positions, but neither did they take center stage. Abrams opposed these and other efforts to restrict women's choices.

One ad that ran only on Atlanta television showed Kemp in step with the #MeToo movement, featuring the endorsement of a victim of sexual violence. A major concern for women is the safety of their children while at school. One Kemp ad, fueled with a budget of $1.8 million, attacked Abrams for voting against harsher penalties for those involved with sex trafficking. The woman in the ad expressed concern about her child's safety when at school, referenced the Abrams's vote, and concluded with "I don't know what Stacey Abrams was thinking. But I know she's too extreme for Georgia" (Bluestein 2018h). Abrams explained that she opposed the bill because it limited judges' discretion.

When seeking the GOP nomination, Kemp, like the other candidates, supported passage of a Religious Freedom Restoration Act (RFRA). Years earlier when the legislature passed a RFRA Governor Deal vetoed it, much to the approval of the state's booming film industry and other economic drivers. RFRA, it was feared, would allow businesses to discriminate against the LGBTQ community, which would lead to boycotts that would harm the state economically just as North Carolina had suffered following passage of its bathroom bill.[6] As he shifted to emphasizing what he would do to promote jobs and economic growth, Kemp recast his stand on RFRA explaining that he would veto any version of this law that did more than simply restate the provisions of the federal statute.

Abrams, joined by a number of pro-business Republicans, saw no need for a state RFRA.

As Kemp downplayed commitment to issues popular with conservative men, he demonstrated commitment to education with a proposal to increase teacher salaries by $5,000.[7] This would have a special appeal to women who dominate the ranks of public school teachers.

One aspect of the Kemp effort that did not change even as the tone of the ads shifted was his emphasis on rural Georgia. Kemp traveled extensively in the many counties outside of metropolitan areas and especially beyond metro Atlanta's expanding footprint. Whites in these communities often carried the same frustrations and fears about change and how to survive it that sent Donald Trump to the White House.

Some Kemp ads repeated the theme that Republicans have used against Democrats for years in Georgia and in many red states. Kemp labelled his opponent as "too extreme" for Georgia, predicting that she would "have Georgia turn into Venezuela" (Blinder and Fausset 2018). As an example of what he and most Republicans considered extremist, Kemp accused his opponent of favoring a single-payer health insurance program that he warned would bankrupt the state. To underscore Abrams's liberalism, GOP mailers showed Abrams along with Hillary Clinton and Elizabeth Warren. Another ad had an excerpt from an Abrams's speech to supporters in which she praised the diversification of Georgia's population, with the implication that she wanted backing from both those legally in the country as well as those who lacked documents to vote. Kemp acknowledged that "Stacey Abrams is very articulate, very smart, but she has just as radical views on wanting to grow government, raising taxes, trying to have these big government policies that didn't work in the Barack Obama administration and are bad for Georgia" (Bluestein 2018a). In contrast the Republican vowed to take a chain saw to government regulation while cutting taxes.

Each campaign raised questions about the unmet financial obligations of the opposition. A Republican Governors Association ad noted that while Abrams owed the Internal Revenue Service $54,000 in unpaid taxes from 2016 and 2019, she lent her campaign $50,000. She also had a student loan debt of $96,000 and owed $76,000 on credit cards (Bluestein 2018c; Prabhu 2018b). Abrams responded in an ad sponsored by the Democratic Party of Georgia. "When my father was diagnosed with cancer and money was tight, I knew that I could defer payment on my taxes, but not on his cancer treatments. I made the right choice—the choice to fulfill my obligations to my family . . . ." She explained that she was not delinquent but making scheduled payments to IRS.

An aspect of Kemp's finances also came under attack. He owned part of a company that produced canola and sunflower oil. The company had fallen on hard times, and Kemp was named in a suit seeking repayment of a $700,000 loan. In an effort to peel off some of the farm vote that had supported Kemp in the primary, the unpaid loan was portrayed as leaving farmers holding the bag. Kemp noted that he was a minority stock holder and not in charge of day-to-day operations of the company.

As the campaign drew to a close, the Kemp campaign weighed in on what had been a key Abrams issue—election security. On Sunday before the election, Kemp announced "AFTER FAILED HACKING ATTEMPT, SOS LAUNCHES INVESTIGATION INTO GEORGIA DEMOCRATIC PARTY," implying that the Democratic Party had tried to hack the registration files (Judd 2018b, all capitals in the original). The impetus for this charge was a warning received by a Democratic volunteer from an individual who discovered when downloading a sample ballot that he could download every file in the election system along with voters' personal information stored in the system such as driver's license numbers. This alert was forwarded to the FBI and to the secretary of state who cleverly deflected evidence of yet another vulnerability in the election office's software by accusing the opposition of potential illegal behavior (Fausset and Blinder 2018; Judd 2018b). The secretary of state did not pursue the claim after the election, and more than a year later, Georgia's attorney general concluded that Democrats had not sought to hack into the voter registration system (Niesse 2000).

Although Kemp did not stress immigration as he had in his quest for the GOP nomination, the electorate clearly identified him as the anti-immigration candidate based on his earlier ads. Of the third of the electorate that identified immigration as the nation's most important issue, 91 percent voted for Kemp. He was also preferred by the quarter of the electorate that pointed to the economy as the biggest issue, a group he won with 58 percent of the vote.

As he had in the GOP runoff, President Trump weighed in on behalf of Kemp. The general election evoked more than a tweet, and just before the vote, the president appeared with Kemp at a rally in Macon. Not wanting to make the election a referendum on the president, fearing that would stampede more Republicans to the polls, Abrams avoided referencing Trump.

Election Outcome

To win, Abrams would have to overcome a 200,000-vote deficit that Democrats at the top of the ticket had lost by in 2014 and 2016. This disparity, while daunting, was less than the margin that had separated the parties at the height of GOP success in Georgia. As Figure 2.3 shows, the GOP advantage peaked in the Bush reelection at 550,000 votes. Two years later Sonny Perdue coasted to a victory with 400,000 more votes than his Democratic challenger.

Kemp extended the GOP gubernatorial winning streak to five elections, securing almost two million votes, more than any previous governor, as reported in Table 2.1. However in losing, Abrams also won more votes than any previous governor and almost twice as many as any Democrat governor. Although the 2018 election drew 135,000 fewer voters than in 2016, Abrams ran 45,722 votes ahead of Hillary Clinton who received 45.9 percent of Georgia's vote to Trump's 51.1 percent. Kemp's 54,723 vote margin was smaller than in any gubernatorial contest since 1994 when Zell Miller (D) edged out Guy Milner by 32,000 votes. The 1.4 percentage point advantage was the smallest in half a century. Abrams reduced the Democratic deficit of the two previous election cycles by almost three-fourths.

The initial count showed Kemp ahead by more than 65,000 votes, yet Abrams did not concede. On election night, even as Kemp claimed victory,

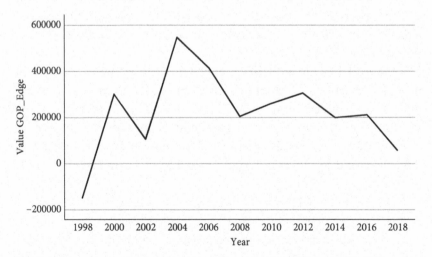

Figure 2.3 Margins of Victory by Republican Candidates at the Top of the Ticket, 1998–2018

Table 2.1 Votes for Governor in 2018 and for President in 2016

	Governor			President	
Name	Vote	%	Name	Vote	%
Kemp (R)	1,978,408	50.2	Trump (R)	2,089,104	51.1
Abrams (D)	1,923,685	48.8	Clinton (D)	1,877,963	45.9
Metz (L)	37,235	1.0	Johnson (L)	125,306	3.1
Turnout	3,949,905			4,092,373	

Source: Created by the author.

Abrams clung to hope that a runoff would be needed. She said, "If I wasn't your first choice, or if you made no choice at all, you're going to have a chance to do a 'do-over'" (Fausset and Blinder 2018). Since she had repeatedly pointed out problems with the electoral operation that she believed made it more difficult for minorities to vote, Abrams vowed to wait until every legally cast ballot was counted. Throughout the course of the state's review of the results, Abrams reiterated the charges she had leveled against Kemp, claiming that some legitimate provisional and mail-in ballots had been excluded (Bluestein 2018g) and alleging efforts by his office to suppress turnout. Her best hope rested on Georgia's requirement that candidates win with a majority. Since the gubernatorial contest included a Libertarian candidate, if Kemp's vote failed to exceed 50 percent, Abrams would get another bite at the apple in a runoff conducted in December. She refused to acknowledge defeat until all 21,000–26,000 provisional ballots and 5,147 absentee ballots that had been rejected were examined.[8] Her campaign telephoned and even went to the homes of voters who cast provisional ballots encouraging them to take the steps necessary to have the ballot counted (Bluestein, Mitchell and Niesse 2018). While Kemp had remained secretary of state throughout the campaign despite Abrams's calls for him to resign, he stepped aside on November 8 and thus did not preside over the recount.

During the recount and careful examination of provisional ballots, Kemp's margin eroded making the possibility of a runoff more likely. However, once all eligible ballots had been tallied, the Republican avoided a runoff by 17,488 votes, as the Libertarian candidate attracted only 37,235 votes (less than 1 percent). Libertarians never run well when the two major parties have nominees but usually attract between 2 and 3 percent of the vote. Four Libertarians running for other statewide offices in 2018 received between 2.2

and 2.7 percent of the vote. Had Ted Metz, the Libertarian gubernatorial candidate, achieved the average of his fellow partisans, 97,235 votes, and had most of that support come from individuals who would have otherwise voted for Kemp, it would have triggered a runoff, perhaps with Abrams going into the second round having a narrow lead.

The narrow win, with Kemp slipping past Abrams by 1.4 percentage points, was in line with pre-election polling. Almost all of the polls taken as Election Day neared showed Kemp ahead, although usually his advantage fell within the margin of error so that the contest appeared to be a statistical dead heat. The final Real Clear Politics average of five polls had Kemp up by 3 points. Two polls had the Republican leading by 2 points, one had Abrams ahead by one while a fourth poll showed the contest tied. The fifth poll, an outlier that proved woefully inaccurate, showed Kemp leading 52–40 percent. None of the other polls had either candidate with a majority. Excluding the outlier, the average for the other four polls gave Kemp a lead of 0.75 percentage points. That figure is very much in line with *all* of the publicly available polls conducted after Kemp won the GOP runoff. Over the course of several months Kemp usually led but never by more than 2 points. Excluding the outlier, the eleven other polls all had the result within the margin of error.

The widespread assumption that the outcome would be close, coupled with the heavy spending on television advertising and mail outs along with extensive media coverage stimulated record high turnout for a midterm election. In Georgia, as is the pattern across the nation, substantial fall off in participation usually occurs between the presidential and the midterm election. Georgia's 2018 election drew fewer voters than in 2016, but with a decrease of only 135,000 participants the electorate for the two years was strikingly similar in size. The 3,946,430 Georgians going to the polls accounted for a 52 percent increase over the participation four years earlier.

The Abrams campaign hoped that Democrats would turn out at rates near that of a presidential year, while Republicans would participate at the much lower midterm rate. If that happened, she would win. Both parties used sophisticated metrics to classify voters and then relentlessly targeted those identified as most likely to favor their candidate (Bluestein 2018f). In the Atlanta suburbs favored by Millennials, the Abrams team used social media to contact apartment and condominium dwellers. These communities often require pass codes to enter, thereby thwarting door-knocking by outsiders. The Abrams campaign recruited residents to solicit support from their neighbors. The GOP mayor of a city with many such communities observed ruefully, "They identified voters in apartments, and then ran the best ground game I've ever seen" (Galloway 2018). Jason Shephard, the GOP chair in Georgia's third largest county, admitted, "Let's be frank: They outworked us. They took their message door-to-door and engaged voters one-on-one. If we are going to get back on top in the suburbs, we need to get just as determined and be willing to invest just as many resources—if not more" (Bluestein 2018j).

One of Abrams's groups, Care in Action, claimed to have texted every registered woman of color in Georgia (Chira 2018). These efforts helped boost Black turnout to 1,141,972, coming within 2,822 of the *total* vote received by Jason Carter's gubernatorial bid four years earlier. Perhaps most surprisingly, the 2018 Black turnout exceeded that in 2016 by 15,410 and came within 41,000 of the record Black vote set in the 2008 presidential election. While Abrams's campaign succeeded in mobilizing African American voters, a 52.6 percent increase over 2014, this was very much in line with the overall increase in turnout.

Offsetting Abrams's success in inspiring Democrats was a late GOP surge triggered by Democratic senators' attempts to block Brett Kavanaugh's Supreme Court nomination following Christine Blasey Ford's allegation of a sexual assault by the teen-aged Kavanaugh. Democratic senators' attacks on Kavnaugh united Republicans (for whom a conservative majority on the Supreme Court is a top priority) and convinced some who might otherwise have sat out the election to vote. Joel McElhannon (2018) of the Kemp campaign reports that their polling showed an uptick in support as Democrats focused on the allegations against Kavanaugh. In Cobb County, Georgia's third most populous, GOP chair Jason Shepherd contrasted the time before and after the hearings. "We were struggling to get phone calls, get people going door-to-door, and [after the hearing] it was a night and day difference" (Chira 2018). Kemp's Operation Red Wall hired fifty workers who knocked on 120,000 doors to boost rural, White turnout (Bluestein 2018j). The backlash to Democratic opposition to Kavanaugh contributed to turnout increasing by more than 20 percent over the 2014 figure in eighty-one counties, all but ten of which voted for Kemp (Bluestein 2018f).

The Fox exit poll identified only 5 percent as first-time voters, which would reflect poorly on Abrams's efforts to expand the electorate. However, 68 percent of these novices voted for her. The CNN exit poll asked a different question, and 17 percent of its sample reported voting *in a midterm election* for the first time. This group divided evenly, with Abrams getting 51 percent.

Yet another source estimated that 540,000 of the 2018 voters had not participated in 2016 and that African Americans accounted for about 40 percent of
these new arrivals (Bluestein 2018f). A Democratic Party data firm, Catalist,
estimated that of the 2.4 million who voted early, about half had not participated in 2014 (Chira 2018). The surge in early voting favored Democrats,
but not by much. Surveys suggest that Abrams's work may have had greater
success in mobilizing voters who do not consistently vote in midterms than
in bringing in individuals brand new to the electoral system. Her efforts contributed to, but cannot fully account for, the extraordinary turnout in 2018,
which broke all records for a midterm.

The 2018 electorate differed from that of 2016 in its racial composition.
The 2016 electorate was 27.6 percent African American, with Blacks constituting the smallest share of the turnout since 2006, as Hillary Clinton failed to
inspire this component of the electorate in Georgia as in most of the United
States.[9] In 2018, Blacks cast 28.9 percent of Georgia's ballots, a figure in line
with the Black vote share in 2010 and 2014. Abrams attracted 92 percent of
the Black vote according to the CNN exit poll. The percent Black in a county
correlated very strongly with the Abrams vote.[10]

Abrams did 2 percentage points better than Carter with Black voters
while the two Democrats each managed about a quarter of the White vote.
However in suburban Gwinnett and Cobb, Georgia's second and third largest
counties, respectively, the Abrams team believes she got a third of the White
vote (Bluestein 2018f). Abrams also exceeded Carter's share of the growing
Latino vote, taking 60 percent compared with her predecessor's 53 percent.

In both 2014 and 2018, partisans cast well over 90 percent of their votes
for their party's nominee. That partisans embrace their party's nominee
surprises no one. All but two counties favored the same party in the 2016
presidential election and the 2018 gubernatorial contest. If the two parties
have roughly equal numbers, then Independents may decide the outcome.
Abrams got the nod from this segment but not a sufficiently vigorous nod
to become governor as Independents favored her 53–45 percent. Four years
earlier Carter lost the Independents 59–28 percent.

The 2018 electorate was 3 points more heavily female than in 2016,
reaching 55.8 percent. While the female share of the 2018 turnout was only
slightly above that for 2014, turnout among Black women increased from
44.5 percent in 2014 to 59.2 percent in 2018; the number of Black women
voting in 2018 was just 600 fewer than in the 2016 presidential election. The
exit poll shows Abrams lost the female vote by a percentage point, but she

trailed Kemp by 6 points among men. There was no gender difference among White voters, but Abrams did 10 points better among Black women (97 percent support) than men (87 percent support).

Age correlated with candidate preference. As have other Georgia Democrats beginning with 2014, Abrams carried the youth vote. Voters under 30 cast 63 percent of their ballots for her while those aged 30–44 gave her 57 percent of their votes. Kemp got 58 percent of the votes in the 45–64 age group and beat Abrams 60–38 percent among the oldest cohort. Table 2.2 compares 2018 with 2014 and shows that the two younger cohorts cast larger shares of the vote in 2018 than previously. The youngest group almost doubled its vote share to 13.5 percent. Moreover the two younger cohorts displayed greater support for Abrams than Jason Carter, the 2014 gubernatorial nominee. The largest cohort, those 45–64 years old, gave a smaller share of their vote to Abrams than Carter. However, the oldest voters, whose share of the electorate declined, found Abrams more acceptable than Carter although this group was the most Republican in each election.

Amount of education correlated positively with Abrams support. The only cohort among whom she performed poorly were the least educated, those who had no more than a high school education who cast 62 percent of their ballots for Kemp. The two candidates split evenly the quarter of the electorate who dropped out of college. Abrams won all of the other groups, with her strongest performance coming among those with advanced degrees, 60 percent of whom favored her. Whites who lacked a college education overwhelmingly rejected Abrams, as they cast 83 percent of their votes for Kemp.

Table 2.2 Age Turnout and Party Preference

Age	2014		2018	
	% of vote	% Democrat	% of vote	% Democrat
18–29	7.0	54	13.5	63
30–44	20.3	54	22.8	57
45–64	44.3	44	39.8	41
65+	28.4	35	23.9	38

Sources:The percent of the vote figures were computed using data collected by the secretary of state based on those who turned out to vote. The percent of each group that voted for the Democratic nominee for governor comes from the 2014 Fox News exit polls and the 2018 CNN exit polls. The 2018 Fox News voter analysis shows Abrams taking 63 percent of those 18–29; 55 percent of those 30–44; 43 percent of those 45–64; and 39 percent from the oldest group.

Abrams did better with White, college-educated voters, but still lost these individuals by 20 percentage points. Her best showing among Whites came from college-educated women, with 42 percent support.

Evangelical or born-again Christians constitute the core constituency for Republicans in much of the South. This group cast 35 percent of the vote in 2018 and Kemp won their support 88–11 percent. Since this group was 6 percentage points larger than the Black vote and almost as cohesive, it provided more votes for Kemp than Abrams got from African Americans who are the Democrats' core constituency. This pattern has persisted in recent elections (Bullock 2018). White Evangelicals played a larger role in 2014 when they cast 39 percent of the ballots, although they were less united behind Nathan Deal who got 82 percent of their ballots.

As in most of the United States and in Western democracies, the electorate split sharply along an urban-rural axis. Kemp, whose first bid for statewide office came in a 2006 campaign for agriculture commissioner which stalled out in the GOP primary, pinned his hopes on running up the vote in rural Georgia. With urban centers expanding and becoming more Democratic, Kemp had to do exceptionally well out beyond the street lights. He courted rural Georgians in multiple bus tours that took him to often-ignored county seats but rarely into metro Atlanta. The heavy emphasis was not a manifestation of anti-urban sentiment, according to a key campaign official, but a recognition of the reality of where Republicans votes could be found. Table 2.3 shows Kemp's vote share outside metro Atlanta hit 61.4 percent, almost a percentage point better than Trump, 2.7 points above that achieved by Nathan Deal in his 2014 reelection, and 2.4 points better than Romney's 2012 showing (O'Connor 2019). Trump also performed well in parts of Georgia not served by high-speed internet connections, but Kemp managed to exceed even the lopsided Trump votes. In numerous north Georgia counties that have few non-White voters, Kemp secured more than 80 percent of the vote. In an extraordinary show of strength Kemp won 89.8 percent of the Banks County vote, eclipsing Trump's impressive 88.3 percent. The 130 counties that backed Kemp gave him 71.4 percent of their votes (Denery 2018). The Kemp campaign's courting of the rural vote, largely to the exclusion of suburbia, worked for the candidate, but the GOP paid a price as it lost state legislative seats in metro Atlanta. Some of those losers bitterly observed that they might have survived had the Kemp campaign helped them half as much as Abrams's urban focus aided Democrats.

Table 2.3 Support for Top-of-the-Ticket Democrats and
Republicans in Metro Atlanta and Elsewhere (%)

Year/Candidate	Metro Atlanta	Rest of Georgia	Statewide
2008			
Obama	51.5	41.6	47
McCain	47.8	58.2	52
2012			
Obama	49.7	40.0	45
Romney	49.1	59.0	53
2014			
Carter	49.0	39.0	45
Deal	48.6	58.7	53
2016			
Clinton	52.3	36.9	46
Trump	44.2	60.6	51
2018			
Abrams	56.5	37.8	49
Kemp	42.5	61.4	50

Source: Dan O'Connor, personal communication.

Abrams excelled in Georgia's core urban counties. She carried nine of
the twenty-eight counties in metro Atlanta by almost 600,000 votes beating
Kemp by more than two to one. Her strongest showings came in majority
Black Clayton (87.8 percent) and DeKalb (83.5 percent) counties. Georgia's
second and third most populous counties, Gwinnett and Cobb, respectively,
broke with recent tradition and narrowly backed Clinton in 2016. Abrams
expanded the Democratic margins in both counties. She took Gwinnett by
45,000 (56.5 percent) compared with Clinton's 19,164 and won Cobb by
30,000 (54.1 percent) while Clinton eked out a win of 7,209. Fulton County,
the state's most populous, rallied to Abrams with 72.3 percent of the vote.
Although she lost 19 Atlanta-area counties, she trounced Kemp in metro
Atlanta taking 56.5 percent of the vote (O'Connor 2019). As reported in Table
2.3, this showing was 4.2 points better than Clinton in 2016 and 7.5 points
above what Jason Carter managed. She won in the counties housing all of the
state's secondary cities: Athens, Augusta, Columbus, Macon, and Savannah.

Outside of metropolitan areas, Abrams carried fourteen counties, all but
one of which was in the Black Belt, a productive agricultural band in which

the African American population was traditionally concentrated. Only two of the non-urban counties in Abrams's column cast more than 10,000 ballots total. Her efforts to mobilize infrequent voters in rural Georgia, a task assigned to three paid staff, paid few dividends as Abrams got smaller vote shares than Carter in 2014 or Obama in 2012 (Suggs 2018; O'Connor 2019).

Upon completion of the recount, Abrams acknowledged that Brian Kemp would become governor, but she refused to concede. She explained that while she recognized reality, she continued to believe that the conduct of the election was so marred by the kinds of problems she had emphasized during the campaign that she questioned the fairness of the process and the justice of the result. "Let's be clear: This is not a speech of concession because concession means to acknowledge an action is right, true or proper. As a woman of conscience and faith, I cannot concede that" (Blinder and Fausset 2018a).

In the end, there were simply not enough provisional or absentee ballots available for Abrams to overtake Kemp. Even awarding *all* of the uncounted provisional ballots to Abrams would have left her 7,800 votes short of forcing a runoff. Adding the 6,994 rejected absentee ballots to her count still could not pull Kemp below 50 percent. Of course, there is no way that all of the rejected provisional and absentee ballots had been for Abrams. The conflict over counting absentee ballots centered on Gwinnett where a federal judge ordered the inclusion of those initially rejected for trivial errors. In the final count, rejected absentee ballots equaled 0.52 percent of the ballots cast (this includes the 1,632 rejected absentee votes) in Gwinnett. That compares with 0.17 percent statewide but is not that much more than 0.41 percent in DeKalb which has been governed for years by Democrats.

Both before and after the election there were complaints about the voting process. A few precincts experienced problems with equipment, and in some locations voters waited in long lines before registering their choices. These difficulties, regrettable as they are, do not appear to have been widespread. The Fox exit poll reports that 62 percent of the respondents found it very easy to vote, and another 25 percent judged the process "somewhat easy." Only 2 percent rated it very difficult. Respondents less positive about the voting process were more likely to favor Abrams who got support from 65 percent of those who judged voting very difficult compared with 44 percent support from those for whom it was very easy. An unknowable component that might have prompted a runoff or, conceivably, delivered an Abrams victory is those who were frustrated by long lines and left without voting.

Abrams's warning that some eligible voters would be thwarted in their efforts to register choices resonated, to a degree, with many Georgians. Just under half (49 percent) in the Fox survey were "very confident" that eligible voters could participate. A quarter of the respondents were "somewhat confident" while 8 percent were "not at all confident." More than 90 percent of those who had just left the voting booth but had serious questions about access favored Abrams. Kemp won the support of 78 percent of those very confident that the eligible could cast ballots. Despite losing, Abrams nonetheless led the Democratic ticket both in the number of votes (1,93,685) and the percentage (48.8 percent). As reported in Table 2.4, the next strongest Democrat, the candidate for secretary of state, trailed Abrams by 33,375 votes. Abrams's vote share is the highest for any non-incumbent Democrat since 1998, when Democrats won multiple offices. Due to Abrams's showing, Kemp did not lead the GOP ticket, finishing 61,689 votes and 2.9 percentage points behind the incumbent agriculture commissioner. The model in Table 1.6 estimates that, ceteris paribus, Black candidates do 3.5 percentage points less well than White candidates. Abrams performed better than the model, as did the 2018 Black candidates nominated for school superintendent and insurance commissioner. The Black candidates polled 47 and 47.5 percent of the vote, respectively, compared with the average for the five White Democratic statewide nominees of 47.9 percent. In Georgia, by 2018, African American

Table 2.4 2018 Statewide Election Results

	Democrat		Republican	
	%	#	%	#
Governor	48.8	1,923,685	50.2	1,978,408
Lt. Governor	48.4	1,828,566	51.6	1,951,738
Secretary of State	48.7	1,890,310	49.1	1,906,588
Attorney General	48.7	1,880,807	51.3	1,981,563
Commissioner of Agriculture	46.9	1,803,383	53.1	2,040,097
School Superintendent	47	1,814,499	50.4	1,944,963
Commissioner of Labor	47.5	1,830,061	52.5	2,019,389
PSC, District 3	47.6	1,838,020	49.7	1,917,656
PSC, District 5	47.2	1,820,868	50.3	1,937,599

Source: Georgia Secretary of State.

Democrats paid little if any racial "tax." Abrams paid none at all and the mean for the three African Americans competing statewide was 47.8 percent. That the Black candidates in 2018 performed as well as their White fellow partisans indicates that White attitudes have changed. This change may have come about as a result of familiarity with African Americans competing statewide. Since the turn of the century just over a third (sixteen of forty-five) Democrats competing statewide have been African American as have four of the nine successful Democratic candidacies in this century.

Table 2.5 presents the results of a model estimating the vote share for Georgia Democratic candidates. For the most part this includes the same variables as used in Chapter 1 except that no Hispanics have run statewide in Georgia, so that variable was deleted. While the minus sign indicates that a Black Democrat did slightly worse than a White Democrat, the relationship is not significant and the coefficient is half the size of its standard error. Only two variables were significant. Democrats ran much worse when challenging a Republican incumbent and Democrats have performed worse since 2002. In Georgia when Black candidates lose, it is due more to their party than their race.

Table 2.5 Correlates of the Share of the Democratic Vote Won by Georgia Democratic Candidates, 1989–2018

	Coefficient	Std. Error
Democratic Incumbent	2.922	2.377
Democratic Statewide Office	−2.44	2.581
Dem. Other Office	−2.247	1.904
GOP Incumbent	−6.145**	2.119
GOP Statewide Office	.476	2.447
GOP Other Office	−2.292	1.957
Black Democrats	−.856	1.758
Democratic Normal Vote	.129	.254
Post 2002	−3.95*	1.838
Constant	46.189	
Adj. R^2	.38	
N	67	

**$p < 0.01$; *$p < 0.05$

Coattails

Abrams failed in her effort to become the nation's first Black, woman governor but her mobilization efforts paid dividends for Democrats running in the Atlanta area. The highest profile victory saw the upset of Rep. Karen Handel in Georgia's Sixth Congressional District by Lucy McBath, an outspoken advocate of restricting access to guns motivated by the killing of her teenage son, shot by a man angered at loud music. McBath, a first-time candidate, succeeded where Jon Ossoff had come up short despite being the beneficiary of more than $30,000,000 spent on his behalf in a 2017 special election (Bullock and Owen 2018). McBath eked out a victory of fewer than 3,300 votes, while Abrams carried the district by about 11,000 votes.[11]

Abrams's coattails came close to defeating the Republican in the district north and east of the Sixth. In the Seventh District four-term incumbent Rob Woodall escaped losing to another Democratic novice by 433 votes, and early in 2019 he announced he would not seek reelection in 2020. Abrams's margin in the Seventh District was almost 4,000 votes. Democrats also picked up fourteen state House districts and a pair of Senate seats in metro Atlanta, many of them in the districts Handel and Woodall represented. These were the biggest setbacks experienced by Republicans since they took control of the legislature in the first half of the 2000s.[12] Republicans held on to fifteen seats, twelve in the House, with less than 55 percent of the vote. Most of these marginal seats are in metro Atlanta. Abrams's surge did not rise high enough to sweep out these Republicans, but in some districts it revealed a vulnerability not previously apparent, making these legislators GOP targets in 2020.

Postmortem

Losing, but especially losing narrowly, causes great pain. Most defeated candidates withdraw from public view, at least temporarily, as they come to grips with the realization that their dreams have not come true and may never materialize. Abrams did not disappear but remained very much in the news. In the immediate afterglow of her strong performance, she indicated that she was pondering whether to challenge Senator David Perdue (R) in 2020, wait until 2022 and a rematch against Governor Kemp, or join the scrum of Democrats vying to challenge President Trump's reelection. Early in 2019, media reports linked her to Democratic presidential front-runner Joe Biden as his running mate, should he be nominated. Her near success and her verbal skills made her much in demand by those seeking interesting speakers. She even appeared on NPR's "Wait, Wait! Don't Tell Me."

The high point came when she appeared on national television to give the Democratic response to President Trump's 2019 State of the Union address. Although the reason for her choice was not articulated, it is suspected that Senator Chuck Schumer (D-NY) tapped her as part of his courtship designed to get her to challenge Perdue. She had the highest name recognition of any of the potential Democratic candidates, and she had demonstrated an ability to raise campaign funds and to mobilize Black turnout to Obama levels. Ultimately she declined to compete for the Senate seat.

Abrams continued challenging what she sees as problems with Georgia elections and established Fair Fight Georgia, which has frequently sued the state. Four months after the election, Abrams continued to believe that her loss resulted from illegal actions by her opponent acting in his official capacity. "The results were purely and fully attributable to voter suppression," she told the *New York Times* (Chira 2019). Abrams's accusations about the fairness of the election have been taken up by public figures around the country. Using language that strikes similar notes to Donald Trump's explanation for why he lost the popular vote, Abrams's allies point to malfeasance by election officials. Democratic senators Cory Booker, Kamala Harris, and Sherrod Brown, have accused Republicans of stealing the election, alluding to Abrams's charges of voter suppression (Thrush and Peters 2018; Fausset 2018c). Hillary Clinton joined in with, "Stacey Abrams should be governor leading that state right now" (Chira 2019). Claims that the election was "stolen" are difficult, if not impossible, to prove. The head of Georgia's Common Cause branch and a former Abrams's staffer acknowledges that "None of our groups has hard data on exactly what happened. We have no way of knowing, no paper trail" (Chira 2019).[13]

Fair Fight Action went to court once Abrams conceded with a sixty-six-page complaint alleging that Georgia's electoral system violates the Fourteenth and Fifteenth Amendments and the Voting Rights Act (Fausset 2018c). The suit asked that the state be barred from purging individuals who had not voted recently and that the 1.4 million who had been removed from the lists be reinstated. The suit also asked that steps be taken to eliminate long lines on Election Day. Another portion of the suit sought to enjoin further use of voting machines that have no paper trail. This became moot in 2019 when the legislature authorized purchase of a touch screen system that prints out a receipt showing the voter's choices that the voter deposits in the ballot box. Finally the suit asked that Section 3 of the Voting Rights Act be invoked to restore Georgia's status as a jurisdiction needing federal preclearance of all changes involving elections before implementation. Georgia had been subject to preclearance of its election-related changes until 2013 when the Supreme Court struck down the Section 4 triggers of the Voting Rights Act for being outdated.

Abrams's claims of voter suppression gained traction when the Democratic majority on the US House Oversight and Reform Committee sought records from Georgia and requested that Governor Brian Kemp and the new secretary of state, Brad Raffensperger (R), appear before the committee to answer questions about the conduct of the 2018 general election and the state's election system more broadly. Of especial concern to the committee were documents concerning the elimination of 1.4 million registrants post-2012, the closure of 200 precincts, the long lines waiting to vote in Atlanta, Kemp's allegations that Democrats had tried to hack the state's election database, and his refusal to step down as secretary of state overseeing the election in which he competed (Hallerman 2019).

The ACLU filed suit in early 2019 charging that the state's four largest counties were unprepared for the surge in turnout and failed to provide enough voting stations, so that the delays in getting signed in to cast a ballot effectively denied some people the right to vote. Officials responsible for conducting elections in Cobb, DeKalb, and Fulton counties blamed the long lines on a lack of voting machines, which they attributed to the hundreds that federal judge Amy Totenberg had sequestered in response to a law suit claiming that the state's voting machines could be hacked. Plaintiffs had asked Totenberg to set aside a sample of voting machines for testing but release the others, a request not honored by Election Day (Niesse 2018b). The issue became moot when the General Assembly replaced all of the state's voting machines. Abrams's defeat did nothing to weaken her fundraising ability. During the first six months of 2019, Fair Fight Action took in $3.9 million, 90 percent of it coming from non-Georgians (Salzer 2019). The group has provided funding for more than fifty candidates, along with groups opposing efforts to limit access to abortion.

Her continued ability to attract substantial funding, coupled with the abortion issue, could prove decisive should Abrams decide to challenge Kemp's reelection in 2022. The governor had promised during the 2018 campaign to support the nation's most restrictive abortion law. In 2019 he honored that pledge when he signed a fetal heartbeat bill—a law that largely banned abortions once a fetal heartbeat could be detected by a physician, which is usually about six weeks into a pregnancy.[14] The legislation narrowly passed in the state House; several suburban Republicans, whose ranks suffered in 2018, avoided voting for the bill. Its passage threatened the lucrative film industry, which pumped $9.5 billion into the state's economy in 2018 and provided 92,000 jobs (Newkirk and Sakoui 2019). Netflix, Disney, and other major studios threatened to pull out of Georgia if the new law went into effect on January 1, 2020. A reduction in the filming of movies and television programs would negate the benefits stemming from the huge tax breaks the state had offered to attract the industry. Implementation of the law was delayed when the ACLU sued to block enforcement, and even the law's supporters acknowledged that the statute would probably have to pass muster before the US Supreme Court before taking effect. Nonetheless, the law provides yet another motivator for urban, well-educated White women—a group that can determine the outcome in close elections. Abrams firmly opposed the law but also opposed threats by Hollywood to boycott the state, urging an alternative strategy of remaining in Georgia and helping in the fight to overturn the statute. Kemp, aware of the electoral consequences of the "heartbeat bill," launched his reelection bid much earlier than previous governors and raised almost three-quarters of a million dollars during the second quarter of 2019 (Fowler 2019).

Despite losing the governorship, observers see in Abrams's near miss the rumblings of dramatic change in Georgia politics that could extend beyond the confines of the Peach State. As Bullock told a reporter with the *Los Angeles Times* right after the election, "there's been a flashing red light for Republicans—be careful! You're running out of votes! Now that flashing red light has been replaced by a siren" (Jarvie 2018b). Raphael Warnock, pastor at Atlanta's Ebenezer Baptist Church where Martin Luther King preached, sees in Abrams's candidacy the birth of dramatic change. "We are seeing unfold before our very eyes a new South that is progressive and inclusive and increasingly embracing of the future. Georgia will never be the same because of her candidacy" (Jarvie 2018b). NBC's "Meet the Press" host Chuck Todd took notice of Abrams's near miss and devoted a section of the March 10, 2019, broadcast to speculating on whether Georgia might vote Democratic in the 2020 presidential election. Emory University political scientist Andra Gillespie concludes, "There is no longer a reason for any concern about Black candidates being viable in statewide races in the Deep South" (Newkirk et al. 2018).

Wrap-Up

Why did Abrams come up in short in Georgia? The simplest answer is that Georgia remains a red state and she suffered the same fate as every non-incumbent Democrat during the previous twenty years. Abrams would give another answer. She would attribute her defeat to unfairness in the electoral system and incompetence that suppressed the minority vote, although hard evidence to support such a claim is scarce.

Despite not winning, Abrams promoted the fortunes of the Democratic Party, advancing the time at which it will begin winning statewide contests and may reclaim majority status in the legislature. She reduced the margin by which top-of-the-ticket Republicans win by almost 75 percent.

The demographic time bomb that Democrats have been awaiting to demolish GOP control did not go off but continued to tick. Abrams scored very well with minorities and rolled up impressive margins among younger votes. She made headway among educated White women, although they, as a group, remained in the GOP corner. She made headway in encouraging infrequent and non-voters to participate. African Americans, inspired by her candidacy, turned out in record numbers for a midterm election but other groups also voted at extraordinarily high rates for a midterm.

The game plan that Kemp followed worked well for him, but this may be the last time a Republican can secure office with a rural coalition. For the better part of a century the rural-urban divide in Georgia has run canyon deep, so Kemp's decision to appeal to small town and crossroads Georgia is nothing new. The Talmadges thrived for decades with a similar game plan. But Georgians increasingly live in high rises and communities with dictatorial home owners' associations. Only an extraordinarily large and cohesive rural vote saved Kemp's bacon, but urban Republicans cautioned that 2018 may mark the last triumph of the red necks (Bluestein 2018i).

There is yet another possibility. The decisive element may have been something completely out of the hands of either candidate. Had Senate Democrats realized that with the nuclear option having been invoked for Supreme Court nominees they had no chance of derailing the Kavanaugh nomination and therefore not tried so hard to defeat it, Abrams and Florida's Andrew Gillum and numerous other Democrats who lost tight contests might be in office today. Making Kavanaugh's confirmation a partisan litmus test awakened largely disinterested Republicans and eroded the enthusiasm gap working to Democrat's advantage. Stacey Abrams succeeded in getting Democrats to vote at presidential-election-year levels. She lost when Republicans also turned out in greater numbers rather than at the usual midterm levels that she had counted on.

In her near miss, Abrams benefitted from several of the conditions that scholars have identified as facilitating Black electoral success. She competed for an open seat and headed a united Democratic Party, while her opponent had emerged from a bitter runoff (Sonenshein 1990; Strickland and Whicker 1992; Jeffries 1999). She had adequate funding and had served an apprentice-ship in the state House, but had not held statewide office as a steppingstone (Sonenshein 1990; Frederick and Jeffries 2009). Black turnout was strong but so was White turnout, and Abrams proved unable to make further inroads among Whites (Grose 2011). As noted earlier, she ran as a progressive, rather than following the advice of some that a Black candidate should adopt the Wilder pose and present as a moderate-to-conservative, focus on law and order, and mount a conciliatory campaign (Sonenshein 1990; Jeffries 1999; Frederick and Jeffries 2009). That she came so close while charting a liberal course may reflect changing expectations among White voters or the greater role played by an expanding minority electorate.

3

Florida

Andrew Gillum Narrowly Loses 2018 Governor's Race

With the assistance of Amy Benner, David Bonanza,
Anthony Cilluffo, and Aida Vazquez-Soto

The 2018 gubernatorial election in the nation's most competitive, most racially and ethnically diverse, and largest swing state generated national and international attention. It was the first time in years that both major political parties had highly competitive primaries. Tallahassee Mayor Andrew Gillum emerged as the underdog victor in the Democratic primary, and Congressman Ron DeSantis upset a favorite son in the Republican primary.

Both candidates attracted national endorsements and visits: US Senator Bernie Sanders for Gillum and President Donald Trump for DeSantis. The two candidates represented the ideological extremes of their respective parties—"the far right and the far left" (Taylor 2018).[1]

Democrats were hungry for a gubernatorial win after having lost five straight. (President Barack Obama had won Florida twice—by 3.8 percent in 2008 and 0.9 percent in 2012—but those were presidential, not midterm, elections.) Republicans counted on the party's history of superior voter mobilization and an anti-socialism message.

Gillum came close to being Florida's first African American governor. Part of the explanation for this lies with the state's rapid growth over the past fifty years, generating significant changes in its population. Florida is now the nation's third largest state; more than one-third of its registered voters are non-White. Moreover, the growing political clout of the younger, more racially/ethnically diverse, and more liberal generations (Gen Xers, Millennials, Gen Zers)[2] has given rise to more diverse candidates throughout the state. In fact, two Gen X African American Democrats ran for statewide office in 2018—Gillum for governor and Sean Shaw for attorney general.[3] Both came up short, but Gillum came closer.[4]

African American Statewide Candidates in the New South. Charles S. Bullock, III, Susan
A. MacManus, Jeremy D. Mayer, and Mark J. Rozell, Oxford University Press. © Oxford University Press 2022.
DOI: 10.1093/oso/9780197607428.003.0003

The contest went down to the wire. Gillum, with his progressive platform and #BringItHome slogan, lost to the Trump-endorsed DeSantis by a scant 32,463 votes out of 8.4 million votes cast, requiring an automatic machine recount under Florida law. The contest had sharp racial overtones, largely driven by candidate commentaries and a proposed constitutional amendment on the ballot to restore the voting rights of convicted felons. Post-election analyses criticized Democrats for inadequate attention to voter registration and mobilization efforts and for poor outreach to Hispanics (Schale 2018; Grunwald and Caputo 2018).

Gillum's 2018 campaign and his new vision for how to achieve statewide Democratic victories in Florida reflect his knowledge of the growth and diversity of the state's racial and ethnic populations, the rise of younger generations, the state's closed-party primary system, the influence of national political figures (endorsements and funding), and the power of an inspirational life message. The Florida of today is quite different for Black candidates than it once was.

Florida's Racial History

The political history of Florida has long been driven by racial and ethnic conflict: for example, the Seminole Indian wars, slavery and emancipation, and Reconstruction followed by segregation, the communist revolution in Cuba, and the Hispanic and Haitian migration to the state. Racial and ethnic politics are projected to become even more important based on demographic projections showing continued growth and diversity of the state's minority populations. From 2019 to 2030, the Black population's share is projected to increase from 16.2 to 17.1 percent and Hispanics from 25.3 to 30.1 percent. The White non-Hispanic share is expected to decline from 55 to 49.2 percent.

Decades of high growth rates have transformed Florida into the proverbial melting pot of cultures. An influx of retirees from the North and immigrants from Latin America, the Caribbean, and more recently from Asian countries has led to Florida being labeled the "immigrant magnet" state (MacManus 2017). Today, one-third of the state's registered voters are *nonwhite*, but this group is hardly homogeneous. Within broad racial/ethnic groups (Blacks, Hispanics, Asians), there are significant socioeconomic and political differences, some driven by country of origin. Florida is no longer a state in which Black-White racial politics dominate.

Florida's Changing Black Voters

As early as 1900, nearly half of Florida's population (44 percent) was African American. Yet Blacks in Florida and elsewhere in the South were socially and economically deprived and politically repressed. Thus, many Blacks left the region seeking better opportunity in the North. During Reconstruction, immediately after the Civil War, Blacks actively participated in the political life of the state. They served in the Florida Legislature, and Floridian Josiah T. Walls became the first African American member of the US House of Representatives from Florida in 1870. Virtually all Black voters and officeholders of this era were Republicans.

But by 1900, White Democrats had recaptured all the important offices. Democratic primaries became the only meaningful elections, and Blacks were officially excluded by a rule requiring all primary voters to be White. Not until the US Supreme Court outlawed the White primary in *Smith* v. *Allwright* in 1944 were any Blacks registered as Democrats in Florida.

The Florida Legislature eliminated the poll tax in 1937, well before the Twenty-Fourth Amendment (1964) to the US Constitution barred it throughout the nation. Black voting began to increase after World War II, especially in the state's larger cities. By the early 1950s, about one-third of the state's eligible Blacks were registered to vote. But in many rural counties, threats, intimidation, and extralegal means still prevented Blacks from registering or voting.

Led by civil rights activists Harry T. Moore, C.K. Steele, and others, Black voting rose in the early 1960s. After the federal Voting Rights Act of 1965, Black registration and voting increased dramatically, as the threat of federal intervention eliminated the last official obstacles at the local level. However, White in-migration to the state, combined with African American out-migration, greatly diluted Black voting strength. More recently, African American political power has diminished because of a growing Hispanic population. The share of Florida's registered voters who are Black increased from 9.4 percent in 1994 to 13.3 percent in 2018, although there has been relatively little change since the 2008 election (see Figure 3.1). Latinos are now the state's largest minority, although they are less cohesive than Blacks in their voting patterns.

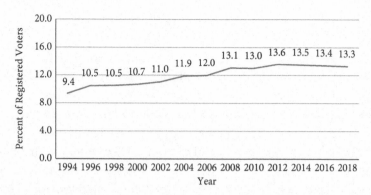

Figure 3.1 Share of Florida Registered Voters in General Elections Who Are Black

The percentage of Black registered voters increased since 1994, though little has changed since 2008.

Source: Florida Division of Elections General Election Book Closing statistics.

Black Trailblazers in Florida Government[5]

Blacks have been elected to office in both houses of the Florida Legislature, to the Florida Supreme Court, and to Congress (MacManus 2015). Gains came following passage of the federal Voting Rights Act, elimination of multi-member legislative districts, and court-ordered redistricting. Blacks have yet to win a statewide executive office—as governor or at the cabinet level.

Legislature
The first gains after Reconstruction occurred in the Florida Legislature. Joe Lang Kershaw was elected to the state legislature in 1968, followed in 1970 by the first Black female legislator, Miami attorney Gwen Cherry. The first Black state senators post-Reconstruction were elected in 1982: Arnett E. Girardeau from Jacksonville and Carrie Meek from Miami. The keys to even greater Black legislative successes were the adoption of single-member legislative districts in 1982 and federal court-ordered redistricting in 1992.

Congress
Black representation in Congress began after the redrawing of district lines in 1992 (required redistricting). In that year, three districts (two in South

Florida and one in Jacksonville) were crafted specifically with the intent to maximize the opportunity for Black representation in the congressional delegation to comply with the federal Voting Rights Act. Three Black Democrats were elected from those districts (Carrie Meek, Alcee Hastings, and Corrine Brown). Today, there are four Black Democrats in the state's twenty-seven-member congressional delegation.

Supreme Court

Governor Reubin Askew (D) appointed Joseph Hatchett to the Florida Supreme Court in 1975. Hatchett became the *first African American to win a statewide office*—not just in Florida, but in the South—when he won a contentious, racially charged election to keep the seat in 1976. (Also in 1976, Floridians changed the law so that future Supreme Court justices were subject to a retention vote only to keep them in office or turn them out.) Governor Bob Graham (D) appointed Leander Shaw to the Supreme Court in 1983. Shaw would later become Florida's first Black Chief Justice. Lawton Chiles (D) and Jeb Bush (R) placed the first African American woman on the Florida Supreme Court, Peggy Quince, in a rare joint appointment in 1998. A fourth justice, James E. C. Perry, was appointed by Governor Charlie Crist in 2009.

Executive Offices

Attempts by African Americans to win gubernatorial and cabinet posts in the post-Reconstruction period have mostly failed. Doug Jamerson lost his 1996 electoral bid to remain as commissioner of education, after appointment to the vacant seat by Governor Lawton Chiles in 1994. Sean Shaw, son of Chief Justice Leander Shaw, lost his race for attorney general in 2018.

Daryl L. Jones, a state senator from South Florida, finished third in the 2002 Democratic gubernatorial primary. In 2006, Democratic gubernatorial candidate Jim Davis selected Jones as his running mate. Had the Davis-Jones ticket won, Jones would have been the state's first African American to be elected statewide to a non-judicial post. But that honor went to Republican Jennifer Carroll, a former state legislator from Jacksonville, who was elected lieutenant governor in 2010 as the running mate of Governor Rick Scott. *It's not hard to see why Andrew Gillum's run for governor in 2018 mattered so much to Blacks and Florida Democrats.*

The Democratic Primary

Under Florida's closed-primary system, only voters registered as Democrats can vote in the Democratic primary; in 2018, it was held August 28. One of the nation's latest, it ended up one of the most competitive and expensive races ever, with a surprising winner—Andrew Gillum. The result was surprising not only because Gillum was Black but also because he had never led in any of the published pre-election polls, and he was the only non-millionaire among the candidates. Gillum, Mayor of Tallahassee, was first to announce his candidacy in March 2017, but he soon found himself in a strong, five-candidate field. He was followed into the race by Chris King, a wealthy entrepreneur from Orlando; Gwen Graham, a former congresswoman and daughter of former governor and US senator Bob Graham; Philip Levine, former mayor of Miami Beach; and Jeff Greene, a Palm Beach billionaire real-estate investor, who in 2016 had lost a primary race for US Senate to African American Kendrick Meek.[6]

From the start Gillum was the underdog, lagging far behind Graham, the perennial frontrunner. Each of the five major candidates entered the race with a calculus of how to build a coalition of Democratic voters that would take them to victory, with around 35 percent of the vote. In the end, Gillum wound up with 34 percent and Graham 31 percent. For Florida Democrats, the key (base) constituencies in 2018 were: women, minorities, young voters, LGBTQ communities, unions, Jewish voters, and environmentalists.

Florida's Democratic Registrants

Florida's registered Democrats are considerably more diverse than either Republicans or NPAs (No Party Affiliation). More than half (52 percent) are persons of color, with Blacks making up a considerably larger share than Hispanics (29 percent vs. 17 percent). Women are 58 percent of the registrants, men 40 percent—a much larger gender gap than among either Republicans or NPAs. A majority of female Democrats are non-White. In age, Democratic registrants are considerably younger than Republicans, but not as young as NPAs (see Figure 3.2). Geographically, two-thirds of all registered Democrats live in the Miami, Orlando, and Tampa media markets—the state's most racially/ethnically diverse.[7] The candidates themselves reflected the party's diversity: Gillum (race), Graham (gender), Gillum and King (younger generations), Levine and Greene (religion).

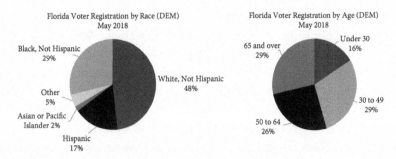

Figure 3.2 Florida Registered Democrats by Race and Age
More than half of Florida's registered Democrats are non-White; nearly half less
than 50 years of age.
Source: Author's analysis of Florida Division of Elections Florida Voter Registration System
(FVRS) data.

It was clear from the outset that Graham looked at party registration,
voting patterns, and turnout statistics and saw gender as key and women
voters as her critical base. "She took every opportunity to remind voters that
she's the only woman running in a five-person field" (Smiley 2018c). Gillum's
strategy of targeting minorities (Blacks and Hispanics) and young voters
was perceived by some Democrats as riskier, based on their traditionally
low turnout rates in midterm elections. But he justified it this way: "We've
been losing this race for governor repeatedly for the last 20 years, for the last
five consecutive races because we have failed to nominate a candidate who
has the ability to move more of our voters who typically don't participate in
midterm elections . . . . Many of those voters are black voters, they're brown
voters, they're poor voters and I honestly feel like I offer the best opportunity in November to win a general election. I believe we have the ability to
move more of those voters to the polls than anybody else running" (Capitol
News Service 2018). Both Levine and Greene hoped to benefit from the large
Jewish vote in Democrat-rich South Florida and that of the area's environ-
mentally conscious Democrats worried about rising sea levels.

Issues and Experience: General Consensus, but
Different Emphasis

Initially, the big issues to Florida Democrats (not in order of importance)
were education, environment, the economy, healthcare, gun control,

minority and voting rights, criminal justice, and immigration. Democrats had relatively little disagreement on these issues. Higher levels of consensus are not uncommon in a highly competitive multi-candidate *primary* in a sharply partisan-divided state. The candidates emphasized different issues, with Graham pushing education, the environment, the economy, and women and children's issues, whereas Gillum focused on education, healthcare, wages, minority rights, and the Stand Your Ground law.

The candidates also heavily touted their experience credentials vis-à-vis their opponents. The mayors (Levine, Gillum) both stressed their unmatched *executive* and leadership experience, while Gillum also claimed his fifteen years in office (2003–2018),[8] first as a city commission member and then mayor, made him the most experienced of the bunch. Graham touted her congressional experience and position as an attorney for the Leon County School District. Greene frequently talked about his negative experiences as a losing candidate, with the state party's outreach, voter mobilization, and financial support (Greenblatt 2018). The candidate with the least experience in the political arena, Chris King, promoted his outsider role.

The Money: Outside Groups Contributed Heavily to Gillum

Although Gillum raised far less than his four opponents, he had significant financial support from activities financed by groups promoting Black candidates and a progressive agenda. Collective PAC, which supports Black candidates, ran attack ads against Graham and funded get-out-the-vote (GOTV) efforts. Billionaire Tom Steyer and his NextGen group spent $1.4 million registering and turning out young voters, especially on college campuses. George Soros also contributed handily to Gillum. Color of Change PAC engaged in door-to-door campaigning for Gillum and hosted numerous events targeted to Black women (Schouten 2018). Phil Levine, Chris King, and Jeff Greene largely self-financed their campaigns. Gwen Graham benefitted from contributions from Emily's List and Ruth's List—both supportive of female pro-choice candidates.

Primary spending for the five candidates clearly showed Gillum in last place (Leary 2018): Philip Levine spent $37.7 million; Jeff Greene $34.7 million; Gwen Graham $16.3 million; Chris King $7.8 million; and Andrew Gillum $6.6 million. Gillum wore these numbers as a badge of honor: "The truth is, money doesn't vote, people do" (Ceballos and Haseman 2018).

TV Ads

Kantar Media's Campaign Media Analysis Group analyzed money spent on TV ads from January to early August and reported that candidates and political groups spent "at least $95 million on nearly 90,000 TV commercials" (Ceballos 2018b). "The deluge of ads in the crowded Democratic primary alone has so far cost at least $48 million, most of it fueled by personal cash from the wealthy crop of primary candidates and The Collective Super PAC." (See Figure 3.3.)

Levine started his ad campaign in January, ran the ads across all the state's ten media markets, and was the only candidate to target Spanish-speaking voters via TV ads. Greene didn't enter the race until June but spent the most—nearly $22 million (Ceballos 2018c). Gillum had limited funds for TV ads. He didn't run one statewide until July 25 (Lemongello 2018).

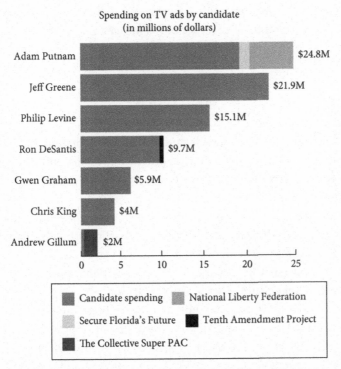

Figure 3.3 TV Ad Spending by Primary Candidates through Early August

Note: Putnam and DeSantis were Republican candidates.

Source: Kantar Media's Campaign Media Analysis Group, as reported by Ft. Myers *News-Press.*

Frontrunner Graham was hit heavily by TV attack ads run by a union supporting Levine (Unite Here) and by her opponents, most notably Jeff Greene. Three weeks before the primary, Greene ran a TV commercial "mauling" Graham for her family's involvement in a megamall project (American Dream Miami) that environmentalists strongly opposed due to its proximity to the Everglades watershed: the ad strongly inferred Graham was personally profiting from the mall. Graham vehemently fought back against Greene's characterization of her as anti-environment, ran a counter TV ad, and said she had "removed myself from my family companies" and put her interests into a blind trust (Powers 2018). To this day, some Graham supporters blame Greene's late entry into the race and his nonstop negative ads for her narrow defeat (Kam 2018).

Gillum was not subjected to vicious TV ads during the primary for two reasons. First, he was considered a long shot, with little chance of winning. Second, none of Gillum's opponents wanted to risk losing the critical Black vote in the general election should they have secured the party's nomination. Gillum's way of capturing Democratic voters' attention via TV was more through debates and local coverage of his in-person appearances. (Gillum had more campaign events during the primary than any of his competitors.)

The Debates

As the campaign progressed, each candidate grew more desperate to break away from the rest of the field. Debates provided such an opportunity. There were five formal debates in 2018. The first three featured just four candidates. Greene joined them in the last two.

Graham stressed her ability to win statewide with her moderate stances and her ability to win over some Republicans, particularly suburban moms. Graham had won a North Florida congressional seat in 2014—"I'm the only one who has beaten a Republican and I beat a Republican in a Republican wave year in a Republican district" (Smiley 2018c).

Gillum attacked Graham for not supporting President Barack Obama enough while in Congress and for not embracing a more progressive agenda. "Her votes . . . 54 percent of the time against Obama was not what I wanted from my member of Congress," he said (News Service of Florida 2018a). As the campaign moved forward, the rest of the field echoed Gillum's attack on Graham's lack of progressive "creds" (Dixon 2018b). But he did it best.

The Polls Missed the Gillum Surge

Published polls showed Graham entering 2018 as the frontrunner. Philip Levine briefly took over the top spot in the polls, which some attributed to his use of his personal wealth to "pour more than $10 million into TV ads" (Dixon 2018b; Wilson 2018). For most of the primary campaign, it looked as though it would be a down-to-the-wire race between Graham and Levine, although Greene looked competitive after he announced his candidacy. Gillum was written off by many, including the media, having received no major newspaper endorsements in his primary run. Some of the newspapers' hesitation was related to an FBI investigation of corruption in Tallahassee City Hall, although Gillum repeatedly claimed he was not a named suspect (Dixon 2018a).

Not once did Gillum lead in any widely published poll (posted on RealClearPolitics)—a big reason few expected him to best Graham. The polls had also failed to predict Trump's Florida victory two years prior. The two back-to-back misses promoted an election-night tweet from the well-respected Miami Herald Tallahassee Bureau Chief: "Can we use this Florida Democratic primary as the final proof that pollsters and political consultants have NO IDEA what voters are thinking and the media is foolish to parrot it?" (Klas 2018).

As it turned out, a private tracking poll conducted for the Gillum campaign by a little-known, progressive-focused survey firm (Change Research) did get it right—but these results were never made public. The firm's co-founder told WFSU-FM that the firm's success is attributable to use of Internet and social media methods targeting underrepresented groups (Hatter 2018). Gillum's targeted voters were Blacks and young Floridians—two such groups.

A few weeks ahead of the primary election, notably after Bernie Sanders's endorsement of Gillum on August 1, Gillum's campaign team began "telling anyone who would listen that their candidate was surging and would end up as the Democratic nominee for Florida governor. Few people listened" (Man and Swisher 2018). Unexpectedly, the surge was real. According to several pollsters addressing a group of Florida political consultants at a post-election conference,[9] focus groups and door-to-door interactive canvassing were much better detectors of Gillum's surge of support, especially among Black voters. (Several consultants in the audience offered an additional indicator—crowd size and energy—reminiscent of Trump in 2016.) Gillum himself acknowledged: "It is hard to reconcile sometimes what you see in polls with what you are experiencing on the streets" (Call 2018b). And it was Gillum's final well-publicized drive across the highways of Florida, designed to push his targeted bases to the polls, that made a difference.

Gillum's "Bring It Home" Bus Tour

From the outset, Gillum campaigned in Black churches and had the support of popular Black elected officials—male and female, notably US Representatives Alcee Hastings and Frederica Wilson, Mayors Wayne Messam of Miramar, Eric Jones of West Park, and Hazelle Rogers of Lauderdale Lakes, and State Representative Shevrin Jones. But it was his in-person visits near the end of the campaign that helped him turn out the Black vote in the midterm election.

At a noon rally in Tallahassee Monday, August 20, (two days after early voting began and eight days before the August 28 primary), Gillum launched his "Bring It Home" bus tour–three stops a day hitting media markets along all three coasts and in Central Florida (Call 2018d). The bus stops were primarily in communities with large concentrations of Black registrants and at venues drawing large crowds of minority and young voters (Man and Swisher 2018). One of the most significant stops was in Daytona Beach at Bethune-Cookman University, an historically Black university. He ended his tour on August 27, first in Gainesville, then at Florida A & M University (FAMU)—his alma mater, where he had been elected student body president (see Figure 3.4).

At FAMU, Gillum put the August 28 primary date in Black history context by noting that on August 28, 1955, Emmett Till had been killed by two White men in Mississippi and on that same date in 1963, Martin Luther King Jr. had delivered his powerful "I Have a Dream" speech. "You can imagine where I'm going with this," he told the FAMU crowd, which responded with loud cheers (McAuliffe 2018).

It was easy to see the payoff of these stops. A post-election analysis by the *South Florida Sun Sentinel* directly linked Gillum's appearance at an NAACP rally held August 28 on a Sunday afternoon in Fort Lauderdale with a surge in Black votes in Broward County (the state's largest Democratic stronghold) and in other big metro areas with large concentrations of minority voters: "Gillum told the audience that it was time to get a seat at the table to bring about real change . . . . The payoff: When Broward posted a big batch

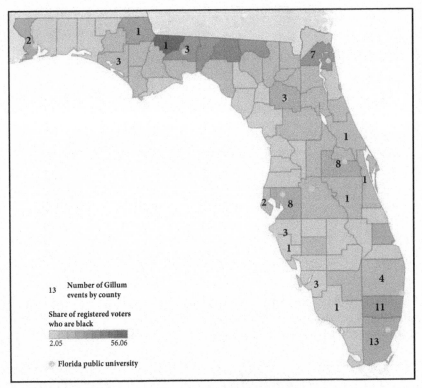

Figure 3.4 Gillum's Events in the Last Three Weeks before Primary Focused on Areas with High Share of Black Voters and College Campuses

Source: Created by author using data from media reports (campaign events) and Florida Division of Elections (race and ethnicity of voters).

of election results Tuesday night, what was a slight Graham lead turned into a slight Gillum lead ... Unofficial results show Gillum won 40 percent of the vote in Broward ... Gillum won all but one of the counties with large urban centers."[10] Gillum didn't rely just on the Black vote. Democratic Hispanics, most notably Puerto Ricans, White progressive Democrats, and college students were also important to his primary victory.

A Closer Look at the Primary Results

Gillum's victory on August 28 came as a shocker to everyone. *Gillum, the progressive, defeated Graham, the centrist* (see Figures 3.5a,b). Gillum never

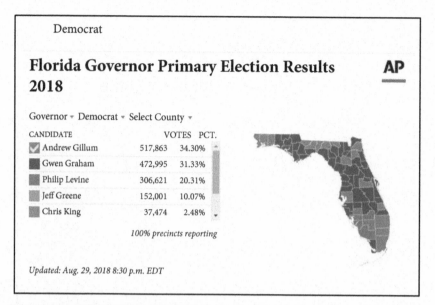

Figure 3.5a Gillum's Victory Focused on Large Metropolitan Areas and Areas with High Black Registration
Source: Associated Press as reported by the *Tampa Bay Times.*

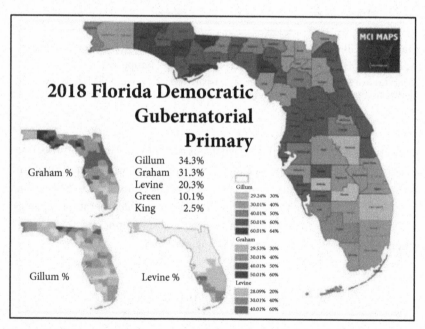

Figure 3.5b Intensity of Support: Individual Democratic Candidates by County
Source: Matthew Isbell, MCI Maps.

led in any poll, was not endorsed by any major Florida newspaper (Ogles 2018) and spent less than any other candidate[11] (Austin 2018). Gillum was aided by the fact that the large South Florida Democratic vote was split among Gillum, Graham (with South Florida family roots), Levine, and Greene. He won eighteen of sixty-seven counties. Levine, the third-place finisher, did best in a few southwest counties where environmental issues were most pressing due to a record-breaking algae bloom.

Gillum won with an unconventional primary campaign—a grassroots effort aimed at young and minority voters who historically have had the lowest turnout rates in August midterm primaries but who voted at higher rates than usual, driven by his charisma, attentiveness to their issues, and his diversity. His strategy reflected a knowledge of Florida's changing demographics and how to communicate with and energize different constituencies. He also benefitted from his opponents splitting the rest of the Democratic base. While it was natural that Gillum basked in his victory, it was short-lived. All it took was a look at the Republican primary election results. Trump-supported Ron DeSantis had swamped longtime Republican favorite son, Adam Putnam.

The Republican Primary

The Republican primary was not as competitive as the Democratic one. It was pretty much over after a December 2017 tweet by President Trump in support of Congressman DeSantis. DeSantis was not even in the race at the time, but he entered it shortly thereafter—unofficially on January 5 on Fox News early morning show, *Fox and Friends*, and officially on January 29, 2018. Most telling was that DeSantis (from Ponte Vedra Beach, the Jacksonville area) made his formal announcement in southeast Florida (Boca Raton) and gave a speech at a Statesman of the Year event in Palm Beach County—intentionally promoting his strong connection to Trump, whose Mar-A-Lago resort is located there.

The polls were never close. Putnam supporters hung on to hope that Florida Republicans would see DeSantis as too right-wing to win. Putnam was long considered a shoo-in for the Republican nomination and next in line for governor. After all, he had been elected to the state House in 1996 (at 22 years of age), to the US House in 2000, and to agriculture commissioner in 2010; he was the only candidate who had won a statewide race. But even with his massive war chest advantage, an extensive grassroots strategy, and the endorsements of major Republican officials, Putnam couldn't compete with a Trump-endorsed Fox News star.

Florida's Registered Republicans

Florida's Republicans are far less racially/ethnically diverse than either Democrat or NPA registrants, and Hispanics make up a much larger share of the party's minority registrants than Blacks. Republicans are also considerably older than either Democrat or NPA registrants. Women make up 50 percent of the GOP registrants, men 49 percent. (See Figure 3.6.) Geographically, Republicans are less concentrated than Democrats, although nearly half live in the famous I-4 Corridor—the Tampa and Orlando media markets (Central Florida).[12]

Putnam's campaign heavily targeted Republican super voters—older, rural, and suburban voters—while DeSantis focused on ramping up turnout among sporadic Republicans, who traditionally vote at much lower rates in midterm elections but really loved Trump: suburban women, gun owners, religious conservatives, agricultural communities, some Hispanics, and working-class Whites. *Both* candidates recognized the popularity of Trump. Putnam repeatedly touted his support for the president on the campaign trial, but DeSantis had Trump's endorsement. At a huge rally in Tampa, Trump labeled DeSantis as "a true leader, a proud veteran, a tough, brilliant cookie" (Caputo 2018c). The day before the primary,

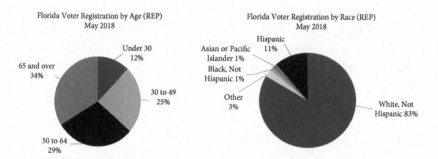

Figure 3.6 Florida Republicans are Older and Overwhelmingly White

Source: Author's analysis of Florida Division of Elections Florida Voter Registration System (FVRS) data.

Trump delivered one final tweet, again emphasizing his total support of DeSantis for governor.

Issues, Money, and Strategies

As with the Democrats, the Republican candidates generally agreed on the major issues of concern to their party members, particularly the economy, education, environment, government regulation, the Second Amendment, and immigration and border security. Their issue positions differed most on the environment (the role of US Sugar in polluting estuaries and causing toxic algae bloom), immigration (E-Verify), the concealed weapons permitting process (Putnam's mishandling of it as agriculture commissioner, not the Second Amendment), and testing requirements under the No Child Left Behind education act (Rohrer 2018; Z. Anderson 2018). Racial overtones were largely missing in the primary, mostly because both candidates expected Gwen Graham to win the Democratic nomination, not Gillum. By far, their biggest battles were more along the lines of who understood Florida issues and "more about gut level GOP politics" (Z. Anderson 2018).

Early on, it was clear that it was a classic insider (Putnam) vs. outsider (DeSantis) race. Putnam's campaign slogan was "Florida First." At virtually every campaign stop, he touted the depth of his knowledge about the state. DeSantis, in turn, cast Putnam as a Tallahassee insider and Tallahassee (the state capital) as a place desperately in need of a cleanup (Smiley 2018a). DeSantis described Putnam as "a career politician." "He is a transactional Republican, and he is the choice for every insider up in Tallahassee. He's the crown prince of crony capitalism. He's the toast of Tallahassee" (Roulette 2018). DeSantis's lead consultant justified his candidate's emphasis on national politics: "We are in a political environment where far more attention is being paid to what is happening in Washington than what is happening in Tallahassee" (Caputo 2018).

There was no contest in fundraising. By mid-August, Putnam had raised $38.8 million, DeSantis $17.6 million. Putnam spent $21.9 million to DeSantis's $10.5 million on TV ads (Contorno 2018a). DeSantis took advantage of free media and the Trump endorsement. The ever-present insider vs. outsider comparisons spilled over into fundraising. Putnam criticized DeSantis for relying so much on contributions from outside Florida. DeSantis, in turn, attacked Putnam for relying more on Floridians with deep pockets than small donors. For much of the primary campaign, DeSantis raised his funds from out-of-state donors, many of whom were small contributors who had received a fundraising letter from DeSantis. As DeSantis continued to lead Putnam in the polls, contributions from Floridians increased (Ceballos 2018a). In the end, it didn't matter. As political editor of the *Tampa Bay Times* put it: DeSantis "spent half as much."[13]

Putnam adopted a traditional grassroots strategy. A flurry of his signature "Up & Adam" breakfasts followed his entry into the race. He was endorsed by forty-five of the state's sixty-seven sheriffs (Dunkelberger 2018). September's Hurricane Irma saw him making numerous appearances in his role as commissioner of agriculture and consumer services. The bulk of his *many* appearances at festivals, county fairs, barbecues, parades, and car shows (Greenblatt 2018) were aimed at key constituency groups in rural and suburban areas.

DeSantis chose a cable-TV centric approach. More than 60 percent of his "appearances" were via the Fox News and Fox Business channels. His most noted TV ad was aired repeatedly as part of regular news coverage on FNC. The ad linked him to Trump's hip: "A new 30-second commercial . . . jokingly shows him teaching his toddler to 'build the wall!' with play blocks, reading 'Art of the Deal' as a bedtime story, teaching his kids to read a Trump campaign sign—'Make America Great Again!'" (Caputo and Cook 2018). DeSantis targeted Trump voters via Fox News appearances, ads, and big-stage events with Fox's Sean Hannity and Donald Trump, Jr. (Man 2018). He was convinced that "Trump's supporters [were] enough for victory on Aug. 28" (Mahoney 2018a). Post-primary revelations of the campaign's internal surveys confirmed the candidate's confidence in this strategy.[14]

Not Even Close

The Associated Press called the race for DeSantis just minutes after the polls closed (Politico Pro Staff 2018). DeSantis won handily in the state's heavily populated coastal areas—home to more older voters, many of whom were retirees who had moved to Florida because of its environmental assets. DeSantis's pledge to do something about algae bloom and red tide and his attacks on Putnam for taking campaign funds from Big Sugar had an impact. Putnam fared best in the more rural, agricultural parts of the state and in Tallahassee. (See Figures 3.7a,b.)

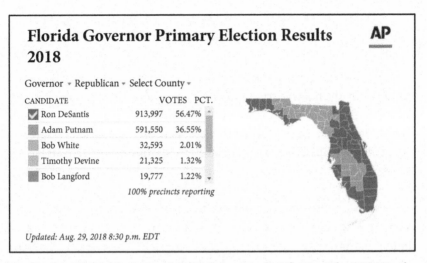

Figure 3.7a Florida Governor GOP Primary Results: The Outsider Wins Easily
Source: Associated Press as reported by the *Tampa Bay Times.*

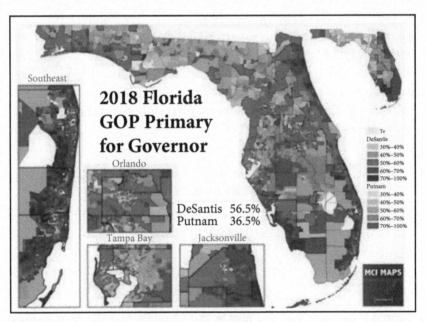

Figure 3.7b Florida Governor GOP Primary: Intensity of Vote by County
Source: Matthew Isbell, MCI Maps.

Analysis of Primary Voter Turnout: Republicans Best Democrats

Heading into the general election, Democrats and Republicans alike were energized by the higher turnout rate in 2018 than in 2014. Competitive primaries on both sides of the aisle were undoubtedly a major contributing factor. Altogether, the seven candidates for governor had raised a staggering $168 million.[15] But as in past midterm elections, the turnout rate for Florida Republicans was higher than for Democrats—37 percent vs. 32 percent. (See Figure 3.8.)

There were also demographic differences in who came out to vote, with a particularly large racial gap. Whites were the most likely racial and ethnic group to vote (32 percent of registered White voters voted), although Blacks were not far behind (29 percent). Hispanics, Asians, and other racial groups were much less likely to vote in the primary (16–17 percent). (See Figure 3.9.) Age differences were also striking. Only 9 percent of registered voters younger than thirty voted, compared with 45 percent of those aged sixty-five and older (see Figure 3.10). There was also a gender gap, with women slightly more likely to vote than men (29 percent vs. 27 percent).

Florida's late primary meant that both campaigns had only a little more than two months to sell themselves to the state's twelve million registered voters. Each candidate was well aware of Florida's history of nail-biter, statewide general elections and growing ranks of independents.

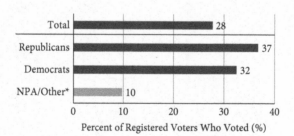

Figure 3.8 Florida Primary Turnout by Party: Higher among Republicans than Democrats

Note: *When only one party fields a candidate for a race, all registrants can vote in that primary (universal primary). Some legislative primaries were contested by only one party.

Source: Author's analysis of Florida Division of Elections Florida Voter Registration System (FVRS) data.

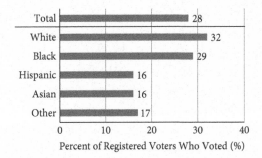

Figure 3.9 Florida Primary Turnout by Race and Ethnicity.
Far more Blacks turned out to vote than Hispanics

Note: Whites, Blacks, Asians, and other races are only non-Hispanic. Hispanics are of any race. Asians includes Pacific Islanders.

Source: Author's analysis of Florida Division of Elections Florida Voter Registration System (FVRS) data.

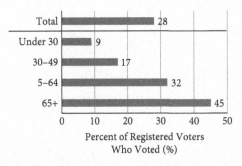

Figure 3.10 Florida Primary Turnout by Age: Significant Age Gap in Voting.
Source: Author's analysis of Florida Division of Elections Florida Voter Registration System (FVRS) data.

Selection of Lieutenant Governor Running Mates

Shortly after the primary, Florida's gubernatorial candidates picked their running mates, a selection usually done with attention to "strategic considerations such as party unity, campaign financing needs, or geographical, ideological, racial/ethnic, or gender balance" (Kilgore, 2018a). DeSantis's selection of State Representative Jeanette Nuñez, Miami, fit that model.[16] She brought gender, ethnic (Cuban American), and geographical (South Florida) balance to the GOP ticket. She also brought in-depth knowledge of Florida issues (something DeSantis lacked) from her experience and her position as House Speaker pro tempore.

In contrast, Gillum chose as running mate his former opponent Chris King, who had finished last in the Democratic primary with less than 3 percent of the vote. The *Tallahassee Democrat* described the selection as "almost as startling as the mayor's [Gillum's] victory in the primary" (Cotterrell 2018). Gillum said his choice of King was more about choosing someone he could trust, feel comfortable with, and who shared his philosophical beliefs than about balancing the ticket (Koh 2018). The choice signaled Gillum's strategy to continue targeting progressive voters in the general election. By all accounts, it was the most liberal Democratic ticket ever in Florida.

Disappointment with Gillum's choice of King over second-place finisher Gwen Graham surfaced soon after the election. In contrast, DeSantis's choice of Nuñez was credited with helping him boost turnout among vote-rich, Miami-Dade County's Republican-leaning Hispanics—a big factor in his victory.

The General Election

Florida's primary election results stunned the nation. The underdogs had won. The *New York Times* headline "A Black Progressive and a Trump Acolyte Win Florida Governor Primaries" said it all (Mazzei and Martin 2019). No one expected the general election to be anything but an epic battle. The stakes were high for both parties—nationally as well as at home. Florida's next governor would be appointing three justices to the Florida Supreme Court and would have veto power over the congressional redistricting plan to be drawn up after the 2020 US Census. And it is always an advantage for a presidential candidate to have a sitting governor of one's own party for guidance on fundraising, issues, and turnout.

Race Arises as a Key Focal Point

Race quickly became an integral part of the general election campaign. The day after the primary, in an interview on Fox News, DeSantis described Gillum and his platform in a way that was labeled racist rhetoric with "dog whistle connotations" by Gillum supporters (Caputo 2018d): "You know, he [Gillum] is an articulate spokesman for those far-left views and he's a charismatic candidate. [However] *the last thing we need to do is to monkey this up* by trying to embrace a socialist agenda with huge tax increase and bankrupting the state. That is not going to work. That is not going to be good for Florida."

Gillum and his supporters immediately seized upon the phrase "monkey this up" as a racial slur, which mystified some of the public. To some, "monkey around with," and similar phrases, is an idiom that means "fooling around with" and "tinkering with." But not to African Americans. In the days and weeks that followed, Gillum's campaign referred to the term as coded language, or "dog-whistle politics" (from a dog's ability to hear what people cannot), meant to refer to Blacks as sub-human.

The DeSantis campaign promptly denied any racial intent and called the racism accusation against him "absurd" (Lemongello and Rohrer 2018). DeSantis himself said the comment had "zero to do with race . . . and everything to do with whether we want Florida to continue to go in a good direction building off the success, or do we want to turn to left-wing socialist policies which will absolutely devastate our state" (Folley 2018). But the damage was done. The misstep was described as "the political equivalent of throwing an interception on the opening play of the game" (Saul, Mazzei, and Martin 2018). DeSantis had to live with constant reminders of his "monkey-it-up" comment throughout the general election campaign (Caputo 2018d).

Thereafter, the Gillum campaign and the media carefully monitored and heavily publicized any race-related comments or activities tied to DeSantis, whether inflammatory anti-Muslim remarks by campaign contributors, tweets by supporters using *monkey* terms, robo calls from fringe groups with racist messages, and activities/comments by groups supporting DeSantis. Each time, DeSantis told reporters to judge his campaign on the issues and *his* statements because he couldn't control other people's social media (DeFede 2018). His campaign spokesperson's standard response was "We've said it before, we'll say it again: we adamantly denounce this sort of disgusting rhetoric" (Caputo 2018d).

DeSantis's Campaign: Plays Catch-Up, Republican Interest Lags

After winning the primary, DeSantis had to play catch-up in the grassroots outreach game. Working hard to win over staunch Putnam supporters who greatly resented Trump's intervention in the primary, his in-person appearances increased, while his Fox News Channel appearances fell off sharply.

DeSantis's campaign was far less issue-intensive than Gillum's. Instead, the Republican chose to focus on Gillum's shortcomings—his platform, an FBI investigation of corruption in the Tallahassee government during his tenure as mayor, and the city's high crime rate. His casting of Gillum as a socialist was a message that resonated well with high-turnout, older, White voters and Hispanics with ties to Cuba, Venezuela, Nicaragua, and Colombia.

For much of the campaign, GOP voter engagement lagged. By the end of September, DeSantis's campaign required a major course correction. He replaced his campaign manager with the well-regarded Susie Wiles. She had run Trump's Florida victory in 2016 and been a top adviser to Rick Scott during his first successful run for governor (Bousquet and Mahoney 2018). When Wiles took over, DeSantis was trailing in all the polls.

National events eventually sparked Republican enthusiasm—specifically, the Kavanaugh hearings and the migrant caravan—along with corruption accusations against Gillum that got considerable attention in the last debate prior to the election (on October 24). Late rallies by Trump in two heavily Republican strongholds (Fort Myers and Pensacola) promoting DeSantis and US Senate candidate Rick Scott ramped up turnout.

DeSantis was unapologetically pro-Trump throughout the campaign, choosing to distance himself from the president only a few times following Trump tweets about Puerto Rico—his opposition to statehood and claims that the number of deaths attributed to Hurricane Maria was inflated. DeSantis, well aware of the growing Puerto Rican population in Florida, did not agree with either statement.

Gillum's Campaign: Follow the Same Course; Full Speed Ahead

After the primary, Gillum was subjected to conflicting advice on what strategy he should follow in the general election. One camp argued for a less ideological approach: "So how can Gillum win? He'll need a large turnout among his base of minority voters and progressives. He'll also need to ex-pand his appeal among moderate Democrats and to seek crossover support from Republicans who are dissatisfied with President Trump" (Austin 2018).

Others cautioned him against pivoting to the center: "We have to give our voters something to vote for, not against ... *We won't be able to win if we moderate our views and make candidates seem like Republican-lite*" (Lemongello and Rohrer 2018; emphasis added). Gillum took the latter path, although he constantly promised to be governor "not just for some, but for all" (Collins 2018). And needing to shore up the Democratic base (women who had voted for Graham), he frequently cited his endorsement of Hillary Clinton in 2016 for which he had been awarded a prime speaking spot at the Democratic National Convention in Philadelphia.

Gillum made his general election campaign more proactive, stressing what he proposed to do in Tallahassee and in Washington to help those left behind ("Bring it home, Florida"): Increase the corporate income tax to spend more on education, reform the criminal justice system, automatically restore felon voting rights, increase the minimum wage to $15 per hour, raise the starting pay for teachers to $50,000, expand Medicaid, support Medicare for All, and protect the federal Affordable Health Care Act, especially coverage of persons with pre-existing conditions.

Gillum's strong anti-Trump language and support of congressional impeachment proceedings and reduced authority for Immigration and Customs Enforcement (ICE) helped draw an even clearer line of distinction between him and DeSantis. So, too, did Gillum's repeated attacks on DeSantis for racially insensitive remarks and past appearances at events featuring White supremacist speakers. These attacks became the focal point of the debates.

The Debates: Late in the Game; Racism vs. Corruption the Theme

There were two debates, both near the end of the campaign: October 21 in Tampa and October 24 in Weston. News accounts described the debates as "highly contentious," "a series of testy exchanges" (Farrington 2018a), and filled with "blistering verbal assaults" (Mazzei and Lerer 2018). Vicious personal attacks generally overshadowed any substantive discussion of issues. In each debate, Gillum focused on DeSantis's alleged racism and strong ties to Trump. DeSantis attacked Gillum for being a corrupt mayor in a city with the state's highest crime rate and for his supposed socialist agenda (Ceballos 2018b).

First debate (CNN)

The candidates did spend some time contrasting their views on issues, but *it was the racial dimensions of the debate that got the most press*. CNN's Jake Tapper, the moderator, brought the race issue to the forefront by asking DeSantis about his "monkey-it-up" comment and his refusal to return a contribution from a contributor who once called President Obama the N-word on Twitter (Farrington 2018a). DeSantis defended himself against racism accusations by citing his experience as a Navy officer and his service in Iraq: "When we're down range in Iraq, it didn't matter your race. We all wore the same uniform, we all had that American flag patch on our arm, and that was the end of the story. I'll be a governor for all Floridians."

Gillum questioned DeSantis's response: "The monkey-up comment said it all and he has only continued in the course of his campaign to draw all the attention he can to the color of my skin. And the truth is, you know what? I'm black. I've been black all my life and as far I know, I'll die black." Gillum continued, saying the "only color the people of the state of Florida care about is the blue-green algae flowing out of the east and west side of this state" (Bort 2018). And he did not let up on the racism charges against DeSantis.

Second debate (WPBF-ABC)

The second and final debate was even harsher than the first. It was "an hour of jugular attacks, with the two men accusing each other of being dishonest and unworthy of leading the state" (Kam and Dunkelberger 2018). As in the first debate, their issue discussions took a back seat to race. Gillum brought up DeSantis's "monkey it up" comment and cited two racist robocalls by a White supremacist group mocking Gillum. (Donato and Swire 2018). DeSantis labeled the calls "disgusting" and challenged the media to investigate who made the calls; "I can tell you, we're not doing it."

DeSantis criticized Gillum for supporting a far-left (Dream Defenders) group's "radical manifesto that attacked our police officers"[17] (Farrington 2018b) and pointed to the group's attacks on Israel (Kam and Dunkelberger 2018). (The Jewish vote makes up around 7 percent of Florida registrants. Both candidates made an appeal to Jewish voters.) But that exchange was mild compared to the one that went viral. It began with the moderator asking DeSantis about past speaking engagements at far-right conferences (Mazzei and Lerer 2018):

DESANTIS: "How the hell am I supposed to know every single statement somebody makes?" "I am not going to bow down to the altar of political correctness."

GILLUM: "My grandmother used to say, 'A hit dog will holler,' and it hollered through this room," he said, spelling out letter by letter the slur Mr. DeSantis's donor used. "*I'm not calling Mr. DeSantis a racist. I'm simply saying the racists believe he's a racist.*" [*Note:* The italicized comment sparked a media firestorm.]

DESANTIS: "I am not going to sit here and take this nonsense from a guy like Andrew Gillum who always plays the victim, who's going out and attacking and aligning himself with groups who attack our men and women in law enforcement, attack our military."

While the racial elements of the debate advantaged Gillum, going forward DeSantis benefitted tremendously from the second debate with Gillum finally admitting that he had been given a ticket to a Broadway performance of *Hamilton* but neglected to ask the details of where it came from. (It had been supplied by an undercover FBI agent investigating corruption in Tallahassee city government.[18]) (Spencer and Farrington 2018). Gillum had been denying it for months, and continued to say his brother had gotten the ticket in exchange for some concert tickets. Some post-election analyses point to the "*Hamilton* ticket revelation" as having helped DeSantis eke out a win. Gillum's alleged corruption was the centerpiece of DeSantis's campaign the final two weeks (Call 2018d).

The Money: A Record-Breaker

The race was an expensive one, not surprising in light of the high stakes. The total raised for all 23 candidates who filed was $132,326,510 (FollowTheMoney.org 2018). The two candidates were nearly equal in the amount of individual contributions they received: Gillum–$18.3M; DeSantis–$18.2M. The big difference was in contributions to their respective political committees: Friends of Ron DeSantis, $40.6M; Gillum's Forward Florida, $36.7M. Contributions to a candidate's affiliated political action committee (PAC) are unlimited, whereas contributions to a candidate are capped at $3,000. Thus, it was hardly surprising that each candidate's PAC generated more money than individual contributors. (Contributions by a political party to a candidate are also unlimited. Party funds tend to support polling, consulting, and campaign staff.) Each candidate also received matching funds from the state: DeSantis $3.2M and Gillum $2.6M (Florida Division of Elections 2018).

A higher percentage of Gillum's individual contributors were from out-of-state (Payne 2018). The history-making nature of Gillum's candidacy drew contributions from many of the same deep-pocketed liberal donors as donated to Stacy Abrams's gubernatorial campaign in Georgia—George Soros, Tom Steyer, Facebook co-founder Chris Hughes, comedian Byron Allen, children's book author Judy Blume, Walt Disney Company executive Kathy Mangum, Hollywood's Norman Lear, movie producer Tyler Perry, and others (Wieder 2018).

Progressive groups behind Gillum included Steyer's NextGen Climate America, Collective Future (promoting Black candidates), and Everytown for Gun Safety Action Fund. Senator Cory Booker (D-NJ) hosted a fundraiser, former New York City Mayor Michael Bloomberg contributed and rallied contributions from gun-control advocates, and Hillary Clinton raised money for Gillum.

DeSantis's campaign chest benefitted from contributions from perennial conservative GOP donors: August A. Busch III; Las Vegas gambling tycoon Sheldon Adelson; hedge fund manager Kenneth C. Griffin; Laura Perlmutter, wife of the former CEO of Marvel Entertainment; the DeVos family, who strongly support charter schools; among others (Payne 2018).

The Ads: Different Strategies

Throughout the general election campaign, ads saturated the airwaves and social media. Between September 3 and October 16, the Florida Democratic Party and Gillum had 7,929 TV ad buys costing $8.3 million. During the same period, the Republican Party of Florida and candidate DeSantis spent $9.2 million on 8,277 ads (Ceballos Oct. 2). From October 30 through Election Day, the two campaigns and groups backing them spent $15.2 million on last-minute TV and radio ads—for Gillum $10.9 million, for DeSantis $4.3 million (Dumenco Nov. 12). The two gubernatorial candidates differed in their ad strategy.

Gillum's ads largely focused on what he would do if elected: address the environmental crisis (clean up red tide and algae bloom), protect public safety (work with law enforcement officials, crack down on violent criminals and gangs), improve education (raise the corporate tax, pay teachers better, provide more vocational education), increase diversity (push for inclusivity and unity), and improve healthcare (provide better access, expand Medicaid). Two healthcare ads were in Spanish.

NextGen Florida spent $1.2 million on digital ads running from late October through Election Day targeting 1.8 million young Floridians. These ads urging young people to vote and to vote for Gillum ran on Instagram, Twitter, Facebook, Tumblr, Reddit, Hulu, Vevo, Spotify, Pandora, Google search, and Twitch (a gaming platform) (Man 2018f).

Other groups ran attack ads against DeSantis for Gillum. American Bridge ran multiple radio and digital ads in the Jacksonville area featuring actor Don Cheadle's voice detailing examples of DeSantis's racist behavior (Pisani 2018). The Gillum campaign also ran an attack ad blasting DeSantis for his congressional votes cutting Social Security and Medicare and raising the retirement age to seventy.

Overall, DeSantis's ads touted his strong ties to President Trump and attacked Gillum for his legal troubles in Tallahassee, the city's high crime rate, a proposed $1 billion corporate tax increase, Medicare for All, and his socialist agenda. On issues, DeSantis's ads and social media mentioned his tough stance on illegal immigration, support from the law enforcement community, pro-school-choice positions, pledge to clean up Florida waters, and support for continuation of economic growth following in footsteps of Governor Rick Scott.

The Grassroots Campaigns

Gillum and DeSantis crisscrossed the state, each targeting key constituencies, often appearing with popular political or entertainment figures, and touting endorsements from influential people or groups. Each had a president by his side at one or more events—Gillum, President Obama; DeSantis, President Trump.

Gillum's Ground Game: Bus Tour, Celebrities, Endorsements
The effectiveness of Gillum's primary bus tour prompted the campaign to once again rely on that voter-mobilization technique. From October 25 to Election Day, November 6, the Gillum "Bring It Home" Bus Tour weaved its

way through thirty counties. Gillum targeted college campuses, accompanied by top political figures. President Obama joined him in Miami; former Vice President Joe Biden at University of North Florida in Jacksonville and the University of South Florida (USF) in Tampa; Bernie Sanders at student rallies at the University of Central Florida in Orlando and USF; Congressman John Lewis, civil rights icon, at Florida International University, Florida Memorial University, and Florida Atlantic University; US Senator Kamala Harris in Miami Gardens; and US Representatives Nydia Velazquez and Darren Soto in Puerto Rican, vote-rich Kissimmee, to name a few. Gillum also made sure to appear at Bethune-Cookman University, Florida State University, the University of Florida, and Miami-Dade College.

Celebrities rushed to appear at young voter–oriented rallies and tweeted support. Former First Lady Michelle Obama headlined a "When We All Vote" rally at the University of Miami, along with actor-comic Keegan Michael-Key and rapper Fat Joe. Near the campaign's end, a group of African American stars headlined Gillum's "Bring It Home" Midnight Rally at FAMU, his alma mater: Sean "Diddy" Combs, DJ Khaled, Rapper Gunna, Grammy-winning R&B singer Monica, CNN political commentator Angela Rye, movie producer Will Packer, and comedian Tiffany Haddish (Waters 2018). Popular activist/actress Gabrielle Union posted frequent endorsements on Twitter.

Gillum's celebrity outreach included Latino stars. Two days before the election, his wife R. Jai Gillum appeared with celebrity Latinas Longoria Baston, Zoe Saldana, America Ferrera, and Gina Rodriguez at an early-vote rally sponsored by the Latino Victory Fund and held in a heavily Puerto Rican neighborhood in north Kissimmee. Actor/entertainer Kendrick Sampson was at the "Unidos por Gillum" event at the famous Ball & Chain nightclub in Little Havana, Miami. Shortly after her testimony at the Kavanaugh hearings, sitcom star Alyssa Milano came to energize voters in Hollywood (she is credited with starting the "#MeToo" movement on Twitter) (Geggis 2018).

Gillum reaped key endorsements from major state newspapers,[19] LGBTQ groups (Equality Florida, Human Rights Campaign), numerous Puerto Rican officials, including Puerto Rican Governor Ricardo Rossello, national gun-control advocate and former Congresswoman Gabby Giffords, the Sierra Club, the I-4 Corridor mayors (Tampa, St. Petersburg, Orlando), major unions (teachers, public employees), and local and state Democratic officials throughout Florida and the nation.

DeSantis's Ground Game: Trump, MAGA Rallies during the
Last Week in Key Places

DeSantis's final pushes were in areas with large concentrations of Republicans and 2016 Trump voters, including typical non-midterm voters. His appearances up and down the state focused on suburban and rural areas. DeSantis's visits were often to campaign offices across the state where he spoke with groups of volunteers, local chambers of commerce, veterans' groups, and local businesses. With the exception of the campaign-ending Trump-led rallies in Fort Myers and Pensacola, DeSantis held far fewer large rallies, which are less appealing to older voters—a key constituency. (Gillum's campaign often pointed to the smaller crowds at DeSantis's events as evidence Gillum was winning.)

Except for Lara Trump (TV producer and wife of Donald's son Eric), DeSantis's supportive celebrities were politicos: Vice President Mike Pence (Jacksonville, Orlando, Pensacola), US Senators Marco Rubio and Lindsey Graham, and former New York City Mayor Rudy Giuliani. Running mate Jeanette Nuñez spent invaluable time in Miami, her home, reaching out to critical Hispanic voters. The Republican Party of Florida featured her in a Spanish-language TV ad highlighting the team's plans for Florida (Derby 2018).

DeSantis received no newspaper endorsements but did draw support from the National Right to Life organization, Americans for Prosperity, *The Jewish Press*, Everglades Trust, fifty-five of sixty-seven Florida sheriffs, Broward Sheriff's Office Deputies Association, Florida Police Benevolent Association (Bennett 2018), and thirty-six Puerto Rican elected officials, including the lieutenant governor (Smith 2018).

President Trump's endorsement mattered most. Trump's appearances with DeSantis at two huge Sunshine State rallies just seven days before Election Day ramped up support and turnout. (The president was there to support both DeSantis and Governor Rick Scott, a candidate for the US Senate.) Each of the MAGA rally locations was chosen for a reason. The Fort Myers area, heavily Republican, was one of the state's areas hardest hit by algae bloom and red tide; voters there were angry about slow responses to the problem, albeit more at Scott than DeSantis. Deep-red Pensacola and the rest of the Panhandle were still reeling from the aftermath of Category 4 Hurricane Michael, threatening turnout.

Trump, in his role as the "Closer in Chief" (Mahoney 2018b), gave the Fort Myers and Pensacola MAGA rally-goers plenty of reasons to vote for

DeSantis, calling Gillum a "radical socialist," citing Democrats' open borders immigration policy as leading to Central American migrant caravans, and the party's support for higher taxes. These big crowds gave the DeSantis campaign a glimmer of hope that he could pull it off, even though throughout the general election campaign, polls had shown Gillum in the lead almost all the way.

General Election Polls: Gillum Slight Favorite Most of Race

A *Miami Herald* analysis of the polls taken a month after the primary ended led to this headline: "Florida Democrats Confident at Halfway Point as Andrew Gillum Rides High in the Polls" (Smiley 2018d). Privately, Gillum acknowledged the shortcoming of polls (Smiley 2018d). The most controversial poll was one conducted by CNN and released just hours before the first debate. It showed Gillum up by 12 points. The results were widely criticized, and ultimately the CNN pollster admitted it could have been an "outlier." The irony is that it helped strengthen the "fake news" description of CNN—a constant rallying cry of Republicans (Smiley 2018b).

A Republican polling firm was the only poll predicting a DeSantis victory. Significantly, it was the last one taken and included responses through the day before the election. Republican turnout on Election Day was considerably higher than Democratic turnout—reemphasizing that polls cannot predict turnout but are merely snapshots in time. The events at the later stages of the campaign sparked more interest (and turnout) among Republican-leaning voters.

The Results: Closest Ever, Recount Required

This time the upset victory went to the Republicans. Gillum trailed most of the evening. At 11 p.m. he gave his concession speech. (Mazzei and Robles 2018). (See Figure 3.11.)

Four days later Gillum reneged his concession in the middle of the mandatory statewide recount, as accusations about vote-counting difficulties swirled: "Let me say clearly, I am replacing my words of concession with an uncompromising and unapologetic call that we count every single vote. I say this recognizing my fate in this may or may not change."[20] It didn't. On

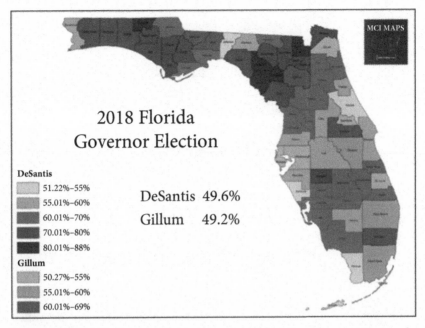

Figure 3.11 Florida General Election Results: Closest Ever; Recount Required
Source: Matthew Isbell, MCI Maps.

November 17, one day before the official deadline for all sixty-seven counties to report results, Gillum conceded for the last time via Facebook and Twitter (Schweers 2018b).

Turnout Up, but More for Republicans

The turnout rate was far higher than in previous midterm elections, reflective of competitive races for governor and US Senate and nationalization of the election. But it was disappointing for Democrats, with turnout higher among registered Republicans (71 percent) than Democrats (64 percent) (see Figure 3.12).

In spite of extraordinary grassroots efforts by Democrats and the potential history-making nature of Gillum's candidacy, turnout fell short among his key constituencies, which had a more negative impact in the two-candidate race than in the five-candidate Democratic primary. Specifically, Gillum "ultimately could not overcome the state's inexorable demographics: Older

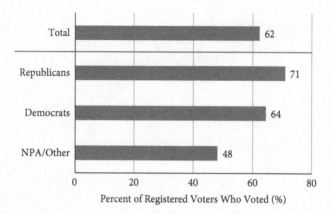

Figure 3.12 Florida General Election Turnout by Party.
Republicans turned out at higher rates than Democrats

Source: Author's analysis of Florida Division of Elections Florida Voter Registration System (FVRS) data.

White voters who lean conservative vote at far higher rates than do millennial and minority voters, whom Mr. Gillum needed to turn out in big numbers to assemble a winning coalition" (Mazzei and Robles 2018).

Hispanic turnout, particularly of Puerto Ricans, fell far below what was expected (Daughterty, Ostroff, and Vassolo Oct 30) (see Figure 3.13). Post-election analyses concluded Hispanic outreach had been too little and too late (Grunwald and Caputo 2018), giving some Hispanic voters the impression that the Black vote was more important than theirs.

While 39 percent of registered voters younger than thirty voted, 76 percent of those ages sixty-five and older did (see Figure 3.14). The gender gap in voting narrowed, with women and men being about equally likely to vote in the general election (63 percent vs. 62 percent).

Geographically, turnout was higher in suburban and rural areas combined (Republican targets) than in urban areas (Democratic targets).

Why Democrats Lost

Losing a close election is sometimes a tougher pill to swallow than being defeated in a landslide. This was not the case for Gillum or the Florida Democratic Party. They viewed the closeness as indicative of a bright blue future for Florida, vowing to leave no stone unturned in examining what

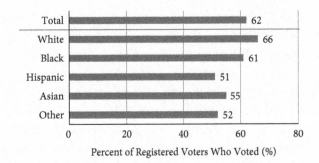

Figure 3.13 Florida General Election Turnout by Race and Ethnicity. Hispanic turnout lagged that of other groups

Source: Author's analysis of Florida Division of Elections Florida Voter Registration System (FVRS) data.

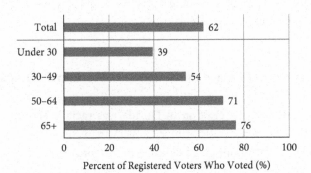

Figure 3.14 Florida General Election Turnout by Age Showing a Significant Age Gap

Source: Author's analysis of Florida Division of Elections Florida Voter Registration System (FVRS) data.

went wrong and how to make course corrections. Post-election analyses by party activists, journalists, and academics have offered up lots of reasons for the loss. The most frequently cited are: failure to register and engage voters year-round; absence of a permanent voter registration effort able to identify emerging communities (Schale 2018); inadequate outreach to Hispanics, not enough face time, ground game too late; overestimation of blue wave of Puerto Rican evacuees from Hurricane Maria (Daughterty, Ostroff, and Vassolo 2018; Grunwald and Caputo 2018); not enough Spanish-speaking candidates to help with voter mobilization efforts (Perry 2018); overes-timation of cohesiveness of young and minority voters; polling that failed to disaggregate the Hispanic vote into narrower country-of-origin groups beyond just Cuban and non-Cuban; overemphasis on immigration[21] as a GOTV tool (Sopo 2018); overestimation of Democrats' cohesiveness on certain issues (healthcare, gun control, climate change); ground game (GOTV) that started too late, focused too much on urban areas and not enough on suburban and exurban areas (Schale 2018); TV ads not as effective at mobilizing Democrats as Republican ads were at energizing Republicans; the FBI investigation of Tallahassee city government corruption related to a development and an ethics investigation of Gillum's travels enveloped him the entire campaign (Austin 2018; Call 2018c); late admission of taking *Hamilton* tickets from an undercover agent after text messages surfaced pushed some undecideds to vote for DeSantis (Sarlin 2018); and underestimation of the power of a Trump endorsement and his ability to turn out his supporters in a midterm and to ramp up turnout in heavily Republican areas via last-minute MAGA rallies (Mazzei and Robles 2018).

Significance of Race in the 2018 Gubernatorial Election

The 2018 gubernatorial election in Florida was racially significant in two ways. First, in the Democratic primary, a Black man considered an underdog for virtually the entire campaign defeated four strong White candidates who had more money, greater name recognition, and a more centrist platform. Second, in the general election—actually the day after the primary—a slip of the tongue by the opponent brought race to the forefront of the campaign.

On Election Day itself, a headline in the *Tallahassee Democrat* captured the ever-present role of race: "Historic Florida governor election mired in name-calling, racist accusations" (Schweers 2018a). But *racist* here and throughout the campaign was largely defined in Black-White terms, not in the multi-racial/ethnic sense that reflects the true population of the state.

What cannot be understated is the fact that an African American came within half a percent of becoming governor of the nation's third-largest state. Andrew Gillum had already made history as the state's first Black candidate for governor. Many observers believe that had he worked more diligently to appeal to Hispanics, especially in voter registration and GOTV efforts, he might have pulled off a victory.

What's also clear is that Gillum's fight was a win for the future. His quick appointments as a CNN commentator, a resident fellow at Harvard Kennedy

School's Institute of Politics, and a board member of a new progressive organization predict his growing influence on the nation's leaders. In addition, his advice to "never give up" remains a powerful rallying cry to the next
generation of Black office-seekers: "I sincerely regret that I couldn't bring it
home for you. [But] are we going to wake up and bask in sorrow and defeat?
Or are we going to get up and reassert ourselves at the mission at hand?"
(Mazzei and Robles 2018). Whether Andrew Gillum opts to again run for
office or chooses to continue on a more media-centric path, it is clear that his
initial 2018 campaign for Florida governor and his handling of serious personal problems mobilized more Blacks, notably more Black women, to run
for office in 2020 and sparked more activism among younger, more diverse,
generations.

4

Virginia

African American Statewide Candidates Navigate a Complicated Past (and Present)

African American candidates for statewide offices in the South have long faced difficult paths to victory, and Virginia, now the most progressive of the southern states, is no exception. Only two African Americans have ever won statewide election in Virginia—one in both 1985 and 1989 and the other in 2017. This paper examines the two candidates' very different paths to winning, separated by three decades of vast social and demographics changes in the Commonwealth that have altered the political environment, although major racial issues concerning African Americans remain. The chapter begins with a review of the Commonwealth's racial history and then of its vast changes in the modern era, followed by analyses of the factors that explain the successful runs for state public office by the two African American candidates, L. Douglas Wilder and Justin Fairfax.

Virginia's Complicated Racial History with Regard to African Americans

Of all of the southern states, Virginia has one of the most complicated histories of race relations. In 1619, slaves from Africa first arrived on the shores of what became the Commonwealth of Virginia. A shameful history followed, of slavery, Jim Crow laws, massive resistance to desegregation of public schools into the 1960s, criminalizing interracial marriage into the 1960s, and textbooks within many of our own lifetimes that taught the blatant lie that the Civil War was about state's rights and not slavery. Voter suppression was highly effective in crushing African American political influence in Virginia for years. An act of the Virginia Constitutional Convention of 1901–1902 circumvented the Fifteenth Amendment to the US Constitution's guarantee of Black male voting rights by imposing a hefty annual poll tax. As a result,

African American Statewide Candidates in the New South. Charles S. Bullock, III, Susan
A. MacManus, Jeremy D. Mayer, and Mark J. Rozell, Oxford University Press. © Oxford University Press 2022.
DOI: 10.1093/oso/9780197607428.003.0004

the vast majority of voting age Black men were stricken from the rolls. It took a constitutional amendment in 1964 (the Twenty-Fourth) to strike down poll taxes. The Voting Rights Act of 1965 struck down literacy tests that had been used to suppress the Black vote. Not long after these federal actions guaranteeing Black voting rights, African American candidates for public offices in Virginia began to experience electoral successes, winning Virginia general assembly seats, becoming city mayors, and being elected onto city councils, as well as attaining other offices.

Virginia also has undergone profound demographic transformations that are changing the nature of racial politics and partisan competition. In 1989 Virginia became the first state in the United States to elect an African American governor, L. Douglas Wilder, himself the grandson of slaves. Wilder had won the office of lieutenant governor four years earlier in an election that leading observers said he would surely lose. In 2017, Virginia elected an African American lieutenant governor, Justin Fairfax, who, in 2021, unsuccessfully sought to follow Wilder's example as a candidate for the Democratic nomination for governor.

For generations Virginia was a part of the "solid [Democratic] South." From the 1870s to the 1950s Democrats won almost all of the major offices in the South. Cracks in Democratic dominance of the region began in the 1950s at the national level; later the civil rights movement began to bring about a shifting by some Southern Whites to the Republicans in some of the southern states (Bullock and Rozell 2012: 12–21). By the 1990s, Virginia had become a Republican-dominated state; in the new century it temporarily moved back to being Democratic dominated. At one point in the 1990s, the GOP controlled the state legislature and the three top statewide offices (governor, lieutenant governor, attorney general). Yet in 2001, the Democrats broke a string of Republican gubernatorial victories, won the governorship again in 2005, only to lose it in 2009 and win it back in 2013 and 2017. At this writing, no Republican has won any statewide election, for either state or federal office, in twelve years.

The Democratic Party in the state today, though, is nothing like the dominant party during the era of the Solid South. Indeed, for many years a Democratic political machine stymied constructive change and kept the party distant from its national organization and leaders. By the 1980s, Virginia Democratic leaders were pointing the way toward a more centrist philosophy that would better promote the party's future chances of winning the presidency. Today though, the Democratic Party at the Virginia state and national level does not look all that different any more.

More than in most states, many residents of Virginia are strongly aware of their political heritage, both good and bad. Citizens and leaders wage political fights over proposals to build homes or retail establishments on undeveloped lands that were once sites of Civil War battles. Virginia in recent years has been almost constantly at the center of intensely heated battles over its many monuments to southern Civil War figures. Some advocate dismantling the monuments, others seek to protect them, and a third group has advocated preserving the monuments by moving them into museums. Battles persist as well over the names of streets and public schools long ago given the names of southern generals of the Civil War. Although demographic changes have altered the electoral landscape and made the state friendly territory for progressive Democrats seeking public office, much of the culture of Virginia remains conservative in the old sense: enamored of tradition and at times resistant to change.

The cultural resistance to accept change has on occasion opened the state to ridicule or at least intense criticism. When Congress approved a national holiday to honor Martin Luther King Jr., the state legislature responded by declaring that date Lee-Jackson-King Day to also honor Confederate generals Robert E. Lee and Stonewall Jackson. African American members of the state legislature responded on that celebrated date by carrying picture posters of their preferred honorees: Spike Lee, Jesse Jackson, and Martin Luther King. In 2000, after seventeen years, the combined holiday practice was discontinued, and Virginia celebrated Martin Luther King Day. Lee-Jackson Day became a separate date of observance in the Old Dominion, and it continued to be held annually the Friday preceding the third Monday of January, the day of the King observance, until April 2020 when Governor Ralph Northam signed legislation ending the official state recognition of Lee and Jackson. For two decades state offices in Virginia were closed on both holidays, although a number of cities—Blacksburg, Charlottesville, Fairfax, Hampton, Newport News, Richmond, and Winchester—did not observe Lee-Jackson Day.

The capital city of Richmond was mired for several years in a bitter debate over where to place a statue to an African American hometown hero, tennis star Arthur Ashe, who had died from AIDS. The city council and residents initially could not agree to place the statue on historic Monument Avenue, which honored Confederate leaders with imposing statues. The city first agreed to place the statue at a public park, but then in light of heavy criticism ultimately honored Ashe with the Monument Avenue location. Since 1993 the city council repeatedly defeated proposals to name a historic street after Ashe. Finally, in 2019 the city council voted its approval.

For decades the state legislature resisted calls to retire the official state song "Carry Me Back to Old Virginny." Although the lyrics had long been justifiably criticized for being a glorification of slavery, many lawmakers defended its standing in a bow to tradition. After being sworn in to his seat in the state senate in 1970, Doug Wilder introduced his first piece of legislation—to repeal the state song. A firestorm of criticism was unleashed on him for that act, some of it in the form of editorial commentaries and some in hate mail (see Wilder 2018: 1–8). It took years before the state legislature came around to his viewpoint. In 1997 the state legislature struck a compromise in which it approved a measure to designate the song with "emeritus" status and to commission the search for a new official state song.

Former GOP Governor George Allen opened wounds with his declaration in 1995 of a Confederate History Month and his statement that the Civil War was "a four-year struggle for independence and sovereign rights" (Blakemore 2017), but with no mention of slavery. When, in 1998, his successor Governor Jim Gilmore proclaimed the same, civil rights leaders strongly protested and threatened to encourage an economic boycott of the state. Gilmore earned some praise from Black leaders when he championed the proposal for separate official celebrations for Lee-Jackson and for King. Others weren't satisfied, because they would have preferred dropping an official day for recognizing the southern Civil War fighters. Confederate History Month in Virginia ended in 2002 with the inauguration of a Democratic governor, Mark Warner, who was succeeded by Democrat Tim Kaine. During Kaine's tenure in 2007, the Virginia General Assembly passed a resolution expressing "profound regret" for the Commonwealth's role in slavery (Craig 2007). Yet in 2010, newly inaugurated GOP governor Bob McDonnell issued a declaration for Confederate History Month that yet again failed to mention slavery. Under harsh criticism, McDonnell apologized for what he called a "major omission." He later declared he would not issue the declaration again, and thus Virginia's Confederate History Month appears to have died for good.

In February 2017, the city of Charlottesville became a flash point in the US race saga after city council members voted to remove a statue of Confederate Civil War general Robert E. Lee from a city park. Demonstrations by

White supremacist groups followed in the ensuing months, leading to violent clashes at a "Unite the Right" rally in August. A neo-Nazi sympathizer plowed his car into a crowd of counter-protesters, killing one and injuring nineteen others, and two state police officers who had been monitoring the protests from the air died when their helicopter crashed outside the city. The moment called for leadership and moral clarity from the US president, but President Donald J. Trump's response, in which he equated the White supremacist protesters and the counter-protesters as somehow equally responsible for the tragedy, only deepened the wounds. Trump then continued to defend Confederate monuments as heroic and legitimate reminders of our nation's history. It fell to Virginia's governor, Terry McAuliffe, to step up to express the outrage of the nation over the tragic events in Charlottesville after the US president had failed to do so.

That year, Democratic nominee Ralph Northam ran a unifying campaign for governor during which he called out his GOP opponent Ed Gillespie for, like Trump, stoking the worst instincts of many voters on sensitive issues of race and immigration. Northam won handily with heavy African American turnout and support. Attorney Justin Fairfax became the state's second African American state elected official when he won his own race for the office of lieutenant governor that year.[1] The celebration of an election outcome that for many symbolized a new racial harmony in the state was unfortunately short-lived as both men became embroiled in separate controversies and calls for their resignations merely one year after being inaugurated. A news organization revealed that Northam's medical school yearbook page featured a deeply offensive racist picture of two men, one in Black face and the other in a Ku Klux Klan (KKK) outfit. And then, when it appeared that Fairfax would ascend to the governorship as many speculated Northam would resign, two women accused the lieutenant governor of past sexual assaults.

The reactions to these controversies contrasted significantly along racial lines and created divisions within the Democratic Party coalition. A statewide survey by the *Washington Post* and the Schar School at George Mason University revealed that on Northam, Whites wanted him to resign his office whereas African Americans by a substantial margin did not (Jamison and Clement 2019). Further, on the question of whether Virginians accepted the governor's public apology, Whites were evenly divided but African Americans were, again by large margins, willing to forgive the governor. With no more detailed data to analyze exactly why African Americans were more willing than Whites to support and forgive a White governor who had made a deeply offensive racial transgression in his past, it is reasonable to conclude that many Whites believed they had to take a stand, on behalf of Black citizens, against a history of racism in the state, whereas many African Americans, accustomed to such behavior, were willing to accept an apology as sincere and move on. The governor's favorable record in his public life on issues of racial justice likely earned him much of that forgiveness. The very strong tradition of belief in redemption and forgiveness coming from the African American churches surely was an important part of the reaction of the Black community as well.

At one point soon after the yearbook story broke, it appeared that Northam was indeed preparing to resign his office, paving the way for Lieutenant Governor Justin Fairfax to become Virginia's second Black governor. Although most other state party leaders had called on Northam to step down, Fairfax was careful not to directly call on Northam to resign. The lieutenant governor referred to the racist yearbook photo as "a searing reminder of the modern legacy of our nation's original sin," and he issued a statement that, between the lines, could be read as encouraging Northam to step down: "At this critical and defining moment in the history of Virginia and this nation, we need leaders with the ability to unite and help us rise to the better angels of our nature. Now more than ever, we must make decisions in the best interests of the people of the Commonwealth of Virginia" (Nirappil 2018).

A woman Fairfax had met at the Democratic National Convention in 2004 then came forward to claim he had sexually assaulted her in a hotel room. Quickly following the accusation came many calls for him to resign, with #MeToo movement activists largely at the forefront of the reaction. That the accuser appeared to many a highly credible person with nothing to gain from going public was enough substantiation for many who called for the lieutenant governor to step down. The *Washington Post*/Schar School poll was taken soon after this allegation and it found a public largely willing to allow for more facts to emerge before concluding whether Fairfax was guilty or not. In response to the question of whether citizens were satisfied with Fairfax's response to the allegation, two-thirds said that they did not know enough to form a judgment (81 percent of African Americans). An interesting racial divide though emerged in the survey on Fairfax with African Americans by a 2–1 margin saying that having Fairfax as governor would help alleviate the racial divisions in Virginia and Whites by a margin of 47–41 percent saying that it would not.

Soon after the survey, a second accuser came forward to say that Fairfax had raped her in college years ago. Again, some found the accuser credible as she had communicated in email to a friend in 2017 that she would not help an effort to promote Fairfax's candidacy because of what she said he had done to her. It did not appear an opportunistic act of accusation, nor did the person have anything to gain from going public. With two credible persons making these stunning accusations, and Northam's decision to not step aside, all talk of Fairfax becoming governor subsided.

The #MeToo movement demands for Fairfax's resignation became deafeningly loud as the lieutenant governor insisted on his innocence and even alleged that he was possibly the victim of a political hit by other ambitious Democratic politicians. But here the story got especially complicated, as a largely White female driven #MeToo movement response ran into an angry African American community that demanded some kind of due process for Fairfax before mere accusations ruined his career and life. A long history in the state of unfair treatment of Blacks in the judicial process, not to mention the lynching of many African Americans in the South on the basis of mere accusations with no judicial process years ago, is intensely known and felt in the Black community. African American leaders spoke up loudly that Fairfax was entitled to a presumption of innocence until proven otherwise, and thus White feminists and African Americans in the Democratic Party coalition collided.

At one point when it actually appeared that both Northam and Fairfax were likely to resign, attention turned to the third in the line of succession, the Democratic attorney general Mark Herring who also had won election in a landslide in 2017. Herring called on the governor to resign when the story of the medical school yearbook page broke, but soon after admitted that he had worn Black face at a party in college when dressing up to imitate a famous Black rap singer. Since Herring's transgression was as a nineteen-year old undergraduate, whereas Northam's was as a twenty-four-year old medical school student, most respondents in the *Washington Post*/Schar School poll treated the two differently. Opinion overall was evenly split as to whether Northam should resign his office, whereas a very large majority said that Herring should not resign.

Further heightening racial tension was that calls for the two White statewide elected leaders to step down began to simmer down right at the point when calls for Fairfax to resign escalated. To be sure, Northam and Herring admitted to inappropriate behavior from many years ago, whereas Fairfax faced two accusations of rape—hardly comparable circumstances. But the optics of the two White men under fire for actions to which they had admitted keeping their offices while the African American, merely accused of wrongdoing and then possibly being forced to step down, was not lost on the Black community. All three leaders retained their positions, and calls for them to resign eventually stopped. The governor of Virginia is prohibited from running for reelection by state constitutional design, and few see any realistic chance for Fairfax to rebuild his reputation sufficiently to be politically viable again. He vigorously denied the accusations, took and passed polygraph tests, and then campaigned unsuccessfully for the Democratic nomination for governor in 2021.[2]

Although the trajectory of racial progress in Virginia has been a positive one in recent decades, recent controversies demonstrate that race remains a highly visible issue in the Commonwealth. Attitudes between Whites and Blacks do not follow easily predictable paths, as evidenced by the public reaction to the controversy over Northam's yearbook page. To further unpack the complexities of racial politics in Virginia requires a brief rundown of some of the state's relevant history on race relations and elections.

The Changing Politics of Race and Party Competition

In his seminal work *Southern Politics in State and Nation*, V. O. Key Jr. described Virginia as a "political museum piece." He added that, "of all the American states, Virginia can lay claim to the most thorough control by an oligarchy" (Key 1949: 19). At that time, the Democratic political machine of Harry F. Byrd dominated state politics. Byrd served as governor of Virginia from 1926 to 1930 and as US Senator from 1933 until he retired in 1965. He assembled his machine from the county courthouse organizations of the landed gentry, who preferred stability over economic growth and were fiercely committed to racial segregation (see Heinemann 1996).

The machine succeeded in part by restricting participation: in 1945, just 6 percent of the eligible adult population voted in the gubernatorial primary—in a one-party state, the only election that mattered (Sabato 1977: 110). Frank Atkinson described how the state literacy requirement restricted participation by Whites as well as Blacks. He noted that prospective registrants had to answer extraordinarily difficult questions: for example, how many people signed the Declaration of Independence, or to name the counties in the Twenty-Seventh Judicial District (Atkinson 1988).

Although the Democratic Party had a minority faction of "anti-organization" members, Key described them as "extraordinarily weak, [having] few leaders of ability, and [being] more of a hope than a reality" (Key 1949: 21). Republicans were few and far between, and their candidates had no hope of winning a general election. In this way, Virginia resembled many other southern states—overwhelmingly conservative, overwhelmingly Democratic (Bullock and Rozell 2018).

During the 1950s, Virginia's Democratic machine led a massive resistance to school desegregation, choosing to actually close the public schools rather than obey a federal court order. Although the initial response by Governor Thomas B. Stanley to the US Supreme Court's *Brown v. Board of Education* (1954) decision rejecting segregated public schools was to pledge cooperation, after substantial political fallout he reversed and declared he would "use every legal means at my command to continue segregated schools in Virginia" (Muse 1969: 7).

Like other southern states, Virginia supported Democratic presidential nominees throughout the early part of the twentieth century. The state's electorate defected to the Republicans only in 1928, when the Democrats nominated a Roman Catholic, Al Smith, who opposed prohibition. But Byrd himself feuded with Franklin Roosevelt and Harry Truman and dissented from the growing Democratic support of greater civil rights for Blacks. Byrd openly expressed his contempt for "Trumanism" and signaled to state Democrats that it was acceptable to vote Republican at the presidential level (Heinemann 1996: 255–264).

In the 1944 presidential election and thereafter until 2008, Virginia supported Republican presidential candidates in every election except the Lyndon Johnson landslide of 1964. In their classic study of southern politics, Earl and Merle Black show that in the period between 1952 and 1964, Virginia was more supportive of Republican presidential candidates than any other southern state (Black and Black 1989: 266). Many of the conservative Democrats of the Byrd machine were more comfortable with Republican presidential candidates than with their more liberal Democratic opponents. In the post-Byrd era, Virginia for years remained solidly Republican at the presidential level. In 1976 Virginia was the only southern state to back GOP nominee Gerald Ford over Jimmy Carter. When many other southern states were backing Democrats Bill Clinton and Albert Gore in 1992, 1996, and 2000, Virginia backed George Bush, Bob Dole, and George W. Bush.

After World War II, the population growth in the southwestern coal mining counties, the naval activity around Norfolk and Newport News, and the growing number of government workers in the northern Virginia suburbs of Washington, DC, changed the demographic makeup of the state and weakened the Byrd machine. The influx of Black voters and the elimination of the poll tax after passage of the Voting Rights Act further weakened the machine. Byrd machine candidates faced intraparty challenges, most notably incumbent Democratic Senator A. Willis Robertson, father of Rev. Marion G. "Pat" Robertson, lost a primary election in 1966.

As the national Democratic Party moved to the left, many of the more conservative members of the Byrd machine turned to the Republican Party. Moreover, the influx of relatively affluent professionals into northern Virginia and of pro-military citizens into the Norfolk region provided growing numbers of Republican voters. In 1969, with the Byrd machine in disarray, Virginia elected as its first Republican governor, Linwood Holton, a progressive on race issues who drew attention by enrolling his daughter in the predominantly Black Richmond public schools. The Republicans won again in 1973, with a candidate who took a less progressive stance on race issues, and in 1977, with a moderate candidate.

By the late 1970s, Republicans held both the US Senate seats and nine of Virginia's ten seats in the US House of Representatives. Virginia moved toward the Republican ranks more rapidly than did other southern states. Between 1951 and 1980 Virginia elected more Republican governors than any other southern state.

The period of Republican control ended in 1981, when Democratic Lieutenant Governor Charles S. "Chuck" Robb won the governorship as a fiscal conservative with progressive views on race and social issues. Robb's philosophical positioning proved to be an ideal combination for the evolving Virginia electorate, as he courted Byrd Democrats and some Republicans with strong appeals to fiscal conservatism and energized the moderate and liberal wings of the Democratic party with progressive appeals on race, education, and social issues.

The 1980s, the Reagan-Bush era, were the heyday of success for the Virginia Democratic Party at the state level. In the 1981, 1985, and 1989 elections Democrats swept all three statewide offices (governor, lieutenant governor, attorney general). At the time, it appeared that the Democratic Party dominance of the Old Dominion was unbreakable.

Historic Breakthrough: Electing Doug Wilder in 1985 and 1989

In 1985 the incumbent attorney general Gerald Baliles, like Robb before him, ran for governor as a fiscal conservative with progressive views on race and social issues. He easily defeated a much more conservative opponent who closely aligned with the state's growing religious right movement. Most significantly, Virginia attracted national attention for electing a Black and a woman to the other state offices. State senator L. Douglas Wilder, a grandson of slaves, confounded analysts by handily winning the lieutenant governor race, making him the first Black elected to statewide office in Virginia. State delegate Mary Sue Terry won the office of attorney general, making her the first woman elected to state office in Virginia.

The significance of Wilder's victory in 1985 to racial politics in Virginia cannot be understated. At the time Wilder was substantially more liberal than the leadership of the state Democratic Party. It was no secret that such figures as Governor Robb had serious reservations about Wilder's electability and some even tried to recruit other leading Democrats to challenge him for the nomination. But when Wilder won the nomination, Robb and other leading Democrats solidly backed his candidacy, despite some predictions that a Black candidate would sink the entire statewide ticket.

Getting to the point of party leaders lining up for Wilder was not easy. In the 1980s in Virginia, the politics of the state were widely understood as conservative-leaning and culturally resistant to change. A Democratic Party statewide ticket that included an African American and a woman caused a major stir. Donald P. Baker, the *Washington Post* Richmond, Virginia, bureau chief during Wilder's campaigns, and a longtime chronicler of state politics, reported that supporters of Democratic statewide candidates in 1985 were often open in expressing that they had stronger reservations about Wilder's candidacy than Terry's. In their view, race was a larger barrier to election than gender. Governor Robb's press secretary George Stoddart stated: "For better or worse, this is still Virginia. That makes it very difficult. Once you get beyond the state senate or maybe a congressional district, it becomes very difficult for Black candidates" (Baker 1989: 173). The incumbent lieutenant governor Richard J. Davis, while contemplating a run for the Democratic nomination for governor, expressed a wish that another Democrat would get in the race for lieutenant governor to challenge Wilder. Davis's campaign manager Bobby Watson noted that "many in Dick's campaign did not feel the state would back a Catholic, especially a liberal one [Davis], a Black and a woman, and in the back of our mind, that someone else would pop up there and the nightmare of Doug Wilder being on the ticket would go away." Watson claimed that potential donors to a Davis campaign said "they weren't going to waste their money if Dick was on the ticket with Doug" (173). Governor Robb, then the most popular figure in Virginia politics, expressed the opinion that a challenger to Wilder for the party nomination would be beneficial, "particularly given the doubts that have been raised." Upon Wilder's announcement, Robb stated that he was "not certain that Wilder, or any Black candidate, can command a majority, but I would hope we've come to the point in Virginia where that can happen" (Baker 1989: 177). Delegate Owen Pickett, the former state Democratic Party chair, piled on: "Unfortunately, I sense racism creeping into voting patterns. And if my perception is correct, putting a Black on the ticket would crystallize that feeling" (177).[3]

Wilder was intensely aware of the reservations about his candidacy expressed by party officials and activists and believed he could make his own case effectively to the voters. To a state AFL-CIO convention that had just endorsed his candidacy Wilder said, "the biggest problem I see is getting out to the people so they can see I'm not the monster that some have tried to depict me as" (Baker 1989: 174).

The most controversial display of Democratic Party leadership efforts to keep Wilder off the ticket was led by the state party chair, Alan A. Diamonstein, who convened a meeting of eighteen White, male Democratic Party members of the House of Delegates. One legislator described the sentiment of the meeting: "The consensus was that with Wilder on the ticket, Democrats can't win . . . It was generally perceived to be a very big problem." Among the ideas presented at the meeting was getting one of the Democratic candidates for the gubernatorial nomination to announce instead for lieutenant governor in order to stop Wilder from being on the ticket (Baker 1989: 178). Upon learning of the meeting Wilder fumed: "Let's get it out on the table now, let's not kid ourselves. The problem is that I'm Black and that is just anathema to some people. Party leaders and the politicos are the ones who bring it up, not the John Does on the street" (179).

Wilder particularly turned his ire on the elected party members and leaders who expressed reservations about his candidacy to reporters under the condition that they would not be quoted by name. He mocked them as saying "It's not me, I have no prejudices at all. It's that redneck, that nameless faceless redneck" who won't vote for a Black candidate. "These people who don't want to be quoted—I won't say they are cowards—but these people who say blacks can't win, they go back to their respective areas and ask blacks to vote for them" (Baker 1989: 179).

Statewide media, though, widely quoted by name the University of Virginia political scientist Larry Sabato when he boldly stated that Wilder's odds of winning were worse than 100 to 1. Sabato based his prediction on his view that the Democratic Party was doomed to failure in Virginia unless it recaptured the White vote, and of course this conclusion assumed that there would be a widespread refusal by Whites to vote for a Black candidate—the same concern expressed anonymously by the many Democratic officials Wilder had referenced. Sabato noted that no Democrat running statewide had won the White vote in the previous eighteen years. He went on: "There's no issue like the race issue in Virginia. The party might be in a stronger position were it seen to be standing up to some of its constituency group members—be it women, be it teachers, blacks. The party is seen as captured by these groups" (Baker 1989: 175). After setting the odds at worse than 100 to 1, the political scientist added that "the odds are much greater that he would sink the ticket" (175). The comments exacerbated an already overheated climate regarding the impact of Wilder's race on the elections, and at the candidate's urging campaign manager Paul Goldman turned up the heat again when he angrily denounced the political scientist as "in danger of becoming the Dr. Schockley of Virginia" (Yancey 1988: 59). Not to be outdone, the candidate himself fumed "unless Democrats in positions of leadership counter the nonsense issued by the likes of that professor at UVA, it will do more damage than my candidacy or any future black candidacy could have. I have never known a more blatant, direct, and even open racist preachment that the Democrats should kick blacks in the behind" (Baker 1989: 175; Atkinson 2006: 55–56).[4]

A common tact among some of Wilder's critics was to plead that their opposition to his candidacy had nothing to do with race but was because he was a political liberal running in a conservative state. Wilder had a retort for those who used the word "liberal" in this manner: "That's a code word for racism" (Baker 1989: 181). Indeed, Wilder's retort had some credibility given that there were no such eager efforts to derail White liberal candidates seeking statewide office that year. Yet his campaign manager Paul Goldman later said that Wilder's racism charge against those who said he was too liberal actually was a calculated political move to get opponents to back off from criticizing the candidate's record as outside the mainstream (Atkinson 2006: 62). "It was like a brush back pitch," Goldman reported (Yancey 1988: 150).

The efforts to get Wilder to back down from running for statewide office in 1985 took some extreme turns. Wilder reported that one potential campaign donor offered him a half-million-dollar contribution for a congressional run in 1986 if he would step down from running for lieutenant governor, and another offered to help raise money for him if he would step down and instead run for lieutenant governor four years later (Baker 1989: 181).

The civil rights leader Rev. Jesse Jackson later weighed in, saying that whereas African Americans had been loyal to the Democratic Party, there was often a lack of "reciprocity" and he noted Wilder's political journeys as proof: "When Doug thought about running for Senate in 1982, he met resistance. Every time he came up with the idea of running, he met resistance. The challenge to White Democrats is to be reciprocal in voting. To be expansive, to be inclusive, to be fair. They have been the beneficiary of black investment and now blacks are demanding a fair return on their investment" (Baker 1989: xii).

Wilder's victory permanently put to rest the question of whether an African American could win statewide office in Virginia. When others went out of their way to draw attention to Wilder's race, he campaigned throughout the state as a traditional southern politician and even ran televised advertisements in rural communities featuring a rotund White police officer with a thick southern accent offering his strong support for the Democrat. As Wilder later put it, the hugely popular advertisement showcased effectively that he could reach out to people others had said were unlikely to vote for him: "It established an issue for me that Republicans usually have going their way, strong on law and order. Adler [the police officer] was the image of a guy who was not supposed to be supportive of my candidacy. He destroyed the myth that the Joe Adlers wouldn't support me. He was mainstream-blue-collar and rural" (Baker 1989: 207).

Wilder's victory was relatively narrow, when compared to his ticket mates. He won by about 4 percentage points over his GOP opponent, whereas the gubernatorial nominee Baliles won by 10 percentage points and attorney general nominee Terry by 22 percentage points over their respective opponents. When asked whether he thought race was a factor in his narrow win, Wilder simply said it wasn't an issue at all, but rather that he had spent less on campaigning than either of his ticket mates (Baker 1989: 212). Wilder did win 44 percent of the White vote—an accomplishment that gave some substance to his insistence that others had made too much of race as a factor in the outcome.

The reporter Donald P. Baker articulated an explanation of White support for Wilder that lent credibility to the views of those who said that the Virginia election had proven that a "New South" was in the making: "Self-conscious about their shameful history in race relations, many in Virginia were anxious to prove that the state's reputation as a bastion of the Old South, preoccupied with the past, was no longer accurate. With Wilder's election, they could exorcise a collective guilt and claim the mantle of a New Dominion in the New South" (Baker 1989: 294).

The Republican politician who would ultimately be Wilder's opponent in 1989, J. Marshall Coleman, praised the Democrat's historic win as evidence of a changing Virginia: "It's an accumulation of demographics, of the changing face of the electorate. If the state were all 71-year old White men, Wilder wouldn't win. Wilder's and Terry's victories are to Virginia what John Kennedy's victory was to the nation" (Baker 1989: 212).

What continued nonetheless to make many Democrats uncomfortable about Wilder was his preference to play by his own rules and not be guided by the party leadership or other public figures, in a political culture that at the time seemed to demand deference to the more established politicians. Wilder in statewide office made it clear that he would chart his own path politically, and he undertook a heavy travel and speaking schedule as he had his eyes on the governorship.

The lieutenant governor openly criticized the national Democratic Leadership Council, a group of prominent party moderates then led by Robb, as a pseudo-Republican organization. He also leveled criticism at Rev. Jackson's "Rainbow Coalition" as too tied to liberal orthodoxy and hurting the Democratic Party's chances of winning elections. While serving as the lieutenant governor, he was very critical at times of Governor Gerald Baliles's leadership and policy priorities, particularly on transportation investments and taxes. To many Democrats, having a lieutenant governor not in step with the governor was somehow a violation of the political norms of the time. Then Wilder and Robb openly feuded with each other with a testy exchange of letters that went public in which Robb characterized the lieutenant governor as not a good team player and Wilder vented his anger at Robb for allegedly taking too much credit for the lieutenant governor's victory.

Although Wilder was at times openly disdainful, when Robb left office in January 1986 he was enormously popular—so much so that in 1988 incumbent GOP US Senator Paul Tribble chose to step aside rather than be challenged by Robb. The Republicans, resigned to their fate, nominated a weak candidate who had never held elected office—African American minister Rev. Maurice Dawkins. Dawkins claimed that he could put together an electoral majority by appealing to both Republicans and Democratic-leaning Blacks with his philosophy of inclusive conservatism. At the GOP nominating convention that chose Dawkins, delegates and party leaders openly boasted that they had upstaged the Democrats by nominating an African American a year before the likely selection of Doug Wilder as the Democratic nominee for governor. Supporters flashed "Let's Make Headlines" signs, a clear reference to Dawkins becoming the first African American nominated for the US Senate in Virginia since Reconstruction.[5] At a post-convention press conference the next day a reporter asked Dawkins if it was realistic for a Republican, even a Black one, to appeal to Black voters long tied to the Democratic Party. Dawkins retorted that the Black community was not "monolithic" and that "We're a lot like White folks in that regard."[6]

Dawkins campaigned vigorously in Black churches and urban communities throughout Virginia trying to promote a message of self-reliance and an anti-welfare state. Ultimately his conservative message was a difficult sell in the Black community. He attracted only 16 percent of the Black vote (and just over 30 percent of the White vote) and 29 percent overall against the popular former governor. Ultimately, Dawkins's doomed candidacy did nothing to steal the spotlight from Wilder's run for governor a year later.

In 1989 Wilder led the statewide Democratic ticket as the gubernatorial nominee. Many party leaders continued to harbor reservations about his electability and pinned their hopes on Attorney General Mary Sue Terry until she made it known that she would not run for governor, but would seek reelection as the attorney general. Once Wilder's nomination was inevitable, major party leaders all backed his candidacy. Despite his clear victory in 1985, many critics again speculated that his race would prohibit him from winning the governorship of the former confederate state. The logic of this concern was that the position of governor is so much more important than that of the lieutenant governor, as the latter has few substantive powers other than breaking tie votes in the state senate.

Wilder's candidacy attracted substantial national and international attention because he stood to become the nation's first elected Black governor.[7] That a grandson of slaves stood to accomplish this goal in the state that was the capital of the confederacy made his possible election all the more intriguing.

What became clear during the campaign was that despite all of the attention paid to Wilder's race and the possible temptation for the GOP candidate J. Marshall Coleman to subtly inject racial appeals—a year after the odious George H. W. Bush presidential campaign ads that depicted a menacing looking Black criminal, Willie Horton—neither candidate drew strong attention to that factor. Indeed, during the campaign and especially during his term as governor, Wilder was more likely to endure criticism from prominent Black leaders for downplaying race or for not having been a leader in the civil rights movement than from opponents for exploiting race for political gain. A detailed content analysis of media coverage of Wilder's campaign concluded that there was little evidence in Wilder's appeals of "catering" to Black voters, and that he strategically directed his messages primarily to attract majority White votes (Jeffries 1997). Coleman did hit Wilder hard during the campaign as a "soft on crime" liberal who opposed the death penalty, and some saw subtle racial appeals in that tactic. But support in Virginia, like much of the nation, for tough sentencing of criminals was popular in the 1980s. Wilder's campaign somewhat inoculated him from such criticism by his taking of strong "law and order" positions and extolling his military record as a Bronze Star Medal recipient in the Korean War.

Wilder once again worked to shed his liberal image and ran a thoroughly centrist campaign with open appeals to Virginia's established culture. His abortion rights message, for example, was best exemplified in the campaign advertisement extolling the state's long history of support for individual rights and freedoms, and it showed images of historic sites such as Thomas Jefferson's Monticello and the national flag. It was an advertisement a libertarian could love and even some conservatives who adhere to a generally consistent belief in non-intrusive government.

When it came to Virginia's conservative culture and past history, Wilder defied the expectations of many of his detractors. In one very calculated campaign stop, Wilder had dinner with a supporter whose front yard sported a Confederate flag on a flagpole. The candidate reported to those covering the event that the homeowner "told me what the flag meant to him, and assured me that it had nothing to do with me . . . [And] he made a nice contribution to my campaign." In another scripted event, Wilder had his picture taken by a reporter while standing in front of a Confederate flag at a rural general store. Wilder told the reporter that "I've come to learn that the flag represents Virginia's heritage, its history, not activism for the cause" (Baker 1989: 188). Reporters asked Wilder all the time about the race factor in the election. He downplayed it at every opportunity. In his words: "I will not suggest that anyone who votes against me is racist. I don't want anyone to vote for or against me because of my race. It's not a political consideration. I ascribe it to irrelevancy" (188).

Wilder won the election by the slimmest margin for a statewide race in Virginia history. With a record turnout of nearly 1.8 million voters (66.5 percent of registered voters), Wilder won by only 6,741 votes. The outcome actually triggered a recount that ultimately assured Wilder's victory. On election night exit polls projected that Wilder would win by a margin of at least 5 percentage points and some news stations early on stated that he had won comfortably, only to backtrack later on as the precincts reported a too close to call election throughout the night. Journalists and pollsters said later on that many of the voters had lied in exit polls in order to appear racially progressive.[8] That explanation, although credible, angered many citizens who felt that by injecting racial motivations to voting patterns, the state's accomplishment in electing a Black governor had been tainted. The state's flagship newspaper, *The Richmond Times-Dispatch*, ran a political cartoon featuring a cigar-chomping White man with a KKK outfit telling the exit pollster that he just voted for Wilder. Further possible evidence of racial motivations in voting was that Wilder at the top of the ticket ran far behind the Democratic candidates for lieutenant governor (Don Beyer) and attorney general (Mary Sue Terry), both of whom won by very comfortable margins. There were no coattails in his election, except perhaps "reverse" ones.

Despite the closeness of his victory and speculation that racially motivated voting nearly cost him the election, the national media celebrated Wilder's win as a historic achievement. The November 20, 1989, editions of three national news weeklies prominently featured stories on Wilder's victory with the titles, "The End of the Civil War" (*U.S. News and World Report*), "The New Black Politics" (*Newsweek*), and "Breakthrough in Virginia" (*Time*).

As state and national media and commentators made much of the historic breakthrough in Wilder's election, the candidate himself made little of the role of race in his victory. Voters too apparently downplayed race as a motivating factor in their decisions on which candidate to support. A CBS

News/*New York Times* exit poll on election day asked voters "Was Douglas Wilder's being black a major reason why you voted as you did for governor?" Clearly this question could not elicit a positive response from those who did not want to reveal that race mattered to their voting decision. Tellingly though, 78 percent said that race was not a reason at all, 12 percent said it was a "minor" factor, and a mere 8 percent admitted it was a "major" factor (Sabato 1990b: 5).

A study of Wilder's election concluded based on voting data that it was Wilder's "pragmatic approach to winning" and ability to reach out to various segments of the populace that carried the election for him, as his political appeal went well beyond minority voting (Schexnider 1990). That conclusion is soundly supported by the evidence.[9] Wilder won the votes of 25 percent of self-described conservatives and he won one-third of the votes of those who supported Republican George H. W. Bush for president in 1988. Wilder's victory drew in part on the increase in in-state migration, as this component of the Virginia electorate increased by about 14 percent between 1980 and 1990 (Jeffries 1997: 72) and nearly 44 percent of Wilder's voters had spent most of their childhood years outside the state (Schexnider 1990: 154). Wilder also was the beneficiary of the youth vote, as he won the votes of 57 percent of those who were 18–29 years of age (Jeffries 1997: 124). The gender gap favored Wilder as well: he commanded 53 percent of the votes of women, whereas his opponent Coleman had a similar percentage among male voters (Sabato 1990a: 2). Finally, the black vote went massively for Wilder: 96.4 percent, with a turnout rate of 72.6 percent of registered voters—about 8 percentage points higher than White turnout (Sabato 1990a: 4–5).

The Virginia Democratic Party surely had much to celebrate from its sweep of statewide offices in the three 1980s elections. Yet there was evidence of a Republican resurgence at the grassroots as the party worked vigorously to recruit good candidates for local offices. The Republicans in the 1980s had continued their steady, incremental gains in membership in the Virginia General Assembly, enough so that by 1989 party members could discuss with credibility the possibility of someday taking control of one or even both legislative chambers. In 1967 the Democrats controlled thirty-four of forty Senate seats and eighty-five of one hundred seats in the House of Delegates. By the end of the 1980s, the GOP had picked up four seats in the Senate and twenty-five in the House, giving them ten of forty and thirty-nine of one hundred seats respectively. It appeared that a few good election cycles could give the GOP control of at least one legislative chamber for the first time since Reconstruction.

Aiding the GOP cause, Wilder had a troubled governorship during a period of economic recession. The era of state budget surpluses and economic growth had ended, and Wilder had to govern during a period of government retrenchment. State agencies and employees had become accustomed to better-than-usual government support from the Democratic administrations of Robb and Baliles and expected more of the same from Wilder. With entirely premature thoughts of national office, Wilder committed his administration to a no-tax-increase pledge and vowed to cut government spending to keep the state budget balanced, as required by Virginia law. He consequently angered traditional Democratic constituency groups, especially in education and social services, as he promoted program cuts in those areas as well as state salary freezes.

As Wilder championed his fiscal conservatism and basked in the praises of such unlikely supporters of the former liberal as the *National Review* editorial board and the libertarian Cato Institute, he planned an ill-fated run for the presidency in 1992. The governor's frequent travels out of state to promote his national profile resulted in an angry Virginia electorate and a popular, mocking bumper sticker that read "Wilder for Resident." Wilder further angered Virginians with his ongoing very public feud with Senator Charles S. Robb and also with state legislators from the northern Virginia region who believed that his policies were slighting the area of the state that had delivered his election.

Indeed, the geographic base for statewide Democratic candidates in the 1980s was in the northern Virginia communities of Alexandria, Fairfax City, Falls Church City, and Arlington, and along what is known as the "urban corridor"—a densely populated stretch of land from these northern Virginia communities, south to Richmond, and east along the coast in the Hampton Roads-Tidewater region. The modern Republican base began west of the urban corridor and covered almost all of the state's rural areas. On election night in 1989, television maps of voting showed a thin stretch of land along the urban corridor that voted for Wilder while the vast geographic portion of the state chose Republican J. Marshall Coleman.

Although Wilder left office with ebbing popularity, he could credibly claim some important accomplishments. He indeed kept the state budget balanced for four years and never raised the state income tax. He took the leadership in successfully promoting adoption by the General Assembly of a one-gun-per-month limit bill. That he did so in a state with a strong pro-gun rights tradition was no small feat. During Wilder's term the Democratic-controlled state legislature and the state GOP feuded over redistricting proposals that ultimately resulted in the creation of a Black majority district. Consequently, in 1992 Democrat Robert C. Scott of Newport News became the first Black elected to Congress from Virginia in over a century.

Wilder next sought political office in 1994 when he ran for the US Senate as an independent candidate against incumbent Chuck Robb, Republican Oliver North, and former attorney general and gubernatorial opponent J. Marshall Coleman who, like Wilder, ran as an independent. It was an extraordinary campaign that featured two tainted major party nominees, as revelations of extramarital affairs diminished Robb's once high popularity in the state and Oliver North carried the stigma of his central role in the Iran-Contra scandal in the Reagan White House. Wilder claimed that he had to run because the two major parties had failed in nominating candidates tainted by scandals and that Virginia had become a national "laughingstock"—a reference to late-night comics having lampooned the state in their monologues. After Robb tried to come clean about his extra-marital relationships, issuing a letter in which he said "I let my guard down," comedian Jay Leno joked that that was "Washingtonese" for "I let my pants down" (Rozell and Wilcox 1996: 164). North's campaign in particular attracted far-reaching and unflattering media coverage of the state's political situation.

For a while it appeared Wilder might surprise political observers yet again. In early June a Mason-Dixon Political/Media Research poll had the four candidates in a statistical tie. Wilder had amassed an impressive number of signatures on a petition to qualify for the November ballot—far more than required by state law (Rozell and Wilcox 1996: 165). Wilder again ran a campaign outside the conventional norms of Virginia elections. He sounded closer to Republicans than his own party at times and even seemed to jab the Democratic nominee Robb more than the two Republicans running for the seat. In one candidate debate when a moderator asked North to respond to charges that he was too closely aligned with the religious right movement, Wilder jumped in that it was "hypocritical" for liberal Democrats who had no reservations about their own candidates appearing at Black churches seeking votes to then suggest it was not legitimate for conservative evangelicals to organize politically out of their own churches.[10]

Although he campaigned vigorously for the seat, Wilder eventually dropped out in the face of declining poll numbers and fundraising. By September when he dropped out, Wilder had slipped to fourth place. What especially hurt his campaign were perceptions that he was only hurting the chances of the incumbent Democrat Robb to win, and possibly would cause a North election to the Senate. When African American political leaders and prominent pastors abandoned Wilder's campaign and endorsed Robb, the signal to Wilder was too strong to ignore. His departure, and eventual endorsement of the Democratic Party nominee, ultimately had a large impact on Robb's reelection.

Wilder nonetheless achieved another historic first when the voters of Richmond elected him mayor in 2004. He thus became the city's first elected mayor in sixty years, as previously the position of mayor had been selected from one of the nine city council members. A successful 2003 referendum to allow direct voting for mayor, led by former Wilder campaign manager Paul Goldman, paved the way for Wilder, who won the following year with 79 percent of the vote. He had a somewhat contentious term in office and in 2008 announced he would not run for a second term. Wilder today teaches part-time at the school that bears his name, The Wilder School of Government and Public Affairs at Virginia Commonwealth University in Richmond.

Wilder's two statewide victories in particular paved the way for African American candidates in Virginia. Once dismissed as not electorally viable—with many party leaders opposed to him saying it was really all about his policies and had nothing to do with his race—Wilder proved more than three decades ago that in the South, an African American can win statewide. And yet, no African American would be elected statewide in Virginia again until nearly three decades later.[11]

A 1997 scholarly analysis of the factors that led to Wilder's victories indeed projected that despite demographic changes occurring in the Commonwealth, the prospects for future Black statewide candidates there did not look at all promising. The authors based their assessment on data showing that demographic changes leading up to Wilder's elections had little to do with his electoral successes (Clemons and Jones 1997). Two decades after this study appeared, vast demographic changes, beyond what any observers could have easily predicted, changed Virginia's politics profoundly and made the state increasingly friendly territory for minority candidates for public offices.

2017: Electing Justin Fairfax

Justin Fairfax made his first run for public office in 2013 when he sought the Democratic nomination for attorney general at thirty-three years of age. Fairfax had worked as a federal prosecutor, as an associate of a law firm, and on campaigns for several Democratic candidates. Although he lost the nomination to Mark Herring, he surprised many political observers by running a very closely competitive race, losing by only about 4,500 votes of over 141,000 cast. Herring was an incumbent state senator with a long career in local and state politics, and most had assumed he would easily win against the young upstart Fairfax. But Fairfax proved an adept campaigner and fundraiser, and he garnered the influential endorsement of the *Washington Post* editorial board (*Washington Post* 2013). As the three Democratic statewide candidates swept to victory that year, Fairfax contemplated his next statewide run. When Herring made clear his intention to run for reelection, Fairfax announced his candidacy for the lieutenant governor position in 2017.

As Fairfax made his political move, it appeared to many that the Democratic Party establishment was repeating its three-decades ago reaction to Doug Wilder. The state party in 2016 invited Fairfax's then most formidable likely opponent for nomination to a prominent speaking role at its annual convention, but did not extend an invitation to Fairfax. A leading state party official accused Fairfax of dividing the party with his candidacy, a statement that led to charges of party leaders trying to scuttle the campaign of an African American candidate to favor a still unannounced White one. The state party then apologized for the comment. A *Richmond Times Dispatch* story described the tensions over Fairfax running again for state office as "it hasn't been simple for Fairfax to crack through the Virginia establishment of his Democratic Party, which currently occupies all five statewide offices with White men . . . Fairfax has not been a part of the club" (Wilson 2017). Once again, as with Wilder three decades earlier, opponents of Fairfax pleaded that their concern about a Fairfax nomination had nothing to do with race and everything to do with a preference to nominate a candidate with a better chance of winning the general election.

The state party ultimately failed to recruit any other formidable candidate to run for lieutenant governor; Fairfax ended up running against two relative unknowns and won nomination with 49 percent of the vote. The path to victory for him looked promising, as the political environment in the state the year after the presidential victory of Donald J. Trump was highly favorable to Democrats whose grassroots activists were hyper-motivated. Further, the Republicans had nominated for the office a far-right candidate, state senator Jill Vogel, who had made her mark by introducing legislation in 2012 to require women seeking abortions to undergo a transvaginal ultrasound procedure. National political commentators and even prominent late-night comedic talk shows lampooned Vogel's proposal, to devastating effect.[12]

Despite the favorable circumstances, Fairfax found himself in a tough race made all the more complicated by another poorly calculated response to his candidacy by his own party backers. At the request of the Laborers' International Union of North America (LIUNA), the Ralph Northam for governor campaign released a campaign flyer featuring himself and attorney general nominee Mark Herring—two White men—but not Fairfax. LIUNA had endorsed the two candidates for state office, but not Fairfax due to a difference over policy. The flyer, though, set off protests by Fairfax supporters. The director of the Loudoun County NAACP expressed a common frustration: "A lot of us feel the Virginia Democratic Party has never been a very inclusive group, and they always kind of marginalize African Americans without providing any grounds for advancement." Fairfax himself slammed the decision to leave him off the flyer as a terrible signal to the party's commitment to African American voters: "This should not have happened, and it should not happen again, and there needs to be robust investment in making sure that we are communicating with African American voters and we are engaging our base" (Nirappil 2017).

Former governor Doug Wilder weighed in late in the campaign by endorsing Fairfax but making no endorsement of the other two Democratic candidates for statewide office. He made little secret of his reason, citing the 2016 state party convention snub of Fairfax as well as the campaign flyer incident. "Justin, in my judgment has not been dealt a good hand," Wilder told reporters (Cain 2017).

Fairfax won the election by a comfortable 5.5 percentage points, although he trailed Northam's margin of nearly 9 percent. Although the Republicans had run hard-right campaigns for both governor and lieutenant governor, even in a Democratic sweep election some of the electorate split their ticket and voted Democratic for governor but not for lieutenant governor. Whether some of the split party voting was due to discomfort with Fairfax because of his race, is a matter of mere speculation.

Conclusion: Comparing/Contrasting Wilder's and Fairfax's Victories

There are important comparisons and contrasts between the electoral experiences of Wilder and Fairfax. Three decades separated their elections.

In state political terms, they ran in two very different eras. According to the US Census data, when Doug Wilder was inaugurated in 1990, the state's population was 77.4 percent White, with a relatively small, but uncounted by the census, non-White Hispanic component (Gibson and Jung 2002). By the time Justin Fairfax announced his candidacy for lieutenant governor, the non-Hispanic White population was 56.1 percent, and the Hispanic (of any race) population stood at 13.9 percent. The African American component of the population across the two periods had grown modestly from 18.8 percent to 20.3 percent, while the Asian population surged from 2.6 percent to 7.7 percent (CDC 2018). The fast-growing diversity of the Virginia population, centered around the urban areas of northern Virginia in particular, and the propensity of minority voters to support Democrats, created a much more hospitable electoral environment for Fairfax than Wilder had faced in the 1980s. Nonetheless, both African American candidates ran behind the rest of their respective Democratic tickets led by White candidates.

Wilder, once a gadfly liberal state senator who often agitated the tradition-bound and conservative Democratic Party establishment in Virginia, ran for lieutenant governor and for governor as a moderate and he even presented himself as an advocate of the state's historic traditions of freedom and liberty in the gubernatorial contest. While his GOP opponent Coleman opposed abortion rights, Wilder turned the tables with a brilliant television advertisement that depicted historic locations in the state that evinced old Virginia while the voice over extolled the candidate as the true defender of human freedoms and against government intrusion in peoples' lives. As outside pro-choice groups angrily intoned against the GOP nominee's abortion position as hostile to women, Wilder struck a middle position framed as maintaining continuity with the state's old traditions.

Wilder's opponent tried repeatedly to cast the Democratic nominee as weak on crime and a threat to the rights of gun owners. Wilder again struck moderate positions on both issues and his campaign responded by highlighting his past support from law enforcement organizations. Wilder's "law and order," conservative-sounding campaign message was more reminiscent of GOP campaigns in the South than that of a Democratic Party nominee.

Wilder's opponent also tried to tag the Democratic nominee as a radical "tax and spend" liberal. "We don't need Wilder taxes and Wilder spending" he repeated on the campaign trail. A clever line, but Wilder himself gave no ground to the accusations that he was going to heavily tax citizens or blow up the state budget with big spending programs. He navigated both issues carefully with a pledge to not raise income taxes, and he repeatedly reminded voters of the state's constitutional mandate to maintain a balanced budget. Wilder's major tax reform proposal was hardly radical: eliminate the state tax on the sale of prescription drugs to seniors.

African Americans strongly supported Wilder's candidacy, but they had little visibility in his campaign. Indeed, when former presidential candidate and civil rights leader Reverend Jesse Jackson offered to make campaign appearances to help mobilize Black support for Wilder, the candidate very publicly snubbed the civil rights icon by making it clear that Jackson was not welcome in the state during the campaign. Wilder and Jackson were long-time friends, going back to their college days in the early 1960s. But in the 1980s Wilder believed that Jackson's liberal populist message and often combative rhetoric were politically out of place, even toxic, in Virginia.[13] Wilder ultimately pinned his gubernatorial hopes on holding the liberal base, while attracting conservative Democratic voters, then still very abundant in Virginia, as well as independents. Harris Miller, the Democratic Party chair of Fairfax County, put it best at the time: "Jesse Jackson believes in a populist political revolution. Doug Wilder doesn't see the world in terms of an upstart revolution; he's a pretty conservative politician, opposed to many of the things Reverend Jackson espouses" (Melton 1989).

Wilder's campaign reflected the realities of the time. The Virginia in which he ran in the 1980s was a vastly different place than it is today. Wilder thus campaigned as a pragmatic moderate, even conservative on many issues. He was aware of the past characterizations of himself as too liberal. Running to become the first African American elected as a state governor, he steadfastly downplayed race. A veteran of the war in Korea, Wilder touted his national service credentials in response to those who tried to paint him as a radical politician posing as a moderate.

As governor, Wilder attracted the ire of liberal members of his own party and of state employees. He froze public spending, refused to raise taxes to cover a budget shortfall, and lambasted his Democratic Party predecessors in state government for having been profligate spenders who bequeathed him a budget unable to sustain even a mild recession. Conservative commentators praised his leadership, and he soon embarked on an ill-fated 1992 presidential campaign running as a party centrist.

The 1989 election map in Virginia has some notable similarities with and contrasts to the electoral map of more recent Democrat victories in

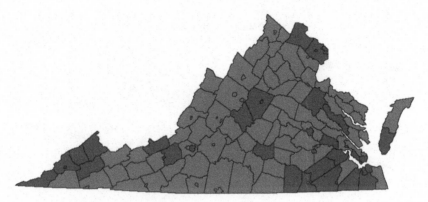

Figure 4.1 1989 Virginia Gubernatorial Election Map

the state (Figure 4.1). The urban crescent from northern Virginia through Hampton Roads and into inner-city Richmond and college towns such as Charlottesville remain strong Democratic territory, although they have become an even deeper "blue" (Democratic) today, as evidenced by the 2017 election maps (Figure 4.2). The outer suburbs of northern Virginia remained Republican territory at that time and the deep southwest, rural coal-mining communities were still strongly Democrat leaning.

The color schemes of the 1989 and 2017 maps do not align perfectly, with the latter being more detailed regarding regions' voter margins. The key differences, though, are clear in that rural, union-dominated areas of the southwest changed from very Democratic to heavily Republican and the "red" areas of the state overall became a much deeper red, whereas the "blue" areas saw the vast majority of the population growth of the state and turned a much deeper blue. For an African American Democrat to win in 1989 required a very different electoral strategy than in 2017. Winning in 1989 required a difficult political balancing act to maintain simultaneously the support of urban/suburban voters in regions with a high population as well as enough working-class rural voters. By 2017, a pure partisan-based urban/suburban vote strategy could win statewide for Democratic Party candidates. Political polarization in Virginia, as in much of the country, has significantly altered the electoral map.

Between 1989 and 2017 Virginia had changed politically. Previously the most Republican-voting state in the nation in presidential contests, by the time Justin Fairfax ran for lieutenant governor, Virginia had voted Democrat for president in three consecutive elections (2008, 2012, 2016). Barack

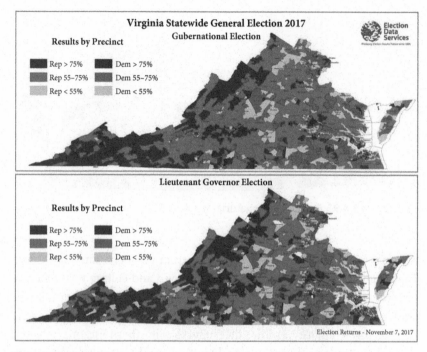

Figure 4.2 2017 Virginia Gubernatorial and Lieutenant Governor
Election Maps

Obama won the state comfortably in his two presidential races. Those were
significant accomplishments when considering that, prior to 2008, and going
back to 1952, Virginia had voted Democrat for president only once—in the
1964 Lyndon B. Johnson landslide, and only by a slim margin. Virginia was
the only southern state to abandon native son southerner Democrat Jimmy
Carter in his run for the presidency in 1976. As evidence of the massive
change in Virginia, forty years later, in 2016, it was the only state of the Old
South to vote for the Democrat, Hillary Clinton, for president. Democrat
Joe Biden carried Virginia by more than 10 percentage points over President
Trump in the 2020 election—the fourth consecutive Democratic presidential win in the state. Entering the 2021 elections, Republicans had not elected
anyone statewide in Virginia for twelve years. National political observers
colored Virginia blue. With these developments in mind, it is easy to understand how Justin Fairfax won election running a very different kind of campaign than Doug Wilder's in the 1980s.

Wilder had to counter images that others had of a "radical Black" or "angry Black man" and he did so by showing deference to Virginia history and customs and touting his military background and moderate-conservatism. Fairfax did not have so much of this hostile environment to counter. Virginia had become much more diverse, with vast population growth led by minority populations, and the election of a Black candidate in the state that had elected Wilder statewide twice and voted twice for Barack Obama for president was not a novelty. Fairfax thus ran a campaign on such themes as criminal justice reform, gay and lesbian rights, raising the minimum wage, affordable college education, Medicaid expansion, and pay raises for public school teachers and other state employees. Wilder, by contrast, held so firm to his fiscal conservatism that teacher salaries were frozen during his years as governor, tuitions at state colleges and universities rose nearly 50 percent to make up for large state funding cuts, and social services throughout the state saw cuts in budgets. He did not promote reforming the criminal justice system or funding affordable college education for all.

In short, each candidate crafted a campaign that suited the political environment of Virginia at the time he ran for office. In that sense, the contrasts in their styles and in their issues are a reflection of their differing times in politics. The other limitation in drawing comparisons is that Wilder rose to the state's highest office, Fairfax only to lieutenant governor. In Virginia elections, candidates for lieutenant governor—a part-time office with little formal power—receive little attention from a public focused on the gubernatorial race, although that certainly was not the case with Wilder's campaign in 1985. Democratic nominee Ralph Northam's gubernatorial landslide anchored Fairfax's election that year, although curiously Fairfax ran several percentage points behind Northam. Similarly, in 1989 Wilder ran far behind the other two Democratic statewide candidates.

Wilder's elections opened the path for African American candidates in Virginia. But it was nearly three decades before another African American would win statewide office in the Old Dominion. Wilder made one more run statewide in Virginia, when he launched his independent campaign for the US Senate in 1994 against incumbent Charles S. Robb. For Wilder, it was a difficult effort given that Robb, a political centrist, occupied similar philosophical territory. Furthermore, Wilder had become politically unpopular during his governorship, especially because he had almost immediately looked to a presidential run and there was a widespread perception that governing the state was not his highest priority. Wilder dropped out of the US Senate race that Robb ultimately won (Rozell and Wilcox 1996).

Fairfax, though, succeeded without positioning himself as a moderate-conservative. He ran on an authentic progressive agenda campaign and, unlike Wilder, he did not distance himself from prominent African American civil rights leaders, but instead embraced them. Whereas Wilder had allowed himself to be depicted with a Confederate flag and said that he was not offended by what he called a symbol of historic heritage, in 2018 Fairfax refused to preside over the state senate—the customary role of the lieutenant governor—during annual tributes to Confederate generals Thomas J. "Stonewall" Jackson and Robert E. Lee. Wilder the pragmatist took the politically necessary path in Virginia in the 1980s in order to get elected. Fairfax rode a wave of progressive growth in the current Virginia electorate.

Virginia is a vastly different place politically today than it was three decades ago. Wilder's election to lieutenant governor attracted widespread national attention. Fairfax's election to that office barely registered any attention at all outside of Virginia. From now on, it may become routine that minority candidates, African Americans and others, are competitive in the state's elections.

5

South Carolina

Jaime Harrison Comes Up Well Short[*]

> This was the seat of Ben "Pitchfork" Tillman, who would go to the floor of the US Senate and talk about the joys of lynching black folks. But on Nov. 3, the people of South Carolina are going to close the book on the old South and write a brand new book called the new South.
>
> —Jaime Harrison, October 17, 2020

> We're not going to let our life and our way of life go away Tuesday, and that's what's on the ballot.
>
> —Lindsey Graham, October 31 or November 1, 2020

In one of the most widely watched, analyzed, and expensive US Senate campaigns in history, Democratic nominee Jaime Harrison came up surprisingly well short in his bid to become the second African American elected to the US Senate from South Carolina. Democrats nationally had pinned their hopes on flipping the US Senate seat in South Carolina, given three-term Republican incumbent senator Lindsey Graham's profile as one of the staunchest defenders of President Donald Trump.

Many, including Harrison himself, saw South Carolina's race as something bigger, part of a larger story about the changing racial politics in the South. In a nationally televised interview connected to his announcement of joining the race, Harrison said:

> We are on the verge—we saw with Stacey [Abrams, of Georgia], we saw with Andrew [Gillum, of Florida]—*we are on the verge of a renaissance in the South,*

[*] Anthony Cilluffo is co-author of this chapter.

African American Statewide Candidates in the New South. Charles S. Bullock, III, Susan A. MacManus, Jeremy D. Mayer, and Mark J. Rozell, Oxford University Press. © Oxford University Press 2022. DOI: 10.1093/oso/9780197607428.003.0005

a new South, and I really hope people will help join me in this effort ... we really are on the verge of changing something, and we've seen it even in recent elections in South Carolina. [We won elections here even though] the pundits in DC didn't think we had a shot because they think, "It's ruby red South Carolina, they can't win anything." *Well, we're winning in South Carolina. It's all about investing and fighting.* (Harrison 2019a; emphasis added)

The presumption among many Democrats was that Graham's close relationship with the president, as well as the senator's big national profile and perceived indifference to state and local issues in South Carolina, created an opportunity to gain a Senate seat. Harrison raised the most money of any US Senate candidate in the nation in 2020, over $131 million. Public opinion polls had the race projected to be close—with some polls even showing a slight Harrison lead close to the official Election Day (FiveThirtyEight 2020). The final projections by Real Clear Politics and the Cook Political Report were that the race was a "tossup." And yet, Graham won re-election by a landslide 10 percentage points.

How can we explain the huge disconnect between such widespread expectations of a very close race and the actual very different outcome of it? Does the strong rejection of Harrison's candidacy offer particular insights into the role of race in South Carolina electoral politics?

State Background

Long a part of the "solid South" dominated by the Democratic Party, since the 1980s South Carolina has been a solid Republican stronghold. As scholar Scott E. Buchanan (2018: 45–49) notes, by some measures South Carolina is the most Republican of all the Deep South states. Consider: Since 1964, only once has South Carolina voted Democratic in a presidential campaign, and that was 1976 when native son southerner Jimmy Carter won the presidency and all of the southern states, except Virginia. In 1968, it was the only Deep South state to vote for Richard Nixon for president, choosing the GOP over independent segregationist southerner George Wallace. Since 1964, Republicans have held at least one US Senate seat, and since 2005 they have held both. Since 1995, the GOP has held a majority of the US House of Representatives districts in the state. Further, the GOP gained control of the lower house of the state legislature in 1994 and the upper house in 2000. Only once since 1986 has the Democratic Party won the governorship, and in the past decade the GOP has swept all of the statewide elected offices.

Buchanan (2018: 46) explains that the dominant conservative ideology of the state has been consistent over time, but the parties changed, with the Democrats having shifted increasingly Left and the GOP further Right. Consequently, any Democrat running to unseat Graham began with a very disadvantageous political context. The reactions of two scholars in the state, just a month before the official Election Day, were telling. Said Danielle Vinson, at Furman University in Greenville, SC: "I have never had a conversation about a South Carolina Senate race like this in my entire 25-year history of being a professor in the state. We have not had a competitive Senate race until now." But then David Woodard of Clemson University (and part-time Republican consultant, including to Graham), who said that South Carolina is "so red it is sunburned," told the *Greenville News* that he did not believe Graham was "in any trouble whatsoever" (Brown 2020). In Graham's previous three campaigns for the Senate seat, he easily won.

Further complicating the race for Harrison was that President Donald Trump consistently held strong leads in the state, and there was very little effort there by the Joe Biden campaign. Thus, Harrison had to count on a substantial percentage of split-ticket voting, which was always unlikely to happen given that polarization has radically increased straight ticket voting in recent elections (Kilgore 2018). The *New York Times*/Sienna poll in October 2020 pointed to another deep challenge for Democrats in the Palmetto State. In all of the Sun Belt states other than South Carolina, college-educated White voters favored Biden over Trump in the presidential race. Yet in South Carolina, Trump held a 12 percentage point lead over his opponent with those voters. Among Whites without a college degree, Trump led by a whopping 77–18 percent (Martin 2020). Additionally, Trump's core constituency, White evangelicals, comprised 44 percent of the South Carolina vote in the previous presidential election, and they voted 88 percent for Trump over Hillary Clinton. The Black vote was an impressive 94 percent for Clinton, although Blacks comprised only 19 percent of the electorate (Bullock et al. 2019: 70).

South Carolina is the slowest growing of the "growth states" in the South. Its population growth has been substantial in recent decades, just not as robust as in the other five growth states. Since 1950, Florida has added twenty-one congressional districts, Texas fifteen, Georgia four, Virginia two, and each of the Carolinas has added one. Among those states South Carolina has the lowest percentage of college-educated residents and the lowest median income (Bullock et al. 2019: 6–9, 42–45). Finally, in recent years leading up to the 2020 elections, Republicans lost seats in the state houses of five of the six growth states—the exception being South Carolina (Bullock et al 2019: 73). Thus, among the categories suggesting increased partisan competition and electoral prospects for Democrats, South Carolina is the least hospitable territory among the southern growth states.

Like most of the South, South Carolina has a long and complicated history of race relations. In the early twentieth century the state Democratic Party used the White primary to exclude Black voter participation, and although the US Supreme Court in 1944 ruled the practice unconstitutional, suppression of Black voting continued such that barely more than one-third of Blacks were registered to vote by the time of passage of the Voting Rights Act (VRA) of 1965 (Fauntroy 2012: 455). After passage of the VRA, Black voting registration and participation went up substantially, and for Barack Obama's presidential campaigns in 2008 and 2012, there was near parity in the rates of voter participation between Whites and voters of color (Buchanan 2018: 50–52).

Race in South Carolina has become much more complicated. The election of a Black Republican to the US Senate from the state in 2014 and again in 2016 suggests that partisanship sometimes dwarfs race for some White South Carolina voters. Tim Scott, appointed by the governor in 2012 to fill a US Senate vacancy, won landslide re-election campaigns in 2014 and again in 2016, each time receiving about 60 percent of the vote, and did much better among White voters than he did among those of his own race. Previously, Scott had won election to the US House of Representatives in 2008, and was re-elected in 2010 and 2012, in a majority White district. Former Governor Nikki Haley, also a Republican, is of Indian descent. She won the governorship in 2010 and 2014, winning substantial support from White voters both times.

Demographics of South Carolina Electorate

As mentioned earlier, South Carolina has grown over the last several decades, but not as much as neighboring Southern states. Official voter registration from the South Carolina State Election Commission (n.d.) bears this out. Total registered voters increased from 2.3 million in 2000 to 2.6 million in 2008, 3.2 million in 2016, and 3.5 million in 2020.

Although the state is growing, the racial and ethnic composition of its voters has not changed much since 2000 (see Figure 5.1). The share of registered voters who are persons of color has remained fairly stable since 2008, when it was 30.3 percent. In 2020, it was 30.2 percent. The share of voters of color usually increases in presidential election years. This pattern stopped in 2016, when the share of voters of color *fell* slightly from 2014 to 2016 and did not change much in from 2018 to 2020. However, all of these shifts are relatively minor, and the overall stability in the share of voters of color in the electorate over the last two decades is remarkable.

The growing population but relatively constant racial and ethnic composition shows that South Carolina's population change is much different from that of other Southern states, such as Florida, Texas, and Georgia. Many of the people who move to South Carolina from Northern or Rust Belt states are conservatives who do so specifically because of the state's right-leaning politics (Fausset 2020). Also, unlike Florida and Texas especially, South Carolina "remains defined very much in terms of a Black-and-White binary, with Whites in the majority," according to Caroline R. Nagel at the University of South Carolina at Columbia (qtd. in Fausset 2020). Among the entire state population (not just registered voters), 65 percent of South Carolinians are non-Hispanic White, 27 percent are non-Hispanic Black, 6 percent

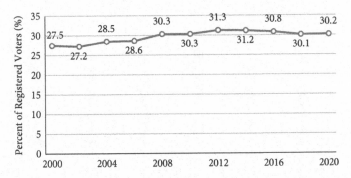

Figure 5.1 Proportion of South Carolina Registered Voters Who Are Voters of Color

The proportion of registered voters of color in South Carolina has increased in most in presidential election years, except in 2016 and 2020.

Sources: Author's analysis of South Carolina State Election Commission Voter History Statistics for each respective general election (https://www.scvotes.gov/data/voter-history.html). Accessed April 1, 2021.

are Hispanic, and 2 percent are Asian or Pacific Islander (South Carolina Revenue and Fiscal Affairs Office n.d.a).

South Carolina usually has a substantial racial and ethnic turnout gap (see Figure 5.2). In general elections since 2000 (presidential and mid-term), White voter turnout was on average 5.2 percentage points higher than turnout among voters of color. In the 2016 presidential election, White voter turnout was 8.2 percentage points higher. The important exceptions were 2008 and 2012, both presidential elections with Barack Obama on the ballot, when voters of color turned out to vote at higher rates than White voters. Although Obama did not win South Carolina in either election, higher turnout among voters of color contributed to him receiving a higher share of the vote in both 2008 (44.9 percent) and 2012 (44.1 percent) than Hillary Clinton in 2016 (40.7 percent), John Kerry in 2004 (40.9 percent), or Al Gore in 2000 (40.9 percent). Importantly for Harrison's bid, voters of color turned out at a notably lower rate than white voters (66.3 percent vs. 73.9 per-cent). While the racial and ethnic turnout gap was smaller than in 2016, it was larger than in the 2004 election and far from that of Obama's elections. As analyzed further later in this chapter, Harrison's failure to turn out South Carolina's voters of color at high rates contributed to his loss.

The South Carolina electorate is aging, representing perhaps the most dramatic demographic shift with political ramifications (see Figure 5.3).

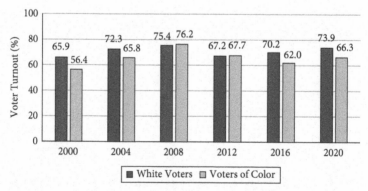

Figure 5.2 South Carolina Voter Turnout by Race and Ethnicity
Turnout in South Carolina was higher for voters of color than for White voters in both presidential elections in which Barack Obama was a candidate.

Source: Author's analysis of South Carolina State Election Commission Voter History Statistics for each respective general election (https://www.scvotes.gov/data/voter-history.html). Accessed April 1, 2021.

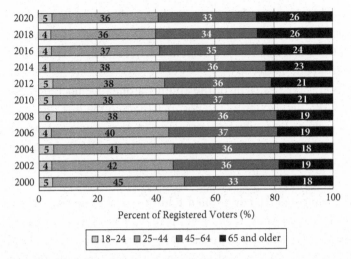

Figure 5.3 South Carolina Registered Voters by Age
The South Carolina electorate is aging, though the trend slowed in 2020.
Source: Author's analysis of South Carolina State Election Commission Voter History Statistics for each respective general election (https://www.scvotes.gov/data/voter-history.html; accessed April 1, 2021).

In 2000, the electorate was evenly split between registered voters aged 18–44 and those aged 45 and older. Just twenty years later, voters aged 45 and older comprised 59 percent of the electorate. The fastest growing age group is those aged 65 and older. They have increased their registered voter share every election since 2000, except for 2020, when they stayed at 26 percent.

Taken together, South Carolina presented clear demographic headwinds to a Harrison upset victory. The state's new residents did not appreciably change the state's racial and ethnic makeup, in sharp contrast to other Southern growth states. Instead, the changes are consistent with a substantial share of the state's new voters being older, White voters, who are more likely to lean Republican.

Harrison Background

Harrison, an attorney educated at Yale University and Georgetown University Law Center, entered this campaign as a first-time candidate for public office. He had nonetheless substantial political experience as a Democratic Party staffer and official and as a lobbyist. He briefly served as director of floor operations for House of Representatives Majority Whip Rep. Jim Clyburn, and later as executive director of the House Democratic Caucus, and as vice chair of the South Carolina Democratic Party. Later he worked as a lobbyist for the firm Podesta Group.

Harrison served as chair of the South Carolina Democratic Party from 2013 to 2017, his election to the post making him the first Black to chair a South Carolina state political party. He also served as an associate chairperson of the Democratic National Committee (DNC). He ran for the position of chairperson of the DNC in 2017, but ultimately withdrew his candidacy and endorsed the eventual victor Rep. Tom Perez.

In the campaign, Harrison often told the story of his own difficult upbringing by a single mother and grandparents. "I was raised on a dirt road in Orangeburg." He was first in his family to attend college, earning a scholarship to Yale University. In speeches he spoke of his story as "emblematic that the American dream is alive and well . . . .We are about to close the chapter on what I call the Old South, and we are going to write a whole new book called the New South, a New South that is bold, that is inclusive and diverse" (Brown 2020).

Harrison frequently highlighted his biography in the campaign, focusing on the details that would resonate most with South Carolina voters. "Born to a teenage mom in Orangeburg, raised by his grandparents, he overcame poverty," started one of Harrison's ads focusing on his biography (Harrison 2020c). The ad continued:

> Jaime Harrison, running for the Senate to restore hope to a broken political system . . . as a son of rural South Carolina, he understands our lives: what it means to go without healthcare, attend an underfunded school, live in places that feel forgotten by the people in power. That's why Jaime's plan does what he's always done: brings people together, Democrats and Republicans, who don't always agree, to work for all of South Carolina. To Jaime, it's not about left versus right, it's about right versus wrong.

Harrison Strategy

Defeating incumbents in Congress is always difficult. Defeating a three-term senator is especially difficult under usual circumstances. Harrison thus entered the campaign as a definite underdog and would have to make the case for voters to remove an incumbent with a long track record representing the state.

Harrison's strategy was to build a new winning coalition: get high turnout from voters of color, have independent voters break his way, and persuade enough college-educated Republicans, especially women, to vote for him. Discussing his own strategy, Harrison said:

> So we are looking at building the coalition that Lindsey Graham ... used to have [before he became one of Trump's closest supporters], one where we will have almost unanimous support from the Democratic Party, one where we will beat him with independents in the state, and one where we will find moderate Republicans who are tired of the heightened partisanship and the sycophantism that Lindsey Graham has conducted. (Axelrod 2020)

Harrison explicitly sought to replicate the political realignment in other southern states, including Virginia and Georgia. "The South is having a renaissance: We can replicate the blueprint created in states like Georgia," he told supporters in a fundraising email (Fausset 2020).

Graham's strategy was to preserve the coalition that won him his previous Senate elections: High turnout and support from the state's conservative plurality—especially White Evangelical Christian voters—while at least splitting the independent vote.

The challenges were not all on Harrison's side; Graham also faced obstacles in the election. In previous contests, particularly 2014, Graham faced primary challengers from his right, attacking him for his membership in the "Gang of Eight" that supported comprehensive immigration reform in 2013 and for supporting Obama's nominations of Elena Kagan and Sonia Sotomayor to the Supreme Court (Martin 2013). He faced six opponents in the Republican primary in 2014 but won easily with 56.4 percent of the vote. He went on to win the general election easily, with 54.3 percent of the vote, while his challenger got less than 40 percent.

In 2020, Graham's challenge was on his left, not his right. During his third term in the US Senate, Graham went from a vocal critic of Trump to one of his closest allies in the Senate. Trump was popular in South Carolina, so Graham's move appeased the GOP base—he received 67.7 percent of the vote in the 2020 Republican primary against three challengers. Instead, his rightward pivot seemed to have opened the one-time moderate to a general election attack from the left. Also, unlike a Trump supporter who had always been on the far right, Graham was potentially vulnerable to the charge of being a flip-flopper. Graham had also been remarkably blunt in his anti-Trump statements during his aborted run for the GOP presidential nomination in 2016. The run itself was also a possible weakness for Graham, as it was profoundly unsuccessful and for months took Graham's focus off what every incumbent politician does naturally to help ensure re-election.

Harrison's strategy in part was to make the case that the incumbent senator had gone too national and thus had ignored the state the people elected him to represent. "He has simply lost touch with the people of this state," Harrison said. Relatedly, Graham was running a campaign that the senator claimed was a bulwark against the national Democratic Party promoting "the most radical agenda that I've ever seen," which Graham said included the Democratic National Convention platform advocating that the District of Columbia become a state. Harrison retorted to the extremism claim that, "whereas Lindsey Graham is trying to scare [voters] to vote for him, I am trying to inspire people to vote for me" (Brown 2020).

Both candidates recognized that their race had been nationalized and would be decided by issues that divided much of the country in 2020. "This is not a South Carolina race anymore. This is a national race," Graham said. By early October, news reports pointed out that campaign contributions to Harrison and Graham from California alone had outpaced contributions from South Carolina residents (Brown 2020). As Harrison was outpacing Graham in fundraising, the incumbent actually went on Sean Hannity's Fox News program to plead for money from the national conservative audience: "I am getting overwhelmed, Help me. They're killing me moneywise. Help me. You did last week. Help me again" (Farhi 2020).

The national Democratic Party policy platform was not popular in deeply conservative South Carolina. Harrison's campaign tried to avoid specific policy positions, especially those associated with progressives. His Rural Hope Agenda—a cornerstone of his campaign—focused broadly on narrowing inequalities between urban and rural communities in access to healthcare, economic opportunity, infrastructure, and education, while proposing a "Farmer's Bill of Rights"—all local issues (Papantonis 2020). He opposed defunding the police: "I oppose all of these efforts to defund the police, but we can't be blind to the idea that there needs to be some reform in our policing" (qtd. in Papantonis 2020). He also opposed the Green New Deal, saying it is "expensive, not feasible and highly partisan" (Lovegrove 2020c).

Harrison also largely avoided directly criticizing Donald Trump, knowing the president was popular in South Carolina and almost certain to beat Joe Biden there. Even Harrison's criticisms of Graham regarding Trump were not over his support of the president but his conversion from being a vocal Trump opponent to a close supporter. Harrison created several ads that contrasted Graham's own words against Trump before the 2016 election and supporting Trump after the 2016 election, saying "Lindsey will say anything, but he does nothing for South Carolina" (Harrison 2020b). "[South Carolinians] know character matters here in this state. This is a values-based state. That's what motivates people, values. And character is a huge part of that. . . . We believe we can make the case that Lindsey Graham has been a failure to South Carolina. And it's time to upgrade," Harrison said (Capehart 2020).

Emblematic of Harrison's political tightrope act in the race is a statement he made at a rally. He pointed out that several million dollars earmarked for a local military base had been diverted to construct the wall at the southern border (without mentioning the border wall directly), and he asked the crowd: "When Senators [Fritz] Hollings and Strom Thurmond were around, do you think they would've ever allowed any president . . . to take money from a military base in South Carolina to use for an administration project? No. Not only no—hell no. . . . But Senator Graham is as quiet as a church mouse" (Desiderio 2020).

This statement is remarkable for three reasons. First, Harrison, the first Black chair of the South Carolina Democrats, invoked former Senator Thurmond—a staunch segregationist—in a positive light for the money he brought to the state. South Carolina's racial history interacted with the election in complicated ways. Second, Harrison avoided specifically mentioning that the money was taken for the wall at the southern border, which was popular in South Carolina, instead painting it as an "administration project"— nefarious big government overreach. Harrison needed policy contortions to appeal to South Carolina's conservative electorate as even a moderate Democrat. Finally, the statement avoids noting that Graham's supposed betrayal of South Carolinians was in support of Donald Trump, which would have hurt Harrison's chances of attracting votes from Republican ticket-splitters. Instead, it was framed as part of Harrison's strategy of discrediting Graham by portraying him as ineffective and out of touch.

Another Harrison ad contrasted Graham's supposed support for "big corporations," while South Carolina "was dead last when it came to small business loans." The narrator, a middle-aged White woman with a local accent, finishes by saying, "I've always voted for Lindsey Graham, but he has changed. So it's time for a change." Interestingly, the fifteen-second social media spot did not mention Harrison or include any campaign images, although it was posted on Harrison's Facebook account (Harrison 2020a).

Avoiding polarizing issues was part of Harrison's strategy of threading the needle on attracting the support of independents and moderate Republicans in Trump-supporting South Carolina. This was a delicate strategy with several risks. Harrison opened himself up to attacks that he would be little more than a rubber stamp for national Democrat's agenda. "To all the folks in California thinking you're going to sell your agenda here, you're going to fall short. They see in my opponent a reliable ally for their agenda. He's not a middle-of-the-road person," Graham said during the campaign (Desiderio 2020).

The other risk of Harrison's strategy was how national events would interact with it. Following the killing of George Floyd by a Minneapolis police officer and nationwide social justice protests, defunding the police became an issue in the campaign. Defunding the police was a very unpopular policy proposal among the more conservative voters in South Carolina. Harrison officially announced his opposition to defunding the police, but his opponents still pegged the issue to him. After the election, Rep. Jim Clyburn (D-SC-6), the US House Majority Whip, a leading voice among South Carolina Democrats and mentor to Harrison, said that: "Jaime Harrison started to plateau when 'defund the police' showed up . . . That stuff hurt Jaime" (Clyburn 2020).

To rally conservative voters, Graham had several factors in his favor. First was his steadfast support for President Trump, who remained deeply popular with the GOP base. Second, as chair of the Senate Judiciary Committee Graham had a national platform from which to lead the confirmation process for a conservative jurist nominated by the president late in the election cycle. Third, the unprecedented efforts by national Democrats and contributors to turn South Carolina blue may have backfired by giving Graham an issue to deepen his connection with South Carolina's voters. Finally, the Democratic narrative that Graham had lost touch with the state may have backfired with some South Carolina voters who knew Graham very well from his previous elections and saw him as one of their own. The enormous amount of money contributed to Harrison from outside the state ultimately weakened the Democrats' strategy of presenting him as more focused than Graham on state and local issues in South Carolina.

Graham also sought to make the national money coming into the race an issue, accusing out-of-staters of trying to by the election for Harrison.

At a debate during the election, Graham brought up the issue: "Let's talk about money and politics. Where the hell is all this money coming from? What is it about South Carolina that has attracted almost $100 million into Jaime Harrison? Mr. Harrison's coffers? They hate me. This is not about Mr. Harrison. This is about liberals hating my guts" (Bean and Reagan 2020).

Election Campaign

Jaime Harrison announced his candidacy on May 29, 2019, in a video posted to YouTube that previewed his campaign strategy (Harrison 2019b). It started with his biography, while Harrison stood outside his childhood home, saying:

> Comic books. That's how I learned to read. Being born to a sixteen-year-old mom and raised by my grandparents in Orangeburg, we made do with the opportunities we created for ourselves. Because that's all we had . . . My grandparents didn't have much, but they raised me right. Taught me what most South Carolinians know, character counts.

The video later turned to his opponent. "Lindsey Graham's story is just comical." Like many of Harrison's later ads, it contrasted Graham's own words about Trump before 2016—"I think he's a kook"—with his words after 2016—"I am all in, keep it up Donald!" "Here's a guy who will say anything to stay in office," Harrison tells us. The announcement closes with several of Harrison's key issues in the campaign: rural healthcare, economic issues, "[helping] the people," and restoring trust in elected officials. The ad closes with a quote from the Bible and pictures of Harrison with his wife and sons.

Harrison was not the first entrant vying for the Democratic nomination to face Lindsey Graham. Gloria Bromell Tinubu, a former Georgia state representative and 2014 candidate for South Carolina's Seventh Congressional District, had already announced her candidacy in the primary. The field would eventually expand to four candidates—Harrison, Tinubu, Justin Wooten, and Willian Stone (Dixon 2019). However, the Democratic Senatorial Campaign Committee—the official party arm for US Senate races—endorsed Harrison, sending a message to the other candidates that the party's support would not be forthcoming (Kinnard 2019). The other three candidates dropped out and endorsed Harrison, allowing him to win the Democratic primary uncontested.

In the early phases of the campaign, Harrison made a string of high-profile appearances on national media: *Rachel Maddow* (MSNBC), May 28, 2019; *Andrea Mitchell* (MSNBC), June 11, 2019; and *Morning Joe* (MSNBC), June 19, 2019. He focused on Graham throughout his appearances and started to cultivate the national liberal audience that would later funnel unprecedented amounts of money to his campaign.

Lindsey Graham launched his re-election campaign on March 30, 2019, at an event with Vice President Mike Pence. The event highlighted Graham's closeness with President Trump—Pence lauded Graham for supporting Trump "every step of the way," while Graham pledged to be an ally to Trump if both were re-elected. "President Trump loves this state and he listens to us and he cares about who we are," Graham told the crowd (Young and Marchant 2019).

Graham faced three primary challengers, down from the six he faced in 2014. Two of the three—Duke Buckner and Michael LaPierre—ran to Graham's right, arguing that Graham did not represent the state's true conservative values. The last candidate, Joe Reynolds, ran on an anti-incumbency platform, arguing new legislators were needed to solve the nation's problems (Lovegrove 2020a). Graham received 68 percent of the vote, with the other three candidates splitting the remaining votes.

Many Republicans were frustrated that Graham did not take Harrison's challenge more seriously from the beginning (Taylor 2020). Graham's first attack ad was in June 2020—after Harrison had been running ads for several months. Graham's ad was simple: remind South Carolina voters that Harrison is a Democrat. "Jaime Harrison's TV ads are missing some things. Not once does he mention he's a Democrat," the narrator says (Lovegrove 2020b).

National interest in the race mounted as the race looked more competitive. Public polls showed that while Graham started with an impressive lead at the beginning of the race, Harrison had caught up to Graham by summer 2020 (see Figure 5.4). Although no one poll should be overly relied upon, especially with the relatively small sample sizes in most state polls, the trend in results of several polls can be illuminating. The end of May 2020—when the killing of George Floyd by a Minneapolis police officer dominated the news—was the first time a poll showed Harrison and Graham as even. After

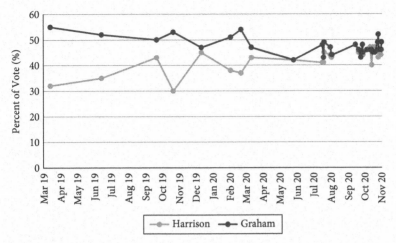

Figure 5.4 South Carolina US Senate Election Polling
Polling showed that Harrison had closed the gap with Graham by summer 2020.
Source: Polls listed on *FiveThirtyEight* poll tracker for SC US Senate Race (https://projects.fivethir tyeight.com/polls/south-carolina/; accessed January 27, 2021).

that, neither candidate created a durable lead, with polls alternating between a small (not statistically significant) lead for one or a dead heat.

The campaign was a winding road (see Table 5.1). Graham was in the national spotlight throughout, including his investigation of the Biden family's dealing in Ukraine (November 2019), voting to acquit in Trump's first impeachment (February 2020), and saying that Congress would reauthorize the $600 per week additional unemployment compensation "over our dead bodies." Graham's polarizing actions brought more attention to the race which, along with the perceived competitiveness and Harrison's personal charm, made Harrison a prolific fundraiser.

By Election Day, Harrison had raised the most money in a US Senate campaign ever to that point, over $131 million. Graham raised the second most, over $109 million (see Figure 5.5). (These records would later be beaten in the January 2021 Georgia Senate runoffs.) Harrison raised a record-setting $70.4 million in unitemized individual contributions—those in amounts less than $200 that come from donors who have given less than $200 in aggregate during the election cycle.

Both candidates relied heavily on out-of-state donors: Harrison raised 95 percent of his funds from outside South Carolina, while Graham received

Table 5.1 Major Events and Fundraising in 2020 SC US Senate Race

Period	Major Events	Fundraising Period (cumulative)
Apr. 1–June 30, 2019	Apr. 6—Former SC US Senator Fritz Hollings died May 29—Harrison announced candidacy May 30—DSCC endorsed Harrison	Harrison: $1.6M ($1.8M) Graham: $3.0M ($9.6M)
July 1–Sept. 30, 2019	July 6—Biden, campaigning in Sumter, SC, apologized for comments on working with segregationists	Harrison: $2.2M ($4.0M) Graham: $3.3M ($12.9M)
Oct. 1–Dec. 31, 2019	Nov. 22—Graham opened investigation of Biden family Ukraine dealings	Harrison: $3.6M ($7.6M) Graham: $4.0M ($16.9M)
Jan. 1–Mar. 31, 2020	Feb. 5—Graham voted "not guilty" on both counts of impeachment against Trump Feb. 29—Biden won SC Democratic Presidential Preference Primary Mar. 11—WHO declared COVID-19 a global pandemic	Harrison: $7.4M ($15.0M) Graham: $5.7M ($22.6M)
Apr. 1–May 20, 2020	Apr. 30—Graham said Congress will extend $600/month unemployment payment "over our dead bodies" May 12—SC legislature unanimously approved bill to expand absentee voting in June primary, citing safety May 17—NASCAR race held at Darlington, SC, one of the first professional sports events post-shutdown	Harrison: $4.2M ($19.2M) Graham: $3.6M ($26.2M)
May 21–June 30, 2020	May 21—Stacey Abrams endorsed Harrison May 25—George Floyd killed by police in Minneapolis, MN May 31-June 1—Charleston County imposed curfew after traffic blocked on I-26 and property was damaged downtown June 7—President Trump endorsed Graham June 9—Primary election June 24—US Senator Tim Scott's (R-SC) police reform bill blocked by Senate Democrats	Harrison: $9.8M ($29.0M) Graham: $4.7M ($30.9M)
July 1–Sept. 30, 2020	July 29—Graham campaign accused of darkening Harrison's skin tone in a campaign ad Aug. 3—Former President Obama endorsed Harrison Sept. 18—Vulgar tweets authored by Harrison campaign staffers surfaced Sept. 18—Supreme Court Justice Ruth Bader Ginsberg died	Harrison: $57.9M ($86.9M) Graham: $28.5M ($59.4M)

Table 5.1 *Continued*

Period	Major Events	Fundraising Period (cumulative)
Oct. 1–Oct. 14, 2020	Oct. 1—Third party candidate Bill Bledsoe unofficially dropped out and endorsed Graham Oct. 3—First election debate Oct. 5—In-person early voting started Oct. 7—*Cook Political Report* rated the race a "toss-up" Oct. 12-14—Senate Judiciary Committee held hearings for Amy Coney Barrett to replace Justice Ginsberg	Harrison: $22.1M ($109.0M) Graham: $14.8M ($74.2M)
Oct. 15–Nov. 3, 2020	Oct. 19—Former President Obama released video supporting Harrison Oct. 26—Full Senate voted to confirm Amy Coney Barrett to US Supreme Court Oct. 30—Final election debate Nov. 3—Election Day	Harrison: $23.1M ($132.1M) Graham: $34.8M ($109.1M)

Note: Listing of major events is not exhaustive and intended only for illustration.

Source: Major events from news reports. Fundraising from campaign FEC reports for each period.

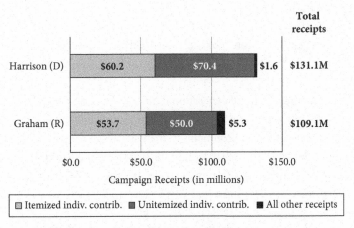

Figure 5.5 South Carolina Senate Campaign Finance

The graph readily shows how Harrison out-campaigned Graham when it came to raising money.

Source: Respective campaign FEC Form 3 post-election reports. Data includes entire 2020 election cycle through Election Day.

91 percent from out of state. Only one of the ten ZIP codes that donated the most to Harrison's campaign was in South Carolina, whereas seven of Graham's top ten were in state (Center for Responsive Politics 2020).

Harrison made national headlines in October for "shattering" the single-quarter fundraising record for a US Senate race, having raised $57.9 million in the third quarter of 2020, far more than the previous record ($38 million) set by Beto O'Rourke in 2018 (Astor, Goldmacher, and Gabriel 2020). That quarter included the surge in donations following George Floyd–inspired social justice protests in the beginning of the period, as well as the death of Supreme Court Justice Ruth Bader Ginsberg at the end of the period, which led to a flood of money to Democratic candidates nationwide (Keith 2020).

Far less attention was paid to Graham's impressive fundraising in the twenty days before the election. The Senate confirmed Amy Coney Barrett as Ginsberg's successor during that period. According to his Federal Election Commission (FEC) filings, Graham raised $34.8 million during those twenty days. To put it in perspective: Harrison during his record-shattering quarter raised an average of about $629,200 a day. Graham in the immediate run-up to the election raised an average of $1.74 million a day. The Supreme Court vacancy was an amazing fundraising boon to both candidates, but at different times in the cycle.

Racial identity and racial issues were key components of the campaign. Early in the cycle, Harrison spoke of race in terms that recognized the diversity of ideas that exist within the Black community in the state:

> I can say . . . there's a lot of generational differences between older African Americans and younger African Americans on a whole variety of issues, from the issues of the environment, to the issue about school and whether we should provide it for free or not, to the issues about equality and rights. There's a lot of diversity within those communities . . . You can't just bring a canned message and think that that's going to resonate in the African American community. (Harrison 2019a)

Issues of race also created difficulties for both campaigns. A Graham campaign ad posted on Facebook generated negative publicity after it was determined that the ad used a visual effect that made Harrison's skin tone appear darker than it did in the original picture. Harrison supporters called the ad "dog-whistle politics." Harrison said, "Lindsey Graham may have darkened my face—but it's Lindsey who the people of South Carolina can't recognize." The Graham campaign said the visual effect used is commonly used in campaign ads, including on an image of Graham a few days before (LeBlanc 2020).

In September, the South Carolina GOP surfaced years-old offensive tweets from two of the Harrison campaign's top staffers, the political director and communications director. The tweets included anti-Semitic, sexist, and homophobic statements. The South Carolina GOP called for the staffers' resignations, but the Harrison campaign disciplined those involved internally without resignations and both staffers issued public apologies (WIS News 10 2020).

Some of Graham's inelegant phrasing on racial issues got attention. At one point he stated: "I care about everybody . . . . If you're a young African American, an immigrant, you can go anywhere in this state, you just need to be conservative, not liberal." And again: "But one thing I can say without any doubt, you can be an African American and go to the Senate, you just have to share the values of our state." In trying to be clever with these statements, the senator appeared to suggest that it is fine to be a person of color or an immigrant in the state, as long as the person is a conservative. "Folks, it's not about the color of your skin or where you came from, it's about your ideas" (Morin 2020).

The death of Supreme Court Associate Justice Ruth Bader Ginsberg on September 18, 2020, shook up the election. In 2019, Graham had been elevated to chairman of the Senate Judiciary Committee—the committee tasked with conducting hearings of candidates for the court and recommending confirmation to the whole Senate. It was generally expected by "strategists in the state on both sides of the aisle [that] conservatives [would] fall in line" behind Graham due to his role in advancing Amy Coney Barrett's nomination (Yokley 2020).

While the Senate confirmation hearings likely helped Graham shore-up conservative support, one gaffe dominated the headlines. In the hearings on October 14, Graham asked Judge Barrett if she was aware of "any effort to go back to the good old days of segregation by a legislative body" (Wise 2020). Harrison immediately jumped on the comment, tweeting "@LindseyGrahamSC just called segregation 'the good old days.' The good old days for who, Senator? It's 2020, not 1920. Act like it" (Harrison 2020d). Graham retorted that the comment was taken out of context and was "made with dripping sarcasm" (Wise 2020). The gaffe did nothing to change the dynamics of the election campaign.

A key moment for Harrison came when former President Barack Obama endorsed Harrison and made an ad for him during the last weeks of the race—just as conservative enthusiasm was at its highest during Barrett's confirmation. Obama only personally entered a handful of the most competitive races nationwide, a sign that national Democrats saw the South Carolina US Senate seat as a top pickup opportunity. "Now you have the power to make history again by sending Jaime Harrison to the US Senate so he can bring some change to South Carolina," Obama said. "If you want a senator who will fight for criminal justice reform, lower college costs, and make healthcare affordable, you've got to vote for my friend Jaime Harrison" (Lovegrove 2020e).

Election Outcome and Analysis

Billed by media, pollsters, and political analysts as one of the most competitive races in the country, the contest turned out to be a landslide re-election for Lindsey Graham, 54 percent to 44 percent (with a third-party candidate who withdrew receiving 1 percent). Harrison made progress toward building a new electoral coalition, but failed to reach critical mass in a deeply conservative state. Graham drew near monolithic support from GOP voters, even though some had questioned whether his transition from opposing to supporting Trump would hurt him with the party's base (Lovegrove 2020d).

Harrison received more votes than Biden did, in the presidential election, in all forty-six counties in South Carolina, while Lindsey Graham ran behind Trump in forty-two counties. Overall, Harrison received about 19,000 more votes than Biden did, while Graham received about 16,000 fewer votes than Trump did. Remarkably, 1,775 more voters took part in the US Senate contest than in the presidential race; typically, statewide elections have fewer participants than the national contest for president. The US Senate race generated more interest in the state, likely due to the widespread belief that Harrison had a better chance of winning the state than Biden did and the fact that both presidential campaigns largely ignored the state.

Ticket-splitting between the presidential and senate races appears to have been uncommon. Harrison needed a significant number of votes from moderate Republicans, especially women, and targeted many of his ads at them (Taylor 2020). Conservatives form a plurality of South Carolina voters; it would have been impossible for Harrison to win without attracting votes from some of them. Even if Biden lost the state (a near certainty), Harrison thought swing voters could deliver him the election. Three facts suggest his strategy did not work.

First, the number of votes received by Harrison and by Biden are incredibly correlated at the county level. Across South Carolina's forty-six counties, there is a 0.9999 correlation between votes for Biden and votes for Harrison. The swing voters Harrison targeted live in different places than each side's core loyalists. If Harrison had convinced a substantial number of swing voters to split their votes, there would be a larger disconnect between the presidential and senate results in the more moderate counties. This did not seem to happen.

Second, straight-ticket voting is becoming more common, not less. South Carolina allows voters to vote a "straight ticket" on their ballot, choosing a single party before getting to any individual race. Straight-ticket voting has been increasingly popular, growing from 45 percent of ballots cast in 2006 to 50 percent in 2016 and 64 percent in 2020. In 2020, 58 percent of straight-ticket ballots were cast for Republicans, compared with 41 percent for Democrats (South Carolina State Election Commission n.d.). Harrison's path to victory required a significant break from a long-term historical trend, both in South Carolina and nationally (Pew Research Center 2020).

Third, the exit poll shows that the parties closed ranks around their nominees (see Figure 5.6). Nearly all Democrats (95 percent) and Republicans (94 percent) voted for their party's candidate in the US Senate race—very similar shares to the presidential race in the state. Only 4 percent of voters who identified with each party crossed lines to vote for the other party's US Senate candidate.

Harrison and Graham evenly split voters who identified as independent— 49 percent each. Harrison depended on this group, courting them with moderate policy positions and portraying himself as the better choice for local interests.

Without Harrison winning either a substantial share of Republican crossover votes or independents—or some combination of the two—the greater prevalence of Republicans in the state made a Graham victory inevitable.

The exit poll results offer other insights into the coalitions behind each candidate. Harrison received strong support from Black voters and Democrats. Voters who identified either the coronavirus or racial inequality as their most important issue were also more likely to support him. Indeed, most South Carolinians (68 percent) say that they think racism is an important problem in the United States; a majority of those (57 percent) voted for Harrison.

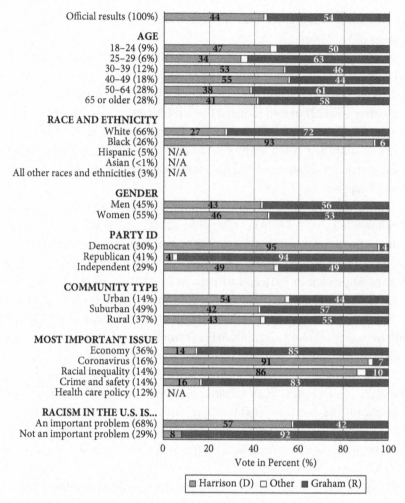

Figure 5.6 South Carolina US Senate Race Votes Differed by Voter Characteristics

Note: Subgroups with N/A are included in the total but are too small to report separately. Number in parentheses after each group refers to their share of all voters.

Sources: Official results from South Carolina State Election Commission, official 2020 general election results (https://www.enr-scvotes.org/SC/106502/Web02-state.264691/; accessed January 18, 2021). Votes by voter subgroups from National Election Pool exit poll conducted in South Carolina by Edison Research, as reported by CNN.

Graham won nearly three-quarters (72 percent) of White voters—with especially strong support from born-again or Evangelical Christians—and Republicans. Voters who were most concerned about the economy or crime and safety also disproportionately supported Graham. About three out of ten

South Carolinians (29 percent) said that racism is not an important issue in the United States, with nearly all (92 percent) voting for Graham.

There was a 3 percentage point gender gap in support for Graham (56 percent of men, 53 percent of women). This was nearly identical to the 4 percentage point gap in support for Trump (57 percent of men, 53 percent of women). The similarity is not surprising given the lack of ticket splitting between the races and the close link Graham drew between himself and Trump.

Harrison did better than his statewide average with voters aged 18–24 and 30–49. Graham did better than average with voters aged 25–29 and 50 and older. Graham's support among older voters is unsurprising, given they are more likely to be non-Hispanic White and lean Republican. His support from voters in their late twenties may have come from voters with connections to the state's large active-duty military population, including around the US Marine Corps base at Parris Island and the state's other large military installations.

The candidates had different geographic bases of strength (see Figure 5.7). Graham did best in the Upcountry region (the Northwest part of the state, in the Appalachian Mountains). This includes the county where

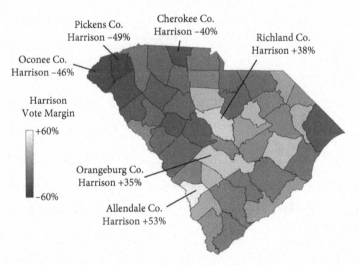

Figure 5.7 Harrison Did Best in Midlands/Central Region, Graham in Upcountry Region

Source: Official results from South Carolina State Election Commission, official 2020 general election results (https://www.enr-scvotes.org/SC/106502/Web02-state.264691/; accessed January 18, 2021).

he did best, Pickens County, which includes his hometown of Central, South Carolina. Harrison did best in the Midlands/Central region, which includes Columbia and Orangeburg. Harrison himself is from Orangeburg and he received his third-highest margin of victory statewide there.

Results do not seem to be closely linked with urbanity. Of the five most urban counties in the state (Richland, Charleston, Greenville, Dorchester, Beaufort), Harrison only won two (Richland and Charleston). However, Harrison also won two of the five most rural counties in the state (he won Williamsburg and Clarendon; he lost Barnwell, Calhoun, and McCormick) (South Carolina Revenue and Fiscal Affairs Office n.d.b).

Instead, race and ethnicity seem to be much more powerful predictors of vote choice in the Senate election (see Figure 5.8). Harrison won every county where half or more of the registered voters were persons of color. Graham won all but three counties where White voters were half or more of registered voters. Importantly, the three majority-White counties that Graham lost (Charleston, Jasper, and Clarendon) are all in South Carolina's Sixth Congressional District, represented by Harrison's political mentor, fellow Black Democrat Rep. Jim Clyburn.

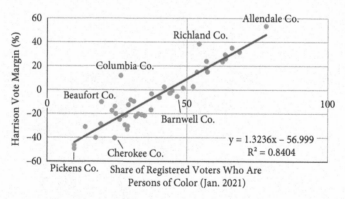

Figure 5.8 Tight Link between County Racial and Ethnic Composition and SC US Senate Results

Note: County voter racial and ethnic composition as of early January 2021.

Sources: Official results from South Carolina State Election Commission, official 2020 general election results (https://www.enr-scvotes.org/SC/106502/Web02-state.264691/). Accessed January 18, 2021. County voter composition from South Carolina State Election Commission, voter registration report, as of early January 2021 (https://www.scvotes.gov/voter-registration); accessed January 19, 2021.

A simple linear trend using the racial and ethnic composition of each county does well at predicting the election results. The model predicts that a 1 percentage point increase (such as from 50 percent to 51 percent) in the share of voters in a county who are persons of color is associated with increasing Harrison's vote margin by about 1.3 percentage points. The model explains about 84 percent of the variation in Harrison's margin. This model does not prove voters' race and ethnicity determined their vote in the Senate election, only that the two are related: there may be another factor, such as party affiliation, that explains the relationship. Because South Carolina voters do not register with a political party, one cannot determine party affiliation through the voter file.

Conclusion

In retrospect, what appeared to many observers at the time of the campaign to be a prime target for Democrats to pick up a US Senate seat turned out otherwise—as should have been predictable. Though many believed the race was competitive, not only was the campaign the most expensive ever for the US Senate at the time, it was by far the most expensive on a cost-per-voter basis. In short, Harrison raised far more than enough money: he ran a good campaign, and yet he lost by double-digits.

Harrison's loss shows how uneven the political evolutions detailed in this volume have been, even across Southern growth states. Even though Stacey Abrams (see Chapter 2) and Andrew Gillum (see Chapter 3) also lost their races, they came far closer to victory and did more to create durable networks for future pathbreaking candidates. By contrast, South Carolina showed that even a personable, nationally rising, star challenger flush with cash and willing to moderate his positions to appeal to swing voters could not overcome ideology and partisanship to defeat a controversial incumbent.

The news is not all bad for Democrats, however. One lasting legacy of Harrison's candidacy is his inspiration to other Black South Carolina Democrats. South Carolina State Senator Marlon Kimpson said, "I know at least two people, including myself, who are considering running for statewide office because of what Harrison has done" (Tensley 2020). They may find support from Harrison himself, in his new position as DNC chair.

Recruiting and "building the next generation of [younger] leadership" is his priority for his term as chair (Schneider 2021).

US Senator Tim Scott, a Black Republican, announced that 2022 will be his last political race (Byrd 2019). The US Senate is currently evenly split by party. Will Scott attract a strong Democratic challenger for his last race? South Carolinians may soon face the state's complicated racial history and politics again.

6

Raphael Warnock

Black Democratic Breakthrough

The arc of Georgia's transformation has become a road map for other
states that are experiencing rapid demographic change and a catalyst
for a new strategy in liberal politics.

—Astead W. Herndon

Raphael Warnock's election and the Democratic takeover of the Senate
in 2021 begin with Johnny Isakson's retirement at the end of 2019. Had
Parkinson's disease not forced Isakson to step aside halfway through his
term, Republicans would have a 51–49 advantage in the one hundred and
seventeenth Congress, and Warnock's "constituency" would still be limited
to the congregants at Atlanta's Ebenezer Baptist Church, the church were
Martin Luther King Jr. and his father once preached.

Governors usually salivate when the opportunity to fill a vacancy falls in
their laps. Rather than keeping his own counsel and then tapping Isakson's
successor, Governor Brian Kemp set up a website and invited anyone who
wanted to become senator to apply. More than five hundred hopefuls
responded. The highest profile applicant, Doug Collins (R), represented the
Ninth District in northeast Georgia. Collins had the enthusiastic support of
Donald Trump, support he earned by being the president's pit bull during
the House debate on Trump's first impeachment. Collins used his position
as the ranking minority member on the House Judiciary Committee to attack the Democratic impeachment effort.

Governor Kemp displayed little interest in Collins's candidacy. Kemp
had his eyes on an alternative: multi-millionaire Kelly Loeffler. The busi-
nesswoman, part owner of the Atlanta Dream women's basketball team,
is married to Jeff Sprecher who, among other things, owns the New York
Stock Exchange. Loeffler had considered running for the Senate in 2014

African American Statewide Candidates in the New South. Charles S. Bullock, III, Susan
A. MacManus, Jeremy D. Mayer, and Mark J. Rozell, Oxford University Press. © Oxford University Press 2022.
DOI: 10.1093/oso/9780197607428.003.0006

but had never sought public office. The forty-nine-year old entrepreneur had impressed Kemp and his wife at a private breakfast as someone who might appeal to White, suburban women, the kind of voter that many speculated would be decisive, as Georgia was becoming evenly balanced politically. Additionally, as a political outsider, Loeffler might tap into the same well of support that put Trump in the White House and in 2014 awarded Georgia's other Senate seat to David Perdue, who was up for reelection in 2020. Loeffler had another attribute, her willingness to self-finance indicated by her commitment to spend up to $20 million of her own money on the campaign. Kemp's decision drew mixed reviews, with moderates in support but conservatives disappointed that he had passed over Collins. When Kemp took Loeffler to the White House, Trump continued to lobby for Collins while questioning Loeffler's loyalty, conservativism, and lack of political experience (Isenstadt and Zanona 2019).

The Jungle Primary

Loeffler would have to secure public support in order to serve all of the remainder of the Isakson term. Georgia law stipulates that an appointee will serve only until the next regularly scheduled election which meant that Loeffler would be on the ballot in less than a year. Moreover, special elections to fill the remainder of a term begin with a jungle primary held on the date of the next general election. Should a candidate achieve majority support, the winner serves the term. But in the absence of a majority, the top two vote getters must compete nine weeks later in a runoff.

The governor hoped that Loeffler would have a clear shot to consolidating the Republican vote in the jungle primary. The new senator quickly tapped her bank account to fund an extensive television ad campaign. She ran ads at a rate not usually seen until near an election in hopes that the display of financial muscle would dissuade Collins or any other Republican office holder from jumping into the primary. That the effort to discourage Collins had failed became apparent when the congressman rejected President Trump's offer of appointment as director of national intelligence. Ultimately twenty-one individuals entered the jungle primary, although most had no prospect of success. Of the six Republican candidates, only Loeffler and Collins had viability.

The first Democratic entrant, Matt Lieberman, could boast that his father had represented Connecticut in the US Senate from 1989 to 2013 and been Al Gore's running mate in 2000. But the younger Lieberman had not run for office before and was relatively new to Georgia and therefore did not have a large following. Ed Tarver, a former state senator who had served as US attorney for the Southern District of Georgia, was initially thought to be viable. Eight Democrats joined the scrum, but the establishment quickly rallied around fifty-year-old Reverend Raphael Warnock. For fifteen years Warnock had led Ebenezer Baptist Church, known as America's Freedom Church. His previous posting had been at New York City's Abyssinian Baptist Church whose pastor, Adam Clayton Powell, was the state's first Black member of Congress. In addition to his ministerial duties, Warnock had headed up Stacey Abrams's New Freedom Project devoted to voter registration. Abrams, whose narrow loss of the governorship in 2018 is chronicled in Chapter 2, recruited Warnock for the Senate seat, rejecting invitations to seek it herself.

Collins had served in the state legislature for six years and his friends there, who included the powerful speaker of the house, wanted to replace the jungle primary and include the contest to fill the Isakson seat on the regular June primary ballot. Governor Kemp, recognizing that his appointee had far less name recognition than the congressman, threatened to veto a bill to move the special election forward, since giving Loeffler more time, until November, to introduce herself to voters was critical to getting public confirmation of his choice. An internal GOP poll conducted in April found that Loeffler's negatives outweighed her positives by 47 to 20 percent (Fandos and Enrich 2020). This poll came in the wake of reporting that after a briefing for senators about the potential for a pandemic, Loeffler and her husband had sold millions of dollars of stocks in companies that subsequently lost value.

Collins's entry into the contest undermined much of what had made Loeffler attractive to Governor Kemp. Confronting a Trump favorite, Loeffler dared not balk at any of the president's incendiary claims, yet her immersion into the Trump world view made her less attractive to the moderate suburbanites she was supposed to win for the GOP. Heath Garrett, Isakson's former chief of staff, summed up the challenge Loeffler faced. "Can Kelly Loeffler run two campaigns at the same time? Can she appeal to the base and appeal to moderate, independent voters?" (Bluestein 2020e). As the two Republicans vied for supremacy, their contest became essentially a GOP primary. Loeffler criticized Collins for doing criminal defense work as an attorney, claiming that as a career politician he had helped career criminals. Collins accused Loeffler of insider trading based on the briefing senators received about the coronavirus. When QAnon believer Marjorie Taylor Greene won the GOP nomination in the Fourteenth Congressional District, both Republicans joined President Trump in extending congratulation. Greene ultimately endorsed Loeffler and the two campaigned together (Fausset 2020a). The Democratic side lacked drama as Warnock went about consolidating support.

Loeffler and Collins calculated that if one of them got the president's nod, that would advance the favored candidate into the runoff. Each denigrated the other as a false conservative. Loeffler claimed to be the only senator who had supported Trump 100 percent of the time and characterized Collins as having a "failed record" and being "one of the most liberal Republicans in the US House" (Hurt 2020; Raju et al. 2020). She ran a set of ads that described herself as "more conservative than Attila the Hun" and featured a character representing the fifth-century marauder voicing displeasure at high taxes and other liberal predilections. Collins and his supporters, as they tried to dig out from under Loeffler's avalanche of ads, claimed that her wealth would prevent her from effectively representing the average Georgian. After Loeffler acquired another jet to get around Georgia more quickly, House Speaker David Ralston observed that most Georgians were still working on their first jet (Bluestein 2020b). Collins criticized Loeffler for having supported Mitt Romney in 2012 and Planned Parenthood.

The presence of two Republican candidates engaged in mortal combat for months helped Loeffler become better known, but it also worked to Warnock's advantage. Loeffler and Collins were too busy attacking one another to pay attention to the reverend. Had either of the Republicans been confirmed in the summer primary, the winner might have defined Warnock as a flaming liberal before he had a chance to introduce himself to the public. While being ignored by the mud-wrestling Republicans, Warnock began his ad campaign in front of the public housing project in Savannah where he grew up. One of a dozen children, he explained that he became the first in his family to graduate college, a first step toward earning a doctorate. In another ad, he told how a twelve-year-old boy was thrown out of a store, considered suspicious because he had his hands in his pocket. Playing off a line that Kamala Harris used in an early debate against Joe Biden, Warnock said, "That little boy was me."

Initially Collins led polling efforts, but by late July, Loeffler had surpassed him since while she was buying ad time at levels not usually reached until deep into the general election, Collins, who is not wealthy, was silent. As the Republicans toured the state—Loeffler in her private jet, Collins in an eight-year old Ford and an Econoline van—seeking votes and questioning the credentials of their opponent, Warnock's numbers rose. First, he overtook Lieberman as the leading Democrat, and by the end of September he supplanted Loeffler as the front runner. Some October polls showed Warnock with more than 40 percent of the vote, while these same polls often showed Loeffler with a modest lead over Collins. Throughout the last month before the vote, Warnock almost always had a lead greater than the margin of error. The average of the final polls posted on Real Clear Politics came close to the vote shares achieved by the Republicans with Loeffler at 24.8 percent and Collins with 21.8 percent. The average substantially over-estimated Warnock's performance, showing him with 40.5 percent.[1]

The two Georgia Senate seats were among ten expected to be competitive. With Democrats needing a net gain of three if Biden won and four if Trump prevailed, spending was heavy; AdImpact (2020) calculated a total of $57 million, most promoting either Warnock or Loeffler. Senator Loeffler spent $16.8 million during the first round. Led by the Club for Growth's $2.4 million, other outside groups invested $4.9 on pro-Loeffler advertising, and Mitch McConnell's Senate Leadership Fund accounted for $575,000 of the outside funding. All told, $32.5 million worth of advertising backed Loeffler's bid during the first round.[2]

Collins lagged far behind, raising and spending less than $7 million of which $3.2 million went to advertising. The disadvantage that Collins confronted becomes evident when compared to the $15,518,681 spent by pro-Loeffler groups attacking him. The Georgia United Victory Fund, created by Loeffler's husband, spent $14.7 million running ads against the congressman—an amount twice the total Collins raised. The $20,041 that the National Right to Life Victory Fund—the only major outside group to support Collins—spent was a drop in the bucket compared to the tidal wave that drowned out his message.

Warnock led the Democratic field in finances, but given the far less serious challenges he confronted, a relatively small $17.5 million was spent during the primary in advertising. Outside groups spent $1.1 million on Warnock's behalf, with $283,000 coming from the Senate Majority PAC.

President Trump, laying the foundation for his subsequent claims that the election was stolen, warned his MAGA-hat-wearing enthusiasts that the absentee process could not be trusted. He issued this warning even as the Republican Party of Georgia filled the mailboxes of its faithful with applications to get an absentee ballot. Ultimately 1.3 million Georgians, or just over a quarter of the turnout, cast absentee ballots.

Georgia law calls for inspection of the envelope containing an absentee ballot to see that the voter's signature on the envelope matches the signature on file. After checking the signature, the envelop is opened and the ballot extracted and run through the scanner, but the results cannot be tallied until after the polls close on Election Day. Heeding their president's warnings, Trump's voters dominated the Election Day turnout, with him winning 61.6 percent of these ballots. Tabulating of Election Day votes and those cast in-person during the twenty-day early voting period progressed quickly, and Trump's lead expanded until it exceeded three hundred thousand. Late arriving absentee ballots were brought to counties' tabulation centers to be processed. As counting of the absentee ballots proceeded, Trump's lead evaporated, and in the early hours of November 6, Biden edged ahead. By the time Georgia was called on Saturday, Biden had a plurality of fourteen thousand votes.

Counting of the presidential votes took precedence over those of the jungle primary. Once these ballots were counted, Warnock led the pack with 32.9 percent of the votes, Loeffler emerged as Warnock's runoff opponent with 25.9 percent of the votes, while Collins came in third with 19.9 percent. Lieberman, who in early polling had led Warnock, wound up with less than 3 percent of the vote and Tarver, the former Augusta legislator, finished fifteenth with barely 0.5 percent. Deborah Jackson with 6.6 percent finished fourth. Jackson had not been included in any polls, attracted no attention from the print press, nor did she have a television budget, yet more than 320,000 people supported her. She had been mayor of Lithonia, a tiny town of about two thousand residents. One possible explanation for her showing is that hers was the first Democratic name on the ballot and may have been the stopping point for Democratic voters who had paid little heed to the contest.

Exit poll results in Figure 6.1 show that Warnock had a remarkable consistency in vote share across the six age categories, getting slightly more than a third from every group. Loeffler performed worst with the two youngest cohorts but got about a third of the vote from all other groups. For none of the cohorts, however, did Loeffler exceed Warnock with her best showing, which occurred in the 40–49-year-old category, being three points less than

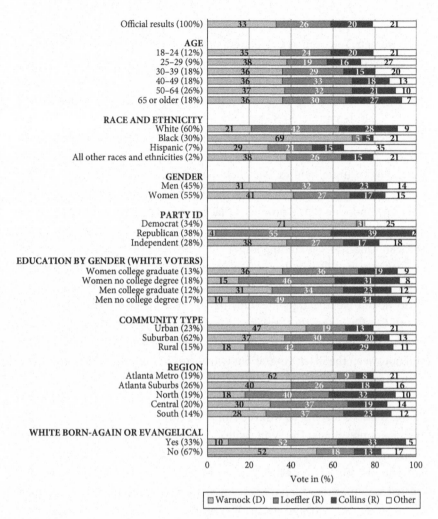

Figure 6.1 Percent of the Vote for Major Primary Candidates by Voter Characteristics

Source: National Election Pool exit poll conducted in Georgia by Edison Research as reported by CNN.

the Democrat. Collins did best with the oldest voters, but in this group, as with the other five, he placed third.

Women are often more supportive than men of Democratic candidates, and so it was in the November vote. Warnock ran 10 points stronger with women, 41 percent of whom voted for him, so that he led Loeffler by 14 points. While Loeffler was selected in part to bring women, especially White, suburban women, to the GOP, she performed 5 points better with men than with women. Yet, even as Loeffler got more support from men than women, she and Warnock essentially tied among male voters.

As would be expected, the Democrat blew away the Republicans among Black voters. However, Warnock's 69 percent of the Black vote is surprisingly small. Joe Biden attracted 87 percent of the Black vote, as did Jon Ossoff in the other Senate contest. Lieberman managed 14 percent of the black vote. Polling done in the months leading up to the election had shown the Black vote slow to unite behind Warnock. An explanation for the hesitancy of some African Americans to rally to the reverend is that they wanted to back a winner and, due to the problems Black candidates have confronted in the past, White candidates may appear more viable. In 2008, some high-profile African Americans, including John Lewis, initially opted for Hillary Clinton. However, once Obama demonstrated viability, Black voters coalesced behind him to a larger degree than behind Warnock. After his strong showing in Iowa and New Hampshire, Obama got 78 percent of the Black vote in South Carolina. Shortly thereafter, when Georgia went to the polls, Obama trounced Clinton among African Americans 87–12 percent. While Warnock did not sweep the Black vote, about two-thirds of the votes he received came from African Americans.

Loeffler took a 42 percent plurality of the White vote, double Warnock's share. If he were going to win the runoff, he would have to do substantially better among Whites. The White vote for the two leading Republicans, 70 percent, would be the upper limit of what Warnock could lose in the runoff and still win. Warnock could take comfort in his performance among college-educated Whites, more than 30 percent of whom backed him. Still, Warnock trailed Biden with this group, as the presidential nominee got 44 percent of the vote of better-educated White women and 40 percent from White male college graduates. For Whites who lacked a degree, Warnock's vote share was 15 percent among women and barely made it into double digits with men.

Warnock got more than 70 percent of the votes cast by Democrats. He also got a 38 percent plurality from Independent voters. Loeffler got a majority of the Republican vote, beating Collins by 16 points. She finished second among Independents, with 27 percent.

Warnock scored pluralities among urban and suburban voters. Loeffler took a 42 percent plurality among rural voters. The countryside rejected Warnock, giving him less than a fifth of their votes, so that he trailed Collins. The Atlanta metro area was where Warnock ran up the score, getting

62 percent of the vote, while the two Republicans ended up in single digits. The Democrat also narrowly led Loeffler in Georgia's suburbs. Warnock ran slightly better in Atlanta's suburbs than in the suburbs generally, with 40 percent in the former and 37 percent in the latter.

Loeffler won each of the three rural segments of the state. In north Georgia, the most heavily White subregion, where Warnock had his poorest showing, the brace of Republicans combined for 72 percent of the vote. Collins had his best showing there, a chunk of which he represented in Congress, but even so he trailed Loeffler. In other parts of the state, Warnock eclipsed Collins.

Critical to Loeffler's success in making the runoff was the strength she registered with White Evangelicals. With these reliable Republican voters, who cast a third of all ballots, Loeffler beat Collins 52–33 percent. As with his inability to win north Georgia, Collins's poor showing among Evangelicals was telling, since he is a Baptist minister who has served as an Air Force chaplain. A majority of all the vote for Loeffler came from the White born-again Evangelicals.

Going into the runoff, Warnock's primary lead looked shaky, since the combined Loeffler-Collins vote easily outpaced Warnock. The combined votes for the six GOP candidates exceed the vote for the eight Democrats by almost forty-eight thousand.

Inspection of other results raised additional concerns about Warnock's viability in the runoff. In the contest for the six-year Senate term, Senator David Perdue led challenger Jon Ossoff by eighty-eight thousand votes. This second Senate seat would also be resolved in the runoff, along with the contest to replace Isakson, since Perdue was 13,471 votes short of a majority. Two Public Service Commission (PSC) seats were also on the ballot. In one of these, Jason Shaw (R) won with 50.1 percent of the vote, while in the other contest, the Republican incumbent would have to compete in a runoff, but had a 49.9 percent plurality. The sum of the vote for Republicans in the fourteen US House contests exceeded that for their Democratic opponents. Republicans also outpolled Democrats in contests for the state Senate and the state House. To summarize, in terms of share of the vote, Donald Trump was the weakest component of the GOP team in Georgia. Except for the presidency, Republicans got more votes than Democrats in every other statewide contest or sets of contests. Had Trump gotten the same percentage of the vote as Perdue or the two PSC candidates, he would have won Georgia. Warnock would have to improve significantly on his November showing in order to win in January.

Runoff Campaign

Runoff elections usually take place two to four weeks after the preceding election. But in Georgia, runoffs for federal offices come nine weeks later, as a result of a court decision that established a requirement for time to disseminate and receive the absentee ballots of military personnel serving overseas. The campaign would extend through Thanksgiving, Christmas, and New Year's Eve, finally wrapping up on January 5, two days after the one hundred and seventeenth Congress convened.

The runoffs for the two Senate seats took on heightened significance when neither party emerged from the November vote with a majority in that chamber. It had been predicted that Democrats would win the Senate by scoring gains in Arizona and Colorado, which they won, and two from among Iowa, Maine, North Carolina, or South Carolina, all of which they lost. Those losses made the Georgia runoffs the center of the political universe. If either of the Republican senators won reelection, Mitch McConnell (R-KY) would continue as majority leader. However if, somehow, Democrats managed to grab both seats, Chuck Schumer (D-NY) would become majority leader, thanks to Kamala Harris's tie-breaking vote. A Democratic majority, even the narrowest one, would facilitate the confirmation of Biden appointees and enhance the likelihood that some portions of the new president's agenda would become reality.

Going into the runoffs, handicappers gave Republicans the edge. Beginning in 1992, Georgia had had eight general election runoffs. Seven of these were partisan, and Republicans had won all of them, including the 1992 Senate runoff, in which Democrat incumbent Wyche Fowler had initially led by 35,000 votes. Republicans had won because they had more success getting their supporters back to the polls for the runoff. While turnout invariably dropped off from the initial vote to the runoff, African American had especially high rates of withdrawal from the electorate.

It was widely assumed that few runoff voters would split their ballots, which pushed the pairs of partisans closer together. At times they campaigned together, yard signs usually listed both partisans, and pairs of candidates had very similar messages. Interviews with members of the candidates' teams indicate that there were more tensions between the two Republicans than on the Democratic side.

The runoffs followed the turnout pattern that usually characterizes these do-overs, but only to a degree. Turnout in the runoff declined compared to

November, but by only 10 percent, a figure in line with the average voter drop off in Senate runoffs held across the South between 1970 and 1986 (Bullock and Johnson 1992) and far less than the declines of more than 40 percent in previous Georgia general election Senate runoffs. An analysis done by the *Atlanta Journal-Constitution* that used state House districts as the units of analysis, found modest declines in much of the four most populous Atlanta counties where Democrats ran up their numbers. Most of rural Georgia, where Republicans must do well to offset losses in Atlanta, saw participation drop by 14–19 percent. With few exceptions, the districts in which drop off exceeded 19 percent were rural (Niesse and Peebles 2021). Interestingly, some of the largest decreases in turnout occurred in the areas where Trump held rallies—Dalton, Rome and Valdosta—raising questions about his ability to mobilize Republicans.

With so much at stake, resources flooded the state. Both parties brought in volunteers from across the country. Republicans, who already had a ground game, welcomed 1,600 battle-hardened staff who had worked on the Trump and Senate reelections in other states and allocated $20 million for the effort (Bluestein and Hallerman 2020). Ralph Reed's Faith and Freedom Coalition brought in 1,400 people who visited six hundred thousand Evangelical families (Bluestein 2021).

Democrats, who had followed Biden's lead during the general election and minimized in-person contacts, now launched door-knocking efforts. A coalition of more than sixty groups promoted Warnock and Ossoff by knocking on seven million doors and engaging in 2.1 million conversations with those whom they found at home (Bluestein 2021). Abrams's New Georgia Project boasted of sending three million texts and placing five million phone calls urging likely Democrats to vote ("So Sweet and Clear" 2021). The Peoples' Agenda reported making a million voter contacts (Suggs 2020a). MoveOn and Bernie Sanders's Our Revolution each contacted their thousands of members (Ember 2020). An Hispanic group set out to contact three hundred thousand households (Suggs 2020b). The state Democratic Party boasted that twenty thousand volunteers had come forward and made 1.5 million contacts while Warnock's volunteers claimed to have placed five hundred thousand calls in one week in December and Ossoff hired two thousand door knockers (Bluestein and Hallerman 2020; Akin and Bowman 2021). Abrams's Fair Fight distributed a million magnets reminding recipients to vote. Volunteers and paid staff for both parties followed up with text messages to likely voters they had contacted.

The deluge of money in Georgia's Senate elections surpassed all previous elections. Loeffler and her husband by themselves invested at least $31 million in her reelection (Bluestein and Murphy 2020). At a minimum, spending on the Ossoff-Perdue contest totaled $459 million, with $382 million going into the Warnock-Loeffler contest. Table 6.1 shows the financial data for Warnock and Loeffler along with that for Collins. According to Federal Election Commission records, Warnock raised 50 percent more than Loeffler and, as of mid-December, had almost doubled the amount she had spent. In addition to the $136 million he spent, outside groups invested another $27.9 million in his campaign. Especially generous were Black PAC, which supports Black candidates urging criminal justice reform and wealth redistribution (which spent $5 million), Georgia Honor ($3.7 million), Majority Forward ($1.7 million), and the Working Families Party ($1 million). Warnock also benefitted from groups that spent $28.9 million to criticize Loeffler, led by Georgia Honor with $15.5 million. The Democratic Senatorial Campaign Committee spent $3.6 million against Loeffler and was joined by Georgia Way, which spent only a tenth as much going after Loeffler ($1.4 million) as it invested in its anti-David Perdue effort. All of the spending by Georgia Honor and Georgia Way came during the runoff (Dumenco 2021).

Loeffler had raised $92 million by mid-December and spent $71 million. Outside groups spent an additional $23.3 million promoting her candidacy, with Peachtree PAC, part of the Senate Leadership Fund, the most generous ($6.5 million). The Republican National Committee, Georgia United Victory Fund set up by her husband, Georgia Balance, and ESA Fund each spent at least $1 million on her behalf. Unlike in Warnock's case, where attacks were far better funded than promotion, attacks on Loeffler were not that much better funded than positive ads, relatively speaking. Outside groups

Table 6.1 Financial Data for Major Candidates (all figures in 1,000,000)

	Raised	Spent	Spent by Others to	
			Support	Oppose
Warnock	$146.2	$136	$27.9	$79.6
Loeffler	$92.1	$70.9	$23.3	$28.9
Collins	$7.3	$7.3	$0.02	$15.5

Source: U.S. Federal Election Commission.

promoting Loeffler by attacking Warnock far surpassed the pro-Warnock groups in spending. Karl Rove's American Crossroads spent $46 million during the runoff in a futile effort to defeat the reverend. Others that generously funded attacks on the Democrat included Peachtree PAC ($12.4 million), the National Republican Senatorial Committee ($9.8 million), Mitch McConnell's Senate Leadership Fund ($2 million), the Republican National Committee ($1.8 million), and the NRA Victory Fund ($1.3 million).

The bulk of the mountains of money spent on this election went into television advertising. With the two Senate runoffs having four well-funded candidates plus multiple wealthy super PACs buying time, some television stations ran five hours of political advertising a day during the runoff (Korte 2020). Warnock's media expenditures in the runoff exceeded those before the November election by a factor of 4.5, while the increase for Loeffler was 2.5; Warnock outspent her in the runoff by almost $30 million (Dumenco 2020).

During one December week, $50 million pumped out eighty-eight distinct ads for the two Senate contests (Corasaniti 2020). In a single commercial break, ads for competing candidates often appeared back to back. When Atlanta television stations had no more space available on news shows, ad placement expanded to children's Christmas specials like "Frosty the Snowman," HGTV, the Golf Channel, the Food Network, and Hallmark movies (Murphy 2020a). As the head of an Atlanta marketing firm observed, "anywhere you can put a political ad, there is one" (Brown 2020). Once space on Georgia stations became fully subscribed, more than $35 million worth of spots on stations that beam into Georgia from Chattanooga, Greenville, and Jacksonville was snapped up (Goldmacher 2020). Even the TV station in Dothan, Alabama, whose signal reaches one small Georgia county, broadcast campaign commercials.

Runoffs are turnout elections. Since participation usually drops in a runoff, the top priority is to get those who voted for the candidate in the first round to come back for the encore. In the two previous Senate runoffs, in 1992 and 2008, turnout dropped by 44 percent and 43 percent, respectively. In 2020, both parties put on a full-court press to get their partisans back to the polls. Political consultants believe that the way to get voters to return for a runoff is to attack the opponent, and the GOP candidates and their supporting cast followed that strategy relentlessly (Herndon and Corasaniti 2020). Fear, not new programs, was believed to be the motivator for Republican turnout. According to GOP communications expert Brian Robinson, "Fear will motivate much more strongly than any other emotion in the runoff" (Nilson

2020). In the first three weeks of the runoff, the GOP ran nothing but ads attacking Warnock (Herndon and Corasaniti 2020). By one count, during the course of the runoff, about 80 percent of the GOP ads and 60 percent of the Democratic ads were at least partially negative, with Loeffler's ads being the most negative of all four runoff candidates (Korte 2020). That Loeffler attacked relentlessly and more than Perdue may be explained by a GOP consultant who opined that with the candidates well known and polling showing little movement, the best hope for Republican success was to take down Warnock.

The most common theme of Loeffler's attacks was that Warnock was a dangerous radical. In their televised debate, Loeffler called Warnock a radical liberal thirteen times and linked him to Fidel Castro, Chuck Schumer, Stacey Abrams, Alexandria Ocasio-Cortez, and Jeremiah Wright—all individuals likely to send shivers down the spines of conservatives (Bluestein 2020a; Herndon and Corasaniti 2020). Her ads suggested that Warnock was educated by communists, guaranteed to set off alarms.

The Republican warnings extended beyond the alleged extremism of the opponents. GOP ads pointed out that the election of the two Democrats would give Democrats control of the White House and both chambers of Congress. One Loeffler ad cautioned that Georgia is "now the last line of defense against socialism" (Bluestein and Murphy 2020). Perdue, who was thought to be better than Loeffler at speaking directly to the camera, warned in one oft-run ad that if unchecked, Democrats would take away private health insurance, allow illegal immigrants to vote, defund the police, gut the military, and pack the Supreme Court. Neither Republican expended much effort in detailing policies they would pursue if reelected.

In January 2020, Loeffler had attended the high profile MLK Day service at Ebenezer Baptist Church, where she praised Warnock who had not yet declared his candidacy (Legum and Zekeria 2020). But things changed after that and rather than speaking to the camera, Loeffler used excerpts from Warnock's sermons in her ads. As GOP communications consultant Robinson had predicted, "There will be plenty of tape with past statements that will probably raise eyebrows with that middle-of-the-road electorate that's the margin of victory in Georgia" (Fausset 2020b). Loeffler drew from the sermons to paint Warnock as anti-police ("he called them thugs"), anti-military ("no man can serve God and the military"), a friend of Fidel Castro, and a fan of Jeremiah Wright—Barack Obama's Chicago pastor whose "God damn America" sermon debuted in 2008 GOP ads against Obama. Loeffler labeled Warnock anti-Israel, a charge that would resonate with White Evangelicals (Hollis 2020a). Some Jewish leaders affirmed Loeffler's claim but others, including one hundred and eighty rabbis and Ossoff, who is Jewish, refuted it (Legum and Zekeria 2020).

African Americans considered Loeffler's taking bits and pieces out of context from Warnock sermons as an attack on the Black church (Corasaniti 2020). Emory University political scientist Andra Gillespie summed up the Black perspective on Loeffler's sermon snippets: "The attacks just look like they're highly, highly racial, and for many African American voters, that's unacceptable" (Williams 2020). Tharon Johnson (2021), a leading Democratic operative and lobbyist, who like Gillespie is Black, agrees that using his sermons to attack Warnock was a mistake. A top GOP campaign consultant concludes that Loeffler spent too much time attacking Warnock's activities as a preacher, since it backfired by motivating Black turnout.

In the closing week of the campaign, Loeffler took a page from Lindsay Graham's playbook and put up an ad on Facebook that darkened Warnock's skin (Sollenberg 2021). Loeffler further alienated Black voters when she criticized the Black Lives Matter movement for promoting "violence and destruction" (Barlow 2020). As part of building her resume as the more conservative Republican, during the primary Loeffler criticized the WNBA for supporting Black Lives Matter. This criticism prompted WNBA players, including those on the Atlanta Dream of which she was part owner, to wear "Vote Warnock" T-shirts during warm ups (Buckner 2021). While Loeffler's criticism of Black Lives Matter got poor press and led to her selling her stake in the team, it gained her Republican voters. Consultants reported that it produced a bump in her polling numbers, because it convinced some Republicans skeptical about this ultra-wealthy, Iowan now living in a $10 million Buckhead mansion that she was indeed conservative.

Warnock was the first candidate on television after the November vote. His initial ad, which drew praise from both sides of the aisle, featured a cute beagle puppy. Speaking to the camera, Warnock correctly predicted that the opposition would lie about him, going so far as to claim that he hated dogs. The last frame showed Warnock lovingly holding the beagle in his arms. The ad was so well received that the puppy appeared in one of Warnock's last ads—a commercial promoting turnout in which Warnock appeared with more and more dogs on leashes who dragged him to the polls (Goldmacher 2021). These ads helped deracialize Warnock.

Warnock criticized Loeffler, as Collins had, for using a private briefing given senators to make money rather than prepare Georgians for the coming pandemic. One Warnock ad pointed out that Loeffler had made no trades during her brief tenure prior to the Senate briefing. Warnock accused Loeffler of blocking unemployment benefits for one hundred and ninety thousand Georgians while taking care of herself by dumping stocks likely to lose value in the pandemic. The *Atlanta Journal-Constitution* calculated that, following the briefing, she sold stocks worth almost $2 million while purchasing $300,000 in other stocks (Hollis 2020b). Perdue came in for criticism similar to that aimed at Loeffler, which prompted Ossoff to refer to the Republican incumbents as the Bonnie and Clyde of political corruption (Allen 2020). As a rejoinder, the Republicans pointed out that multiple entities had found nothing wrong with the trades. To head off future problems, Loeffler and her husband shifted their holdings from individual stocks into mutual funds.

An ad run on behalf of both Warnock and Jon Ossoff described their opponents as two of the wealthiest members of the Senate. In a debate, Warnock injected Loeffler's wealth into the conversation with the assertion that she had purchased the seat (Redmon 2020).

In addition to criticizing his opponent, Warnock endorsed policy changes. If elected, he would press for a new voting rights act, work to get the pandemic under control, expand Medicaid, support additional funding for COVID relief, and reform police procedures.

The Trump Distraction

The hurly burly of the runoff was at times overshadowed by President Trump and his loyalists claiming in any forum available that Democrats had stolen the presidential election. With the Senate runoffs riveting the national media, Trump recognized that his fictitious claims would get more coverage if directed at Georgia so he doubled down on allegations directed at the Peach State. The president's persistent efforts to undo the election failed, much to the disappointment of his fervent followers, but they were critical to Warnock's election. When Trump addressed Georgia rallies, he bragged that not only had he won Georgia but he had won it "big." In reality, Biden beat Trump in Georgia by 11,779 votes. Trump's assertions were shown to be baseless fabrications. The charge that the new voting machines had switched votes from Trump to Biden was disproven when the state re-counted all five million paper ballots by hand. Claims that signatures had not been adequately checked on absentee ballots were disproven when the signatures on a sample of fifteen thousand envelopes found no evidence of fraud and only a couple of minor problems (Niesse 2020a).

Trump retained unblinking loyalty from cult-like Republican voters. Since one negative tweet from the president would put his followers on the sidelines for the runoff, Loeffler and Perdue were attached to Trump like remora to a shark. They slavishly echoed all of Trump's false claims about the accuracy of Georgia's elections, and when questioned, were struck dumb rather than suggest any difference between themselves and the outgoing president (Murphy 2020b). Initially Trump attacked Secretary of State Brad Raffensperger, a Republican. Following orders, the GOP senators issued a call for Raffensperger to resign when he refused to steal the election for Trump. They applauded the challenge filed by the attorney general of Texas that sought to prevent certification of returns from Georgia and other states Biden won. They remained mute when Trump disparaged Governor Kemp, called on him to resign, and pledged to defeat him when he seeks reelection. They remained in Georgia, rather than appear in the Senate and vote to override Trump's veto of the military funding bill. Shortly before the runoff eve rally in Dalton, Trump threatened that, rather than endorse her, he would "do a number" on Loeffler if she did not promise to vote to block certification of Georgia's Electoral College vote on January 6 (E. Johnson 2021). She dutifully made the pledge on stage that night.[3] Although toeing the Trump line and never admitting that Biden had won the presidency, Loeffler tacitly acknowledge that reality when she sought support on the grounds that only a Republican Senate majority would thwart Democrats' liberal machinations.

Two months of Trump's constant claims that the presidential election had been rigged sowed mistrust among GOP voters. Building on the distrust, two of the president's vocal supporters, Lin Wood and Sidney Powell, at a Stop the Steal rally, urged Republicans not to vote in the runoffs citing two reasons. First, Wood asked, "Why would you go back and vote in another rigged election?" (Scanlan 2020). Second, they maintained, the senators "have not earned your vote" since they had not succeeded in blocking or changing Georgia's vote for Biden. Democrat PACs advanced the skepticism with billboard messages: "Perdue/Loeffler Didn't Deliver for Trump, DON'T Deliver for Them" and "Where's Loeffler? Where's Perdue? They have not earned your vote—Lin Wood, pro-Trump Lawyer" (Scanlan 2020). Leading state Republicans sought to counter this crippling message but with mixed success.

With time running out, Trump, in a last-ditch effort, at times begged and at other times threatened the secretary of state. During an hour–long phone call on the Saturday before the runoff, he beseeched Raffensperger to "find" the votes needed to produce a GOP plurality. Unbeknown to Trump, Raffensperger taped the call, which was released by the *Washington Post* the next day.

When not bullying Raffensperger, Trump demanded that Governor Kemp exercise powers he did not have, believing that the governor was beholden to him: six days before the 2018 Republican gubernatorial runoff, the president had endorsed Kemp (Bluestein 2020d). Tracking polls showed a dramatic uptick in Kemp's support in the wake of Trump's backing, although officials with the Kemp campaign claim that he was comfortably ahead before Trump's intervention. When Kemp explained that he lacked the power to award Georgia to Trump, the president asked him to call a special session of the legislature. Several legislators echoed the idea of a special session at which they hoped to overturn the decision of the electorate and name a set of electors who would deliver Georgia to Trump. When Kemp refused to call the legislature into session, Trump turned abusive, calling the governor a fool and a coward and regretting his 2018 endorsement. Trump publicly encouraged unsuccessful senatorial candidate Doug Collins to primary Kemp. Although not supported by any of the statewide GOP office holders, a rump group met in the Capitol in December and selected a set of electors pledged to the Trump-Pence ticket (Haines 2020).

Polling showed that most Republicans accepted Trump's self-serving, distorted view of the election outcome. A statewide survey conducted in late January found that 76 percent of Republicans, but only 4 percent of Democrats and 40 percent of Independents, believed widespread fraud had infected the presidential election (Hood 2021). For those not into conspiracy theories, the president's blatant attempts to rig the election and the discord among Republicans was a major turn-off.

Runoff Election Outcome and Analysis

Polling for a runoff is tricky, since to develop reliable estimates, the pollster has to anticipate the level of drop off in participation. The timing of Georgia's

Senate runoffs made polling even more difficult, since they played out during the holiday season when most people had far more on their minds than the elections. Most of the limited polling conducted showed the absence of a statistically significant difference between the candidates, although one poll showed Warnock leading 52 to 45 percent.

Once the votes were tallied, Warnock won 51–49 percent, with a margin of ninety-three thousand votes out of almost 4.5 million cast. He outperformed Ossoff by 0.4 percentage points. With 51 percent, Warnock got the largest vote share of any Georgia statewide candidate in either party competing in 2020–2021.

As in November, how a person voted correlated with partisanship. A quarter of the electorate cast absentee ballots, and Warnock swept this component, getting 68.2 percent. Warnock dominated absentee balloting, since so many Republicans ignored pleas from their party to use this approach and instead believed Trump's claims that the process was unreliable.[4]

Another two million people (46.3 percent of the turnout) voted early in person, and Warnock narrowly won this group with 51 percent. While the preferences on ballots cast before Election Day would not be known until the polls closed, the characteristics of individuals taking advantage of these opportunities indicated that Democrats were doing an extraordinary job of mobilizing their supporters. Republicans recognized that, to win, they would need their followers to flood the polls on Election Day. They projected that if the number of voters that day fell below seven hundred thousand Warnock would win, but if more than eight hundred thousand people turned out on Election Day, Loeffler would return to the Senate. January 5 saw 1.3 million votes cast, and Loeffler won 63.1 percent of those, but with Warnock harvesting 111,000 votes in Fulton and DeKalb counties, double Loeffler's support there, the Republican came up short.

A criticism often directed at runoff elections is that, while the winner secures a majority, it is a majority of an electorate much reduced from the earlier vote. That was not the situation in 2021. With almost 4.5 million ballots cast, the only election in Georgia history to attract more participation occurred two months earlier when five million people went to the polls. The 2021 runoff attracted half a million more voters than the 2016 presidential election and six hundred thousand more voters than the 2018 gubernatorial election.

Candidate preference in the Senate runoff correlates strongly with age. Warnock did best among the youngest voters winning those aged 18–24 by more than two to one. He won each of the cohorts in Figure 6.2 up to those

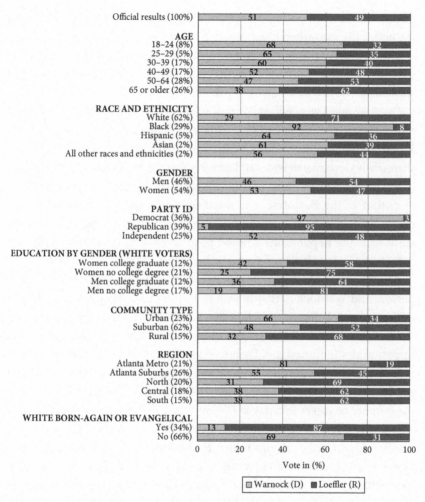

Figure 6.2 Percent of the Vote for Warnock and Loeffler in the Runoff by Voter Characteristics

Source: National Election Pool exit poll conducted in Georgia by Edison Research as reported by CNN.

aged 50 and over, and he was competitive in the 50–64 group, losing them by six points. Warnock performed poorly only among the elderly, losing the retirees by 24 points. Warnock performed better than Biden had in November among all but the two oldest cohorts.

The exit poll shows Warnock coming close to the 30–30 target needed to win. He got 29 percent of the White vote and African Americans cast

28 percent of all votes with Warnock getting 92 percent of that latter vote.[5] He also performed well with Hispanics and Asians where he got at least 60 percent. Critical to Democratic success in 2020 was support among college-educated White women. As Figure 6.2 shows, Warnock won 42 percent support from White, college-educated women. Warnock also won more than a third of White, college-educated men. Whites without college educations, especially the men, showed much less interest in Warnock although he did better than Biden had two months earlier. In November, Biden got 22 percent support among White women without college degrees and a scant 16 percent among non-college White men, several points lower than Warnock's showing.

A gender gap is usual in Georgia elections. Biden lost the male vote by 14 points while women preferred him 54–44 percent. In the Senate runoff, the gender gap amounted to just seven points and, despite competing against a woman, Warnock won the women's vote 53–47 percent thanks to strong turnout and 94 percent support from Black women.

Warnock carried the urban vote, as have other Georgia Democrats during the last two decades, but lost badly in the countryside. The Democrat got two-thirds of the urban vote and did especially well in metro Atlanta, where his support topped 80 percent. Turning from the exit poll results to county returns, the five Atlanta-area counties with the greatest number of Democratic votes provided 51 percent of Warnock's statewide total. He took 70 percent of the votes in these counties with the smallest number of votes coming in Clayton County where he attracted more than 91,000 votes for 88.6 percent of the total. In contrast, Loeffler did not reach 90,000 votes in any of the state's 159 counties with her best showing, 89,480, coming in suburban Cherokee where she got 70 percent.

The exit poll shows Warnock carried Atlanta suburbs (55 percent) but statewide narrowly lost suburbia (48 percent). His weakest performance came in rural north Georgia (31 percent), a very conservative area with few African Americans. An official with the Warnock campaign told us, "We looked at Whitfield County [county seat Dalton where Trump held a rally on the eve of the runoff] and there were essentially no Whites for the Democrats. We don't need those voters therefore why bother? They won't vote for Democrats." There is hyperbole in that statement since Warnock managed 29 percent in Whitfield but there are other north Georgia counties where he was held to less than 20 percent and in his weakest county, he got 11.5 percent.

White Evangelicals constitute the core constituency of the GOP in the South and they came through for Loeffler giving her 87 percent of their votes, 2 points better than Trump. White Evangelicals also cast a slightly larger share of the vote in January than in November. Offsetting Loeffler's strong showing among White Evangelicals was Warnock's performance among the much larger group who did not fit that category, a group that he won with 69 percent. With the cohesion of White Evangelicals almost matching that of Blacks and with White Evangelicals outnumbering Blacks, the former group outvotes the Democrats' core constituency.

The voting patterns in the other Senate race were much like in the Warnock-Loeffler contest. While most voters either picked the two Democrats or the two Republicans, a few split their ballots as evidenced by Warnock running 20,000 votes ahead of Ossoff. Explanations for the disparity point more to differences between the Republicans than the Democratic candidates.

Several factors may have enabled Perdue to outperform Loeffler. Perdue benefitted both from his six years in the Senate but also from sharing the family name of his cousin Sonny Perdue, a very popular two-term governor. With his longer record, Republicans had little doubt about Perdue's conservativism but some, perhaps because of Collins' attacks, questioned whether Loeffler was truly conservative and committed to President Trump (Barlow 2020). Perdue also had an ability to speak directly to the camera in his ads, a skill that Loeffler did not master. Both of the multi-millionaire Republicans sought to portray themselves as rural Georgians with Perdue in a jeans jacket and Loeffler in plaid and a ball cap. Perdue carried this image off better. Politicos in both parties criticized Loeffler, who lives in a $10 million home, for unsuccessfully trying to be something that she wasn't. A Democrat critiqued Loeffler. "Every time she opened her mouth, she sounded like Chicago."

Yet another explanation comes from a survey done shortly after the runoff that found more positive feelings about Warnock than Ossoff. Warnock's favorables outweighed his unfavorables 54–37 percent while for Ossoff the figures were 50–40 percent (Hood 2021). Ossoff's youth and his use of TikTok may have attracted young voters but not been as much of a draw for boomers and older voters. Others suggested that Warnock, with his light-hearted ads, connected better with voters than did Ossoff.

Following the election, both Democrats and non-Trump Republicans attributed the loss of the two Georgia Senate seats and the Senate majority to the president. According to a person close to the Warnock campaign,

"Every time that Donald Trump visited Georgia, our poll number went up. Trump fires up the Democratic base. Without Trump we would have lost." Republicans who pinned the loss on Trump agreed that he fired up voters in both parties. Heath Garrett, Senator Johnny Isakson's former chief of staff and now a campaign consultant who sat out Georgia's Senate elections, reports on work done by GOP number crunchers who estimated that for every additional rural voter that Trump inspired to vote, he alienated more (1.2, to be exact) White Atlanta suburbanites who voted Democratic (Garrett 2021). Activists in both parties agree that the ads run on behalf of the senators and Trump's performance reinforced Democrats' efforts at mobilizing their supporters who might otherwise have sat out the election. A leader on the Loeffler team said, "We hoped that Trump wouldn't come down to Georgia . . . The Dalton rally did us no favors."

Loeffler suffered from charges Trump and supporters like Rudy Giuliani made deriding Georgia's election system as rigged and unreliable. A GOP consultant explained the decrease in Republican turnout: "These voters were wholly behind the president and believed everything that Trump said. Therefore they didn't vote." Democratic consultant Tharon Johnson (2021) echoed the president's consequential role, saying: "People say that Donald Trump was not on the ballot. Yes, he was! His name wasn't on the ballot this time, but when he came down here and with that rally and did all that stuff and had two US senators who felt so beholden to him because they fear him and his base, he gave us an additional reason to come out and vote for the two Democratic Senate candidates." As Mitt Romney observed, "It turns out that telling the voters that the election was rigged is not a great way to turn out your voters" (Fausset et al. 2021). Other potential Loeffler supporters were turned off by his attacks on Georgia's elected Republican leaders, especially those who had found it impossible to vote for Trump in November.

An *Atlanta Journal-Constitution* analysis of voting histories identified 752,000 individuals who voted in November but not in the runoff (Niesse and Peebles 2021). The White dropout rate (11 percent) exceeded that for Blacks (8 percent). The areas of the state in which the most dramatic drop off in participation occurred were solidly Republican. The suspicious voters in the Fourteenth Congressional District who elected QAnon follower Marjorie Taylor Greene experienced some of the largest decrease in turnout. Others who dropped out will come to the polls only if Trump is on the ballot.

In contrast to the feuding Republicans and their poisonous messages about election security, Democrats presented a united front during the runoff, as they went about expanding their component of the electorate. Several bits of evidence document the Democratic success. The runoff electorate included 228,000 individuals who did not vote in November, and these came from groups that tend to vote for Democrats, with 40 percent younger than thirty-five and a majority being non-White (Niesse and Peebles 2021). Tharon Johnson (2021), explained his role in this effort. A super PAC, Battleground Georgia, identified 940,000 African Americans who did not vote in November and concentrated on a quarter of a million of these individuals, deluging them with emails, phone calls, and home visits. Johnson believes that at least one hundred thousand of these individuals voted in the runoff. Since neither senator's victory margin reached one hundred thousand, these carefully cultivated voters held the key to victory. Democrats also reached out to individuals who turned eighteen between the general election and the runoff. The seventy-six thousand new voters who registered in time for the runoff had characteristics associated with Democrats, with 56 percent younger than thirty-five and 54 percent non-White (Niesse 2020a).

Republicans also targeted a set of voters whose characteristics indicated a high probability of voting for the GOP candidates but who were not likely to vote. Of the 360,000 individuals targeted by the Loeffler, ninety thousand voted early and others cast ballots on Election Day. This work proved insufficient but, as the consultant who told us of these efforts pointed out, without this targeted work, Loeffler's loss would have been a blowout.

Trump's incessant claims that he had won Georgia and other states sufficient to get an Electoral College majority weakened what might have been the Georgia senators' strongest pitch. If Trump had conceded defeat, it would have strengthened the warning that Republicans needed to win at least one Georgia Senate seat in order for the upper chamber to block liberal initiatives launched by the Biden administration and rubber stamped by the House. Voters who saw Trump as an agent of God believed right up to noon on January 20 that somehow—perhaps through divine intervention—Trump would serve another term. For those who believed Trump and expected him ultimately to prevail, maintaining a Senate majority was far less important.

By winning, Warnock and Ossoff became Georgia's first Democratic senators elected since 2000, when former governor Zell Miller, who had been appointed to succeed the late Paul Coverdell, won a majority in the jungle primary. Even more impressively, the 2021 victories marked the first time that a Democrat had defeated a Georgia Republican senator since Wyche Fowler denied Mack Mattingly a second term in 1986.

The 2021 Democratic wins, ironically, shared features with Mattingly's (R) 1980 upset win over four-term incumbent Herman Talmadge (D). On his way to the Senate, Mattingly won twenty-nine counties; Warnock and Ossoff won thirty. Mattingly's success rested on running up the score in Atlanta-area urban counties, with 71 percent in Cobb, 69 percent in DeKalb, 68 percent in Gwinnett, and 57 percent in Fulton. Warnock relied heavily on the same four counties taking 84 percent in DeKalb, 73 percent in Fulton, 61 percent in Gwinnett, and 57 percent of the Cobb County vote.

As the appointed senator, Loeffler had an (I) beside her name on the ballot to denote her as the incumbent. Research on runoffs has found that incumbents who finish second in the initial vote, as Loeffler did, face an uphill climb: of ninety-one incumbents for various offices between 1970 and 1986 who finished second initially, only 26.4 percent won the runoff (Bullock and Johnson 1992). Even more troubling for Loeffler, none of the few senators who placed second initially survived the runoff. The fate of Georgia senators in runoffs provided little comfort to Loeffler. In 1992, Georgia's first experience with a general election runoff, Senator Fowler led by thirty-five thousand votes in November but lost the runoff by almost seventeen thousand. Twenty years earlier, an appointed senator, David Gambrell, led the primary with 31 percent of the vote but lost the runoff to Sam Nunn. In 2008, Saxby Chambliss won the general election runoff, but he had led in the November vote and came within nineteen thousand votes of avoiding a runoff.

While the record for incumbents finishing second in the initial vote was not auspicious for Loeffler, she could take heart from other data. The sum of the vote for the six Republicans competing in the jungle primary exceeded the vote for the eight Democrats by forty-eight thousand. Loeffler might have also pinned her hopes on the fact that no Republican had ever lost a general election runoff: whether the Republican finished first or second in November, the GOP carried the day in the runoff. This line of success resulted from Republicans having greater success than Democrats in getting their voters back to the polls—a trend that ended in 2021.

Finally, appointed senators have not fared well when meeting the electorate. A study of senators appointed to vacancies in last half of the twentieth century found that about a quarter lost in the primary and only half of those who survived the intramural contest won the general election (King 1999). Nate Silver (2008) reported on forty-nine senators appointed between 1958 and 2008. All but ten competed for the seat in the next election but seven lost in the primary. Nineteen of the thirty-two survivors won the general election. A dozen of the winners had advanced to the Senate either from Congress or the state legislature. Of those lacking legislative experience, only seven of eighteen won. Novice Loeffler fell into the category with a 39 percent success rate.

The bitter struggle with Collins that Loeffler had to overcome left scars that hobbled her January performance. Incumbent senators who have served one or more full terms but had to fight their way through a bitter primary emerged damaged and often lost reelection (Abramowitz and Segal 1992). Although the November vote was not a GOP primary, it served the function of reducing the field to a single Republican and featured the fratricidal attacks that occur in partisan primaries with opponents questioning one another's credentials, loyalties, and commitments.

To turn back the Collins challenge, Loeffler embraced positions far more conservative than her backers had expected and in so doing alienated the White, well-educated women Republicans saw as potentially critical in the runoff. She was afraid to dissociate herself from Trump, no matter how wild his claims. One of her staffers described the interactions with Trump as "like dealing with a gangster shakedown. Kelly had to repeatedly pledge her fealty to Trump." Another Loeffler staffer said of the relationship with Trump, "We felt handcuffed." Yet on January 6, as he watched the violent takeover of the Capitol, Donald Trump expressed satisfaction in the defeats of Loeffler and David Perdue. They deserved to lose, he observed, because they had not done enough for him (Bostock 2021).

Conclusions

Raphael Warnock is Georgia's first African American senator but he is not the first African American to win statewide office in Georgia. A generation ago, when Democrats still dominated Georgia politics, Thurbert Baker served three terms as attorney general and Mike Thurmond won three elections as labor commissioner. African Americans have won multiple elections as members of the Supreme Court and the Court of Appeals, both bodies being chosen statewide. Baker and most of the jurists began their tenure as appointees, but Thurmond, like Warnock, initially won without the advantage of incumbency.

The 2020 election cycle culminating with the 2021 Senate runoffs demonstrates that Georgia has become a competitive state. If the trends identified in this chapter continue, Democratic strength will increase during the decade. Support for Stacey Abrams, who came within fifty-five thousand votes of the governorship in 2018, along with Warnock's victory suggest that other Black candidates will follow Warnock to the victory stand. How soon other Democrats, Black or White, win statewide depends in part on the degree to which the successes of the most recent electoral cycle were driven by distaste for Donald Trump, who may never appear on a ballot again. The recent elections of Republicans to the PSC, which is a surrogate for a generic ballot, suggest that the GOP retains a slight advantage.

Warnock's win and other recent Democratic successes in Georgia result from two events or trends coming together. One of these is the successful mobilization of the Black vote. Critical to this activity was Stacey Abrams's work over the years of registering Blacks, and the continued efforts culminating in the focus on a quarter of a million potential new voters in the lead up to the runoff. While it is becoming more difficult to get a precise read on the share of the vote cast by Blacks, it appears, from the secretary of state's audit, that in the runoff the Black percentage share was 28.1 percent but may have approached 30 percent.[6] The second element is converting enough of the White electorate. In 2016, Hillary Clinton managed just 21 percent of the White vote, which was 2 points less than the vote for Michelle Nunn in her senatorial bid two years earlier. Abrams also came up short, with about a quarter of the White vote. Warnock and the other Democratic winners approached the target of 30 percent of the White vote by doing well with the better educated.

The Warnock and Abrams's results show that the penalty that Black candidates previously paid, as calculated in Chapter 1, no longer need apply in Georgia. Abrams led the Democratic ticket in 2018 with 48.8 percent of the vote. A second African American, Otha Thornton, who ran for state school superintendent, received 47 percent of the vote, clustered with several other Democrats competing for positions that attract little attention.

Warnock, like Abrams, led the field, getting almost twenty thousand more votes than Ossoff, outpacing his fellow Democrat for the six-year term by 0.4 percentage points. Lost in the blinding light of publicity on the Senate contests was a third position decided in the runoff, a seat on the PSC. In that third contest, a replay of the 2014 face off, long-time Republican incumbent Lauren "Bubba" McDonald beat Daniel Blackman, an African American, by a percentage point. (Blackman ran 1.6 percentage points behind Warnock.) In the 2014 face-off, McDonald had bested Blackman by a margin of 53.4 to 41.8 percent. The recent result is indicative of how party strength has shifted: Blackman was one of four Democrats held to 41–42 percent of the vote. However, the Democrat who tied for the second-largest share in 2014, with 44.9 percent, was an African American. At a minimum, the results of the last two election cycles show that, as the gap between the parties has narrowed in Georgia, Black Democrats are as competitive as White Democrats and may be more popular.

Black nominees have become a staple of Georgia's Democratic Party and will continue to be so. When he runs for a full term in 2022, it is universally expected that Warnock will share the spotlight and perhaps be eclipsed by Stacey Abrams making a second bid for governor.

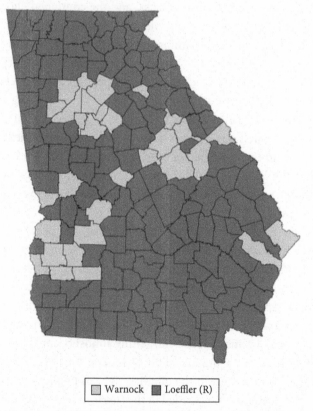

□ Warnock ■ Loeffler (R)

Figure 6.3 Counties Won by Raphael Warnock in the 2021 Senate Runoff
Source: Official results reported by the Georgia Secretary of State.

Warnock's success may be a harbinger not just in Georgia but elsewhere in the South. The near misses of Abrams and Gillum discussed earlier in this volume probably inspired some of the Black senatorial bids in 2020 that included, in addition to Warnock and South Carolina's Jamie Harrison, Mike Espy in Mississippi, Marquita Bradshaw in Tennessee, and long shot Adrian Perkins in Louisiana. *New York Times* writers speculated a week before the 2020 election that if one of these contenders succeeded, it would induce more candidacies. "Should any of them win, though, it would have a catalyzing effect, with more African American candidates inspired to run beyond the confines of a predominantly Black district and party leaders facing pressure to get behind them instead of trying to clear the field for White candidates who may be perceived as safer bets" (Martin and Burns 2020).

7

African American Candidates
Navigate the South

From Whistling Dixie to Winning Dixie

The history of Black presidential aspirations is an almost fifty-year record of mostly failed hopes, with the 2008 nomination and election of Barack Obama as the singular exception, along with his reelection in 2012. However, in 2020, for the first time in history, three credible Black candidates ran for a major party nomination. Although Senators Kamala Harris (CA) and Cory Booker (NJ) and Governor Deval Patrick (MA) were ultimately unsuccessful, Harris emerged as the running mate for ultimate winner Joe Biden. All three Black candidates were counting on support in the southern primaries, and in many ways, their candidacies failed due to an anticipated lack of support from southerners, in particular southern Black voters. Of course, the southern region, the most populous and politically distinct, cannot be ignored by any candidate, Black or White, Republican or Democrat. But for Black Democrats, the southern region has been unusually crucial to their hopes. It is the region where Blacks make up the largest portion of the electorate, in both the primaries and the general election. It is the region where the questions of race have been most dominant in the political system and its history. And it is this region, more than any other, that determined whether a Black nominee would take the top prize in 2020.

Despite being the largest region by population, the South itself also has a long record of dashed hopes on the road to the White House, at least in the period from 1860 to 1964. Prior to that, the South could be said to have dominated the presidency, with eight of the first fifteen presidents identifying as southerners. And since 1964, the South has also been very successful, with candidates from that region winning in 1964, 1976, 1988, 1992, 1996, 2000, and 2004. But from Reconstruction to the civil rights era, the legacy of the Civil War and the brutal apartheid that characterized the South made southerners ineligible for the presidency. Even when Texan Lyndon

African American Statewide Candidates in the New South. Charles S. Bullock, III, Susan
A. MacManus, Jeremy D. Mayer, and Mark J. Rozell, Oxford University Press. © Oxford University Press 2022.
DOI: 10.1093/oso/9780197607428.003.0007

B. Johnson (LBJ) won by a landslide in 1964, some felt that he had run more as a westerner than as a southerner, and moreover had benefited enormously from the halo of John F. Kennedy's (JFK) assassination and the nomination of a Republican extremist. It was not until 1976 that a candidate from the Deep South would go directly to the White House. Before that, immensely talented and widely respected southerners such as Senator Richard Russell of Georgia would not even dare to make a run for the presidency.

Perhaps in part because of this treatment, the South developed a strong regional preference for its own candidates once the door was opened. This regional preference was also produced by the distinctive political history and culture of the South, as well as perceived anti-South prejudice among national elites. Even today, the United States' racial past is uniquely alive in the South, as evidenced by the convulsions over Confederate statues and flags. Candidates from all regions often do best in their home region, but the barrier for outsiders is seldom as high as that facing non-southerners in the South. Even language itself becomes political, as candidates can be accused of trying to "talk southern" in more or less authentic ways. The southern accent, easily the most distinctive US regional accent, has helped candidates when done well. Beyond language, a number of candidates have pandered in almost humiliating ways to demonstrate an affinity for the South, in both primaries and general elections.

Black candidates have faced dramatically different challenges in the South than have White candidates. In part, the challenges resemble those facing any racial, ethnic, or religious minority, in any region. Catholics, Jews, Hispanics, homosexuals, and others who have run or contemplated running have had to contend with prejudice, as have women. Still, the interplay between Black presidential candidates and southern electorates is a particularly delicate and vital one.

For example, one of the emotions forbidden to Black candidates generally is the expression of anger, and this anger is particularly inflammable in the South. Black anger reminds many White voters of White guilt and intrudes on White fragility and fear of racial reparations. The necessity of maintaining racial innocence among Whites is challenged by Black anger, however legitimate (Mayer 2002). Because the South is also the region with the highest concentration of racially conservative Whites (those who oppose efforts to assist Blacks or ameliorate historic inequalities) the shibboleth around Black anger is all the stronger. Thus, a Black candidate, who might be tempted to improve his or her chances in the South with outreach to the Black population via stances on these questions, may also be chastened by fear of White backlash, even in the Democratic White electorate. In most polls, the more centrist White Democrats are present in greatest numbers in the US South. The only White Democrats to win the presidency between 1960 and today were part of the southern moderate wing of the party (LBJ, Carter, Clinton).[1] Until recently, that was the dominant strain in the southern Democratic primaries.

Beneath that dominant voting bloc, though, arose an empowered Black electorate in the aftermath of the 1965 Voting Rights Act. The South remains the region with the highest concentration of African Americans. While border states like Delaware and Maryland are also over 20 percent Black population, it is only in the South where several states have more than 25 percent and all states are over 10 percent. The South thus becomes a vital testing ground for Black candidates for the presidency. The same logic prevailed when JFK was in beauty contest primaries in states with large Catholic voting blocs in 1960. Failing to win their support would have badly hurt his chances, and having that support was crucial to his success. So it is with Black southern voters and Black candidates.

Regional preference. Racial sensitivity. Deep historic scars. The highest concentration of Black population. All of these factors also evolved during the period 1972–2020. This chapter will cover the history of Black candidates for the Democratic nomination running in the South, and how the norms and rules have changed over the decades. It will conclude by examining how the southern primaries played out for Harris, Booker, and Patrick in 2020, and how Harris's addition to the ticket affected Biden's chances in the South.

Chisholm Breaks the Racial Barrier but Fails in the South

The first African American to launch a campaign for the nomination of a major party for the presidency was Congresswoman Shirley Chisholm in 1972.[2] Chisholm was a pathbreaking force in US politics even before this historic run, as her election to Congress from New York City in 1968 made her the first Black woman to serve in Congress. The child of Caribbean immigrant parents, Chisholm had achieved some national stature via her impassioned liberal activism in Congress. Still, her effort at the nomination was considered by many observers to be hopeless, a campaign about breaking barriers, making points, and not about a sincere effort to win. While the 1972 Democratic primaries featured sixteen different candidates of varying degrees of seriousness and viability, the major figures were all White men who had resumes far longer than Chisholm's four years in the House of Representatives. While a few mayors and other Representatives were also in the mix with Chisholm, from the start the assumption was that Senators Ed Muskie (ME), George McGovern (SD), Henry "Scoop" Jackson (WA), and Hubert Humphrey (MN) were the runners to watch, with Senator Eugene McCarthy (MN) and former Alabama Governor George Wallace as potential spoilers. Even Chisholm said during her campaign that her purpose was to "give a voice to the people the major candidates were ignoring." By labeling them "major" candidates, Chisholm was implicitly calling herself a minor one.

Few expected Chisholm to do well in the South, in part because even seven years after the Voting Rights Act, many Blacks remained unregistered. By contrast, White backlash candidate Wallace, whose independent run in 1968 as well as his short-lived 1964 Democratic nomination campaign had been based on race and White rage (Mayer 2002: 47–8, 85), was expected to do well in the southern primaries. But perhaps not; the party had begun to shift on race even by 1972, and Wallace's brand of racial politics might not sell as well now that many White racial conservatives had begun their long shift toward the GOP. If Wallace faltered, North Carolina governor Terry Sanford or Senator Scoop Jackson of Washington, the most conservative Democrat on many issues, were seen as likely to win the White South's support (Mayer 2002: 101–102).

The Black vote on the eve of the Democratic primaries was badly divided, according to some polls. Republican candidate Richard Nixon was keenly interested in who would run against him. Internal campaign documents from late 1971 suggest he feared handsome centrist Senator Edmund Muskie of Maine and Scoop Jackson. Black voters had Muskie as their fourth choice and favored Massachusetts Senator Ted Kennedy (who flirted with running but never entered), Humphrey, and McGovern. Chisholm, who had not yet announced, was not even a consideration at this point ("Muskie Summary" 1971).

The dominant racial issue of the 1972 campaign, in the South and particularly in the North and border states, was busing. While some candidates, such as Wallace, continued to indicate disagreement with integration itself, most of the nation, and most Democrats, were now at least publicly in favor of integration. Yet the nation was sharply against court-ordered busing of school children, particularly White children. The issue bedeviled White Democrats

and divided the Democratic field badly. Even Chisholm was surprisingly am-
bivalent on busing, which while polling badly among Whites, did not have
anything like universal support among Blacks (Freeman 2005).

One aspect of Chisholm's campaign that made it distinctive from all subsequent major party attempts by African Americans for the Democratic nomination was her close association with the feminist movement. Prominent
White feminists Gloria Steinem and Betty Friedan enlisted as Chisholm
delegates, and Chisholm proudly emphasized her commitment to gender
as well as racial equality. After her defeat, Chisholm said that she had faced
greater obstacles in her nomination fight as a woman than she did as an
African American. In part, she said this was because Black men were not
willing to support a Black woman: "Detractors told her that she was a mere
symbol without much substance and that she was getting in the way of viable
candidates. For some she was not Black enough. For others she was too Black
to be taken seriously" (Hunter 2011: 67). While it seems that Chisholm's
strong feminist credentials and her emphasis on her gender gave her another
set of volunteers and a potential base in the emerging women's movement,
the South, among both Blacks and Whites, was then the most traditional region on questions of gender.

Still, Chisholm structured her race around hopes that the southern primaries would be where she pulled away from her all-White group of
competitors. In the first two contests in very White Iowa and New Hampshire,
Chisholm barely registered any support at all (1 percent and 0 percent, respectively). Florida in particular, the second primary and third contest in
1972, was Chisholm's best chance to establish momentum.

The 1972 primary in Florida was also the first time the Sunshine State had
been a player in presidential nomination politics, as the McGovern-Fraser
Commission reforms had empowered states in ways that even party leaders
did not grasp. In that confusion, Chisholm might have been able to eke out
a surprisingly strong showing. Unfortunately, Chisholm was unable to visit
Florida more than twice before the March 14 primary, and had almost no advertising or major endorsements. Her 3.48 percent of the Florida vote was a
crushing early blow to her campaign.

After her failure in Florida, Chisholm struggled to raise money, unite Black
leaders behind her, and gain any media attention at all. She failed for the most
part at all three tasks. As late as August 1972, when the first National Black
Political Convention was held in Gary, Indiana, Chisholm was still being
treated with disdain and sometimes outright derision by prominent Black

leaders, even though she was then still actively running for the nomination (Gallagher 2007: 408). Chisholm's best result was more of a fluke. While she failed to do well in her home state primary of New York, she received 66 percent of the New Jersey primary vote late in the Democratic contest, but zero delegates because of the bizarre rules then practiced.

Why did Chisholm fail to do well in Florida, which would have established her as a much more viable candidate very early on? Why did she fail in all three southern primaries (Florida plus Tennessee with 3.82 percent and North Carolina with 7.51 percent)? The only and first African American running for a presidential nomination failed to rally Blacks in the region where Blacks were most prominent. Why?

First, and foremost, Chisholm was desperately underfunded and never had a chance to build up excitement among southern Blacks or the small group of progressive Whites who might have rallied to Chisholm in the South. Her campaign was run by volunteers rather than paid professionals and had trouble coordinating basic logistics. Her candidacy was never going to be a solid test of whether southern Blacks could be a base for a Black run for the nomination, in the way that labor, environmentalists, urban Catholics, agrarian interests, or other party constituencies had been the base for other candidacies. In part, this was because so many southern Blacks remained unregistered, and among the registered, a tradition of voting in odd things like primaries had not yet emerged.

Second, Chisholm was a candidate for whom southern Blacks would naturally have less affinity. Unlike the majority of northern Blacks, Chisholm had no family roots in the South. As a second-generation Caribbean American, Chisholm lacked the deep historic connection to the South which many other Black leaders had. Even the cadences of Black accents in the North often carry a southern tinge, which translates very well to southern Black audiences. Chisholm lacked that appealing history of southern in her voice.

Finally, Chisholm lacked endorsements or surrogates who could have attested to her authenticity as a potential tribune of Black hopes. The southern Black electorate had only recently and incompletely been enfranchised. There were fewer Black leaders with experience organizing voting coalitions than in the North and Midwest, although the South possessed greater potential for local victories over the long run. The division within the southern Black leadership over her candidacy also contributed to the end of her hopes in the South.

Jackson 1984: A Chicago Resident Embraced by the South of His Youth

Jesse Jackson had a better resume to run in the southern Democratic primaries than Chisholm had. Born in Greenville, South Carolina, Jackson spoke with a natural and resonant southern Black accent. He understood the southern Black church and had worked as a preacher as well as a civil rights activist. He could connect directly to the southern Black church in a way that Chisholm could not. He had fought in the southern civil rights movement, first as a member of the Greenville Eight and then working directly under Dr. Martin Luther King Jr. with the Southern Christian Leadership Conference (SCLC). It was Dr. King who sent him to Chicago, which became his second home, but he never forgot his southern roots, and it showed in every speech he gave in front of a southern audience.

Jackson's 1984 campaign was grounded in anger at the first term of Ronald Reagan (Mayer 2002: 181). Jackson had been rising in the esteem of many African Americans since the late 1960s. He first came to national prominence at the moment of King's assassination, with his dramatic wearing of a bloody shirt, stained with what he claimed was the blood of King, although this claim was contested by other civil rights leaders who were closer to King (both at the moment of King's death and throughout his life). Thus, from the very instant Jackson became a national figure in the Black community, he was polarizing for some established Black leaders. Also burdened with doubts were many traditional power brokers within the Democratic Party, as well as media pundits. While Jackson had a national profile by 1983, he had never run for office at any level of US politics. Up until the election of Donald Trump in 2016, no one had ever been elected president without at least some public service (military, appointed, or elected). Indeed, with rare exceptions, candidates from a major party had all been governors or senators. Jackson, with zero time in any public office, was widely perceived as unqualified by many analysts and elites. As Washington, DC mayor Marion Barry tartly observed: "Jesse never run nothin' but his mouth" (Mayer 2002: 185).

Jackson also faced a White politician with one of the best records on civil rights at the time. Walter Mondale had been with the civil rights movement for decades by 1984, had numerous high-level contacts among the leadership of the Black community, and endorsements and friends in Black communities throughout the nation. He was a known quantity and was assumed to have the Black vote behind him against any rival—except perhaps Jackson.

But Jackson had to consider carefully if the Black vote really would be with him or would be divided as it had been for Chisholm. As one of the key authors of that division, who had refused to clearly endorse Chisholm or even help her much, Jackson knew that a united Black elite could be very helpful and also hard to get. Black leaders met in Chicago in early 1983 to discuss, among other things, whether a run for the presidency was a wise response to Reaganism. Many believed that Black voters had a poor choice between a Democratic Party that took them for granted and an openly hostile Reagan administration. While many names were discussed from among Blacks with electoral experience, none of them were willing to take the plunge. Their hesitancy may, in some cases, have been caused by the awareness that Jackson was likely to run. Getting badly beaten by the charismatic if inexperienced Jackson would be devastating for a more established Black politician.

Shortly thereafter, Jackson began traveling the country, speaking to larger and larger audiences, mostly Black, and the chant would arise "Run, Jesse, Run!" Still, a Jackson run was opposed by important Black politicians like the mayors of Detroit, Atlanta, Birmingham, Philadelphia, and Los Angeles, the heads of the three leading civil rights organizations, as well as the leader of the largest Black labor coalition (Mayer 2002: 181). The head of the Congressional Black Caucus alleged that Jackson lacked follow through and was far more talk than action. Willie Brown, speaker of the California State Assembly and one of the most powerful Black politicians in the country, said "(y)ou can't teach Jesse anything. He never has been disciplined."

Jackson, however, felt that someone needed to challenge the White power structure within the Democratic Party. Jackson, as a Chicago resident, had seen years of neglect and, indeed, abandonment. Blacks were among the most loyal Democratic voters in the Chicago machine, often supporting mostly White slates, but when a Black Democrat was nominated for office outside of Black areas, many Democratic White voters defected and voted for White Republicans. At the national level, Jackson saw similar neglect. In a memorable analogy,[3] Jackson compared Black voters to "concubines" of the White establishment, who were not taken seriously by the Democratic Party. Jackson resolved to force the party to reckon with the power and pride of the Black electorate.

The entrance of Jackson into the race dramatically shook up the race. Mondale, who had served as Carter's vice president, was assumed to be the frontrunner. However, one of the key parts of that assumption had been that none of the other likely candidates were going to threaten Mondale's Black support. With his remaining strength within the party consisting of nearly unified labor backing, the party establishment, a Midwestern base, Carter enthusiasts plus numerous endorsements, Mondale was still formidable, but much more beatable. Indeed, the emergence of Gary Hart as an ongoing threat to Mondale was only possible once Jackson began taking significant portions of the Black vote away from Mondale. Hart, a Colorado Senator with little interest in or experience with the Black community, was unable to make much of a dent in Black support. But with Jackson contesting with Mondale for it, Hart didn't have to.

Jackson's showing in the thirty-three states that held contests for the 1984 Democratic nomination was deeply related to how many Blacks were in the state. A simple bivariate correlation between those states' 1980 census Black population and Jackson's share of the vote has a 0.937 Pearson's coefficient. Indeed, no other variable explains the Jackson vote better than how many Blacks were in the state. That the relationship is this strong despite other powerful influences on nomination outcomes, such as money, media, home state effects, the changing number of candidates during the long primary process, endorsements, and primary rules, is even more impressive. While in a couple of states, like Vermont and New York, Jackson significantly overperformed compared to state Black population levels, mostly likely due to his ideological appeal to White leftists, the norm was to approximate the Black percentage.[4] In the six southern states that held contests, Jackson averaged 24 percent of the vote, while in the twenty-seven non-southern states, he received just under 13 percent. Ultimately, Jackson won Washington, DC, (the only primary where Blacks were in the majority) Louisiana, South Carolina, and split Mississippi with Mondale. The 1984 Jackson campaign was built on Black votes, and most of those votes were in the South.

A few caveats should be noted. The two main rivals for the nomination, Walter Mondale and Gary Hart, were not especially popular in the White South. There was no natural rallying point for White southern voters as there was in the Democratic nomination fights of 1976, 1980, 1988, 1992, and 2000. Other than Mondale, none of the candidates except Jackson had much support in the Black community. Would the same dynamic prevail in the South if those caveats did not apply?

Jackson 1988: Keeping the Black South, Growing Nationally

Jackson spent several years after his 1984 defeat fighting to change the rules of the presidential nomination process. He argued that while he had received over 18 percent of the popular vote in the primaries and caucuses, he received a far lower percentage of delegates due to rules that rewarded statewide winners. Mondale, anxious to assuage Jackson and get his full-throated endorsement for the November election, began the process of giving in on the rules. By 1987, a revised set of rules would be more favorable for Jackson.

And Jackson would be ready. He had learned how to run, how to work local and state politicians, and how to give and collect IOUs like a national politician. He was also far more embraced by established left-wing organizations who had been cautious in 1984. Jackson began to raise money via large donations, compared to his penurious 1984 campaign. Remarkably, he also did something so blatantly political and pandering to the South that it is amazing that it worked so well: he shifted his residence for the purpose of the campaign from Illinois to South Carolina, where he had been born and raised. Of course, Jackson had already claimed South Carolina as his state in 1984, due to birth, and Illinois by residence; this is typical smart politics. But actually shifting your residence between consecutive runs had never been done, and yet attracted little criticism. Jackson had become a far more deft politician, clearly.

Jackson ultimately was part of a three-way race for the nomination, among himself, Tennessee Senator Al Gore, and Michael Dukakis. Dukakis was the frontrunner after winning New Hampshire, and Jackson's strong showing among Blacks in the South prevented Gore from effectively challenging him, while Gore kept Jackson from achieving even more southern victories. The southern tally was mixed: Dukakis only prevailed in Texas and Florida, while Jackson took six southern states and Gore four others. While Jackson also won in Alaska, Michigan, Delaware, and DC, his base of support was still Black votes in the South. The ironic result of the strongest run by a Black candidate for president in the history of either major party was the selection, for the first time since 1972, of a candidate who had won neither the South nor the Black vote. Dukakis was, with the possible exception of McGovern, the least southern-friendly nominee the Democrats had put forward, politically, culturally, and even stylistically. He was also the least able to understand Black political culture or Jackson's demands for respect (Mayer 2002: 215–217).

The data results for 1988 are starkly different for Jackson compared to 1984. While Black population levels were still highly correlated with Jackson votes, the correlation dropped to 0.732. Jackson's support more than tripled or quadrupled in several relatively White states as compared to 1984 and even dropped in a few southern states where Blacks were highly concentrated. This is likely because in those southern states, Gore as a strong moderate White southern candidate turned out many more Whites than Mondale and Hart had in 1984. Also, Jackson's results strengthened as the race went on, thus the order of the voting seems to have been an influence. By the end, voting for Jackson was probably a protest vote against eventual nominee Dukakis as much as anything else.

The story of southern support for Jackson in 1988 was actually one of disappointment when we compare how he improved elsewhere. He received 33 percent of the vote in the twelve southern states that held contests, which was higher than his 1984 results by 9 percent, but he received 27 percent in the remaining thirty-eight states plus DC, more than doubling his support levels from four years before. Jackson in 1988 succeeded at appealing to the left wing of the party nationally, while retaining his base of Black southern support and building somewhat on it. There just weren't enough White leftists in the South to cause Jackson to jump in the polls there.

Barack Obama: Winning in the South, Differently

Barack Obama was closer to Shirley Chisholm than he was to Jesse Jackson on first glance.[5] His roots were in Hawaii and Illinois, and he was educated in Los Angeles and New York City. He was also biracial, with a White mother with roots in Kansas and an African father from Kenya. As one writer deftly put it, Obama had "Kansas and Kenya in his veins . . . Indonesia in his memory, Hawaii in his smile, Harvard in his brain and, most of all, Chicago in his soul" (Lozado 2017). There are few African American leaders who could have six places so central to their existence and family history without one of them being southern. Almost any other Black candidate that could have run in 2008 would have had a southern connection, but not Obama—at least not directly.

Just as Chisholm's Caribbean past sometimes separated her from Blacks with slave ancestry, Obama's White and African heritage raised questions among some potential Black supporters, in the South and elsewhere (Mayer 2013). The tensions in the Black community between those of African American background and those with Caribbean and African roots remain largely unknown to many White observers, but they can have important political implications. The question of Obama's "racial authenticity" was raised by some in the Black community as he contemplated a run for the presidency.

Indeed, Obama himself showed an awareness of this potential political roadblock, in the views of one ex-girlfriend. According to a recent biography by historian David Garrow, Obama was aware that a White wife would be a political obstacle for him in the Black community. However calculating and cold, this is also unquestionably true, and shows Obama's keen political sense. When questions arose about whether Obama was "Black enough" to be a vessel for the hopes of millions of African Americans, the vast majority of whom have the DNA of slaves coursing through their veins, a young Ta-Nehisi Coates defended him:

> Obama is married to a Black woman. He goes to a Black church. He's worked with poor people on the South Side of Chicago. That someone given the escape valve of biraciality would choose to be Black, would see some beauty in his darker self and still care more about health care and public education than reparations and Confederate flags is just too much for many small-minded racists, both Black and White, to comprehend. (Coates 2007)

Obama understood how important the very first point Coates raised in his defense would be. And indeed, in the South, and in other centers of Black population, it was Michelle Obama and her family who frequently attested for Obama once he began running in earnest for the nomination.

Obama also resembled Chisholm more than Jackson in that Obama had actually held elected office, first in the Illinois legislature and then in the US Senate, albeit briefly. But where Obama separated from both is that the crux of his message, from his first appearance on the national stage, was one of inclusion and an end to divisiveness. Jackson famously proclaimed that "hands that picked cotton will now pick presidents!" in speech after speech in 1984 and 1988 (Joyce 1984). This passionate message of Black empowerment, this altar call to Black involvement, was essential to his campaign, and it inevitably cast his candidacy in a racial light, which limited his appeal among Whites, particularly in the more racially conservative White South. Obama had no such core message. His message was unity, hope and change, and . . . himself. What better avatar for racial healing that would not scare White moderates than a man with a White mother and White Kansan grandparents?

Unlike Jackson or Chisholm, Obama would not have money problems in his race for the presidency. Because of his crack staff and his own talent for fundraising, he had the budget to launch a campaign nationwide, and proceeded to do so. Running against Hillary Clinton, who had been planning her campaign for years, and had her husband's vast political and financial network at her disposal, was no easy task. But as with Mondale in 1984, a Black candidate altered the race by removing from a White candidate what had been seen as near certain Black support. As the spouse of a man whose presidency had been so popular with some Black Americans that he had been called by novelist Toni Morrison "America's first Black president," Clinton had been expected to inherit that affection. And while Ta-Nehisi Coates has argued that this was not actually a compliment to Clinton's connection with the Black community but a comment about how he was treated by his enemies (Coates 2015), in the popular imagination, it was widely interpreted as a paean to Bill Clinton's place in the hearts of Black Americans. For whatever reason, the assumption that Hillary Clinton would win the Black vote proved even less true than it had for Walter Mondale. A button worn by some African American Democrats early in the primary said "Don't Tell Momma, I'm With Obama."

The endorsements from prominent Black leaders showed this, including most importantly southern Black Democrats. The Congressional Black Caucus was divided by January 2008, with seventeen for Obama and sixteen for Clinton, with the rest either undecided or with White southern Democrat Senator John Edwards (D-NC) (Hearn 2008). However that was about to change. When Representative John Lewis (D-GA), in many ways the conscience of the civil rights movement in Congress, switched from Clinton to Obama, it sent a giant message heard throughout the Black political leadership. It was one thing to stay on the sidelines, or to support Obama. But to change teams in the middle of the bitterly contested primary suggested that Obama was a rising star, and a likely winner. Lewis said he did so because his home district overwhelmingly supported Obama in the Georgia primary (Zeleny 2008). Especially in the South, Obama's popularity with Black voters put pressure on politicians who had gone with Clinton early. Lewis was not alone; other southern Black politicians also abandoned Clinton as the swelling support for Obama showed up in primaries, polls, and their own town halls.

Another crucial difference for Obama as he competed in the South was the ongoing evolution of the Democratic Party in the region. When Jackson ran in 1984 and 1988, the Democratic Party was still quite competitive in statewide elections in most of the South. The southern Congressional delegations were a mix of White Democrats, White Republicans, and Black Democrats. The White southern Democratic electorate was widely known as the most conservative force in Democratic politics. By 2008, the South that Jackson had run in was gone. Most states were trending Republican in state elections. Congressional delegations were becoming almost binary: White Republicans and Black Democrats. The Democratic primary electorate had gotten Blacker. The White remnant had either become more liberal or was simply the liberal leftover when the conservative and moderate White Democrats headed over to the GOP. Obama, who was not clearly running to Clinton's left or right except on foreign policy, was very well placed to do fine among Whites nationwide, except for the existential question of whether a specific White voter was willing to support any Black candidate at all.

Obama also had what no Black candidate before ever had: a vast collection of endorsements from some of the most prominent White politicians in his party. While Clinton had more endorsements until well into the primaries, Obama's early entrance caused many to wait. When Obama began to do well in early contests and debates, crucial names in the South began to flock to him. But the most important endorsement happened much earlier, in February 2007, when Governor Tim Kaine of Virginia became the first governor (outside of Illinois) to endorse any candidate. The news that a sitting southern governor in an important swing state had come out so early for Obama ricocheted throughout the South and the nation, signaling that one of the smartest young southern politicians saw Obama as a likely winner (Fiske 2007). For a candidate mounting a contest against the spouse of a popular former president who was the frontrunner in most early polls, the Kaine endorsement was vital. The endorsements from Whites culminated in the Kennedy family bestowing its endorsement on Obama, as an ailing Senator Ted Kennedy imbued Obama with the legacy of his martyred brothers.

Ultimately, Obama did well among southern voters, both White and Black, largely for the same reasons he did well with voters of all persuasions across the country. It was fortunate for Obama's hopes that the candidate with the strongest southern credentials, John Edwards, faded so quickly. It was even more fortunate that Hillary Clinton's southern roots were limited to Arkansas. She was much more associated in the public mind with New York and to a lesser extent Illinois, her place of birth. There had always been public ambivalence about her during her husband's many years in Arkansas, and political advisors even persuaded her to give up her feminist embrace of her maiden name and simply become Mrs. Clinton to stop her husband's political opponents from further depicting her as political outsider to Arkansas culture (Maraniss 1996). Had she been a strong candidate in the eyes of White southern Democrats, she might well have won. As it was, Obama was able to compete with southern Whites, while dominating among southern Blacks.

Still, Hillary Clinton did better in the South in her 2008 race against Obama for the nomination than she did elsewhere. Of the twelve southern contests, Obama won seven, while Clinton won five; but outside the South, Obama won twenty-five states to Clinton's thirteen. A means comparison between southern and non-southern state outcomes for Obama shows a closer result, but Obama still did marginally better in the non-South (49.6 percent vs. 54 percent).[6] While there is a small correlation between state Black population and support for Obama, it is not statistically significant.[7] Thus, the data analysis of the Democratic primaries of 2008 confirms that Obama was a very different candidate from Jackson in either of his runs.

Given that Black Democrats were strongly for Obama, it would seem most likely that Obama did benefit from heightened levels of support, excitement, and turnout among African Americans, but that African Americans are located in states with a higher than average number of moderate White Democrats who leaned toward Clinton.

Obama's election, however historic, did not end racial politics in presidential campaigns. Nor did the South suddenly become less distinctive, although its declining distinctiveness has been studied by political scientists and sociologists for decades. Would other Black candidates be able to emulate the Obama success in the South? In 2016, no prominent Black politician ran for the Democratic nomination. That would change in 2019–2020.

The South in the General Elections of 2008, 2012, and 2016

The southern electorate had never had a choice like that in 2008 and again in 2012, when a White candidate faced a Black one in the presidential race. In 2008, Obama carried North Carolina, Florida, and Virginia, while in 2012, he managed only Florida and Virginia. Obama obviously did better in 2008 than he did in 2012, and better in both years than other recent Democratic nominees in the South. Gore and Kerry failed to carry a single southern state in 2000 and 2004, respectively.[8] Obama in 2008 did almost as well as native southerner Bill Clinton in 1996 (who won Arkansas, Tennessee, Louisiana, and Florida) and better than Clinton did in 1992, when he carried only Louisiana, Arkansas, and Georgia.

The comparison between Obama's success in cracking the GOP's hold on the South in 2008 and 2012 with Hillary Clinton's failure in Florida in 2016 is illuminating. Clinton lost every southern state except Virginia, and she had a popular Virginia senator and former governor as her running mate. Trump, a prototypical Northeasterner running with a Midwesterner, did almost as well in the South as had Ronald Reagan, George H. W. Bush, and George W. Bush in their mammoth southern landslides of 1984, 1988, 2000, and 2004. Trump was not just a New Yorker; he was culturally and religiously deeply at odds with what White southern conservatives had traditionally favored. He had recently been pro-gun control and pro-choice on abortion, had appeared in soft-core porn videos, owned casinos, publicly philandered on two wives, and was married to his third, who had modeled in the nude during as well as before their relationship. Credible stories of Trump's philandering just after his third wife gave birth to their child emerged during the general election. He had been openly non-religious for most of his adult life, could not remember a single Bible verse when asked, and famously got the name of one of the most renowned books of the New Testament wrong during public remarks (Bullock et al. 2019: 128–150). Yet, somehow, he won the buckle on the Bible Belt, the southern states.

Also, in a surprise to many observers, Trump managed to do slightly better than fellow-Republican Mitt Romney among both Black and Hispanic voters, based on exit polling (Sakuma 2016). The tiny 2 point rise in support for Republicans among both groups was hardly a ringing endorsement for Trump, but in close southern states like Florida and North Carolina, the combination may have made the difference.

What happened? Why was Obama able to get more than twenty crucial electoral votes from the South in his elections, and Hillary Clinton was not? In addition to the slight rise in support for the GOP among Blacks and Hispanics, one crucial factor was Black voter turnout. The racial gap in turnout had disappeared by 2012 and benefitted Obama in the South and elsewhere. By contrast in 2016, it is estimated that 4.4 million Obama voters stayed home, and more than a third of these non-voting Obama voters were African American. President Trump went so far as to thank the Black community for not voting. "They didn't come out to vote for Hillary. They didn't come out. And that was a big—so thank you to the African American community," he said a month after the election (Bump 2018).

It does appear that Black turnout was a key aspect of the southern results in at least a few states. While overall turnout was high for recent US elections, at 61.4 percent, Black voter turnout decreased, while White turnout increased. Black turnout nationally dropped from the record high of 66.6 percent in 2012 to 59.6, while White turnout rose slightly to 65.3 percent (Krogstad and Lopez 2017). While the decline is interesting in itself, 2016 represents a reversion in an important trend. There had been roughly a 10 point gap in turnout between Blacks and Whites in 1988, but from 1992 onwards, the gap had been closing, until in 2012, and for the first time ever, the percentage of Blacks voting was higher than the percentage of Whites. In 2016, for the first time in twenty-eight years, the non-White proportion of the electorate stayed roughly the same over a four year period, at 26.7 percent, which is even more surprising since the non-White proportion of the population continued to grow at a faster rate.

In at least one southern state that Obama carried in 2012 and Trump prevailed in four years later, the answer may have been new voting regulations. North Carolina radically reduced its early voting opportunities after 2012. Early voting is particularly important for voters who are poor or work for hourly wages. Early voting among Black voters was down 8.7 percent by election day in North Carolina (Roth 2016).

While Trump rose in support among Blacks compared to Romney in 2012 by around 2 points, Clinton fell nationally among Black voters by 5 points. Some Black votes seemed to go to Green Party nominee, Jill Stein, who received only 1 percent of the national vote. Reducing Black turnout overall, and increasing Black support for third-party candidates, was one of the goals of the Russian social media campaign of 2016. In particular, Blacks were targeted with messages that stated that Trump and Clinton were not very different, and Black voters should either send a message by voting for Stein or just stay home (Shane and Frenkel 2018). Stein may have also attracted slightly more Black votes than a usual Green Party candidate, because her running mate was Black. And the decline in Black voting for the Democrat may have simply been a result of the absence of a Black candidate, which electrified Black communities in 2008 and 2012. While it is impossible to say what caused the decline in Black turnout and support for the Democratic presidential ticket, it is obvious that this effect would be greater, ceteris paribus, where African Americans make up a larger portion of the voting

Table 7.1 Democratic Vote in the South, 2008, 2012, and 2016

State	2008 (%)	2012 (%)	2016 (%)
Alabama	38.7	38.7	34.7
Arkansas	38.9	36.9	33.7
Florida	51	50	47.8
Georgia	47	45.5	45.6
Louisiana	39.9	40.6	38.5
Mississippi	43	43.8	40.1
North Carolina	49.7	48.4	46.1
South Carolina	44.9	44.1	40.7
Tennessee	41.8	39.1	34.7
Texas	43.7	41.4	43.2
Virginia	52.6	51.2	49.7
Average of all Southern States	44.65	43.61	41.35

population: the South. As shown in Table 7.1, the Democratic share of the vote declined in almost every southern state. The overall decline was 2.5 percent of the vote share in the South, below the Democratic decline nationwide.

One of the many questions the Democrats were pondering in the aftermath of the defeat of 2016 was where to put their attention for 2020. Should they try to gain back the working class White voters who seemed to be part of Trump's victories in crucial "blue wall" Midwest states like Michigan and Wisconsin? Or should they reach out more to minorities and try to reproduce the Obama coalition? Perhaps not enough attention has been paid to why they declined in the South and failed to take Florida for the first time in three election cycles. As shown in Table 7.1, the average Democratic vote in southern states was down more than 2 percent from 2012 and 3 percent from 2008.

Setting the Stage: The Racial Environment of 2019–2020

One part of the story of the campaigns involving Chisholm, Jackson, and Obama is an examination of the racial environment in which they ran. The degree to which the United States is polarized on racial issues affects how Black candidates run in the South. When racial polarization on Black and White lines runs high, Black turnout may go up, but it may be accompanied by increases in White turnout and by an unwillingness on the part of some White voters to vote for Black candidates or for candidates who are racially progressive in general.

The racial environment of 2020 was highly polarized, although to an extent this is a reflection of the larger partisan polarization that has been going on for more than forty years in the United States. But race in particular seems to have become far more divisive since 2015, perhaps in a way not seen since the civil rights era. Issues and actors that were once considered fringe are approaching the center of US politics. White supremacist groups and racially inspired terrorist acts are attracting the national spotlight. The march in Charlottesville in 2017, in which a counter protester was killed by a White supremacist, along with the inflammatory comments of President Trump, called attention to race in a dramatic way. Similarly, high profile attacks by White supremacist gunmen in Charleston, South Carolina, (in which an angry White racist targeted a Black church intending to start a race war) and El Paso, Texas, (in which a White racist slaughtered Hispanics in order to draw attention to immigration) inflamed the racial divide. Immigration, an issue loaded with racial and ethnic implications, skyrocketed in significance, as the number of apprehensions at the border soared and images of caged Hispanic children were prominent in the national media. Police brutality, an issue with a long history and deep racial importance, attracted greater attention, as incident after incident was investigated and as videos of acts of violence by police against Black citizens went viral.

Above all of these issues loomed the figure of President Trump. From his earliest appearance on the national stage, he has been associated with racial animus. Indeed, he has trafficked in racist conspiracy theories. Throughout Obama's presidency, Trump was the most prominent advocate of "birtherism," the false claim that President Obama was born in Kenya, not Hawaii, and was therefore ineligible for the presidency. As president, Trump injected himself into racially tinged controversies over and over, raising the profile of race in the nation. He crudely attacked Black NFL players who protested police brutality. A president who directly engages on racially charged issues by his own choice is unusual in modern US history. Trump's response to the Charlottesville White supremacist march is particularly noteworthy. He blamed both sides for the violence and argued that there were good people on both sides.

This matters because when the United States is inflamed on racial questions, it may be more difficult for minority candidates, particularly

Black candidates, to thrive, in the South and elsewhere. By contrast, when the nation's attention is on foreign policy or economics, particularly in a crisis, the opportunity for those candidates may rise. Given the current demographics of the nation and the South, no candidate who fails to do well among White voters is likely to succeed in the primaries or the general election.

Booker, Harris, and Patrick: Three Black Candidates Join the 2020 Crowd and Look South

By 2019, the South was showing signs of political change. In particular, the 2018 races for governor in Georgia and Florida suggested the South was approaching a new paradigm, one in which southern Black candidates had a shot at winning statewide elections for top offices. True, this was a glass ceiling that had been broken before, in 1992 by Virginia governor L. Douglas Wilder, a Democrat, and later by Republican Senator Tim Scott of South Carolina. However, these were exceptional; most Black efforts at southern statewide office failed, either in the Democratic primaries or the general election, suggesting that the Wilder victory had been an outlier rather than a harbinger and that Scott was sui generis.

The Stacey Abrams race in Georgia and the Andrew Gillum race in Florida, however, were unexpectedly close. While they both ultimately fell short of the governorship in their respective elections, they demonstrated that the southern electorate had changed dramatically. This also suggested that the Obama victories in Florida and Virginia in 2008 and 2012, and his win in North Carolina in 2008, were beginning to seep down into the statewide electorates of the South. Biracial and multiracial Democratic coalitions supporting Black candidates could win statewide in the South.

But the road to the Democratic nomination had also changed; first, by the remarkable rise of Donald Trump. Trump's victory in the South in 2016 suggests that southern electorates may not be as biased toward southerners as once was the case. Trump was uniquely unfit to do well in the South for a host of reasons: a Manhattan residence, a thick New York accent, a childhood of privilege, the avoidance of military service during war through dubious means, a history of supporting gun control and abortion rights, a distinct lack of interest in hunting, country music, and other southern cultural touchstones, two divorces, internationally reported philandering, appearances in soft-core porn videos (clothed), a model wife who posed nude, and a profound lack of religious faith. Any one of these might have destroyed a candidate's southern hopes, but Trump's success in the South suggests the South has changed in other ways, too (Bullock et al. 2019).

Trump's victory had a second effect, in changing the whole nature of qualifications for running. Trump was the first president to have never served a day in public office. That, combined with a third effect, the white-hot Democratic rage that Trump inspired, produced the largest nomination field in history, with more than twenty-one announced candidates. The South, and the other regions, never had to choose from such a large set of choices.

Perhaps because of some of these forces, for the first time three Black Democratic candidates for president in 2020 emerged: Senators Corey Booker (NJ) and Kamala Harris (CA) and later, former Massachusetts governor Deval Patrick. As we will see, all three had stronger connections to the South than Obama did.

Booker had a father who grew up in North Carolina, and still has family there. His roots in the Black community of New Jersey go deep and aided him in all of his New Jersey elections. Booker also had something that no other Black candidate for nomination has ever had—strong ties to Wall Street. As a New Jersey Senator, Booker raised money from and represented the interests of the financial titans of banking, investing, and insurance. Booker seems to be the rare politician who is at home in both the urban heart of Newark and the ritzy suburbs of New Jersey, where the financial elite often dwell (Grunwald 2019). While Obama eventually had that same ability to cross invisible boundaries easily, he had to develop it over his years working in Chicago, whereas Booker has had it since his first forays into Newark.

Harris has a background that shares some similarities with Obama. She grew up in the San Francisco area—like Hawaii, a bit of a liberal bubble. She moved to Canada, so, like Obama, spent some of her formative years abroad. However, unlike Obama, she attended perhaps the premier historically Black university, Howard. While not a southern institution, it has deep connections to the South, historically and through its alumni network. Crucially, Harris also joined a Black sorority (Goodyear 2019). Black sororities are much more important in the Black community than are similar college organizations in White communities. Harris used her sorority connections in visits to South Carolina, and this gave her a network of supportive Black women all across the South.

Harris also shared with Obama a biracial heritage. In Harris's case, her father was a Jamaican immigrant, and her mother was from India. As with

Obama, a few Black voices, although largely on social media, raised questions about her heritage. Journalists April Ryan and Don Lemon had a remarkable conversation about Harris's background in February 2019, in which Lemon insisted that Harris should say she is Black, but not African American, because she is not someone who "comes out of Jim Crow, out of slavery." Ryan countered by pointing out that Harris identifies as a Black woman, went to Howard, and that should be the end of it. Lemon persisted in finding a difference between Black and African American (CNN Tonight 2019). In a later radio interview with a largely Black audience, Harris was asked questions about the critical voices in the Black community who questioned her heritage. She was asked to respond to people in the Black community who allegedly say "How is she so Black but she married a White guy?" (Pluralist 2019). Harris's answer, that it was just love, and not a plan, seemed to kill the issue in that interview.[9] In this interview, though, as in others, Harris's past as a prosecutor who sent many African Americans to prison came up. Her occupational past seemed to be, over the course of her campaign, much more of a handicap among progressive Black voters and leaders than her interracial marriage.

Patrick's background is a rarity in a modern presidential candidate of any color: a childhood of deep poverty. Patrick's father abandoned the family when Deval was four and only rarely contacted or supported them after that (Patrick 2011). Patrick, partially raised in a public housing project in Chicago's South Side, was selected for a competitive scholarship to elite Milton Academy and from there had a meteoric rise through Harvard, Harvard Law School, and eventually, service as assistant attorney general for civil rights in Clinton's Justice Department (Toobin 2018). In 2006, he became governor of Massachusetts, and won reelection in 2010. Throughout his time in office, he had a relatively deracialized approach to politics, somewhat different from Harris and Booker stylistically (Stout 2015). Patrick has deep ties to the South through his mother's family. In his memoir, he writes of traveling back almost every month in his childhood to his grandparents' ancestral home in Kentucky, as well as the southern flavor of his Chicago neighborhood (Patrick 2011: 12–16).

Still, none of them was a southerner, obviously. Oddly enough, of the more than twenty announced Democratic candidates, only three were from southern states: from Texas, former Representative Beto O'Rourke and former Cabinet secretary and former San Antonio mayor Julian Castro; and from Florida, a gadfly candidate, Wayne Messam, the Black mayor of

Miramar. Had Stacey Abrams of Georgia entered the race, southern Black voters would have had one of their own to choose, but she opted out.

All three candidates put much of their hopes on surviving the very White Iowa and New Hampshire contests so they could make it to South Carolina with its large black voting bloc. All of them had shown in prior races a strong ability to win White votes and the votes of other minorities, but still invested in South Carolina heavily.

South Carolina dominates the southern primaries because it comes first. It has also become one of the most important states nationally after Iowa and New Hampshire. Booker visited South Carolina frequently as his campaign heated up in 2019. He went to small towns and the larger cities, as a way to separate him from rivals who tended to visit the larger population centers only (Lovegrove 2019). Not to be outdone, Harris visited South Carolina several times and received five key endorsements from South Carolina Democrats: three state lawmakers, a 2018 gubernatorial candidate, and a county chair, who all endorsed Harris in early 2019. While none of them had the stature that Tim Kaine had when he endorsed Obama in early 2007, these endorsements might have mattered more in a very crowded field (Marchant 2019).

All three Black candidates faced the same strategic problem—South Carolina Black voters were leaning strongly to Joe Biden. But the early indications of Black support for Biden were tested just before the first Democratic debates in the summer of 2019. Biden unwisely made a statement seeming to boast of his past strong connections with two strident racist southern White Democrats. Biden's tone deaf paean to an era when the Senate ran on courtesy and (usually) genteel racism brought the issue of race to the forefront of the Democratic contest. Both Harris and Booker attacked Biden. Before the debate, Booker was most critical, but only Harris was on the same debate stage with Biden, and she made a national splash with her slashing attack on Biden's record on busing and his close ties to racists during his time in the Senate. Biden's inept response ensured that the issue would resonate for days (Stevens 2019). Some polls showed a drop in Biden's Black support and significant rise in Harris' national polling. But busing was far from the only racial issue to emerge out of the political past.

Unexpectedly, an issue that was considered far too explosive for much of modern US political history was resurrected in the 2020 pre-primary contest: reparations. In part because of an important essay favoring reparations by Ta-Nehisi Coates, reparations became a dividing line among Democrats for the presidency. Booker proposed legislation to study the question, and delicately seemed to favor it in some statements (Rodrigo 2019). Harris also endorsed reparations, although again with some vagueness. She suggested at one point that it might take the form of mental healthcare:

> You can look at the issue of untreated and undiagnosed trauma. African-Americans have higher rates of heart disease and high blood pressure. It is environmental. It is centuries of slavery, which was a form of violence where women were raped, where children were taken from their parents—violence associated with slavery. And that never—there was never any real intervention to break up what had been generations of people experiencing the highest forms of trauma. And trauma, undiagnosed and untreated, leads to physiological outcomes. (Morning Edition 2019)

An issue that was so untouchable that no major Democratic Party figure would endorse it, that the two major Democratic candidates from the 2016 primaries openly opposed, and that the first Black president of the United States also talked down, was now supported by a number of Democrats running for president. This says a great deal about how the Democratic Party had changed in just three years. A party that was progressive enough on race to actively consider reparations might be a party unready to nominate one more White male, particularly an elderly one with some checkered positions on racial matters of the past.

Yet not one of the Black candidates made it to the South Carolina contest. Harris was the first to exit, leaving the race in December 2019 before a single primary or caucus had taken place. Her departure was attributed to the difficulty of raising money as well as her poor showing in the polls. Given that many analysts had seen Harris, with her California donors and her deft showing at several debates, as one of the top-tier candidates, her departure came as a surprise to many (Herndon, Goldmacher, and Martin 2019). Harris had also brought dramatic attention to race during a summer debate, when she brought up Biden's past positions on busing. A flood of donations and support seemed to shift toward her, and Biden seemed momentarily wounded. The real reason for her departure may have been South Carolina and California polls. Harris had largely ignored New Hampshire and Iowa in preference for South Carolina and her home state. But she was failing to break through there, and may have wished to avoid embarrassing results.

Booker was the next to leave, for very similar reasons. Indeed, Booker's chances were always less than Harris's, as he never had the surge into the top tier of candidates that she had. Patrick was now the last major Black candidate left, and yet he was seen as "having virtually no chance" because of his late start and poor name recognition (Smith and Strauss 2020). After a disappointing showing in the New Hampshire primary, Patrick called it quits (Saul and Astor 2020).

What are we to make of the historic presence of three experienced, talented Black politicians all dropping out before a single southern Black voter had a chance to register their opinion on the matter? An old story seemed to be the main cause, in South Carolina, and perhaps across the South. An article in *Politico* suggested that Harris, for whom South Carolina was a "linchpin," faced a "rude awakening": Joe Biden had connections and a large network among Black and White politicians in South Carolina (Cadelago 2019). It seemed that Biden inherited some of Obama's popularity among African Americans. As shown earlier, those who predicted similar loyalty to a White politician among the southern Black Democratic primary electorate for Mondale and for Hillary Clinton in 1984 and 2008 were terribly mistaken. But when Biden won the South Carolina primary decisively, and largely due to the support of Black voters, it suggested that the three Black candidates had chosen wisely. It also suggests the difference between modern Black politicians and less-seasoned pioneers like Chisholm and Jackson. Jackson hung on in 1984 and 1988 long after it was impossible to win, because he wasn't worried about his reputation or his alliances, as most professional politicians would be. The 2020 Black aspirants were behaving like politicians with a future who couldn't risk catastrophic defeats or burnt bridges.

What seems most clear from looking at the history of southern primaries and the current realities of Harris, Patrick, and Booker is that they much more resemble Obama than they do Jesse Jackson in the 1980s. While they focused on Black voters in South Carolina, even there none of them ignored the southern White electorate as Jackson had largely done. The South has changed, the rules have changed, and the candidates have changed. The angry protest moment that was necessary in 1984 and 1988 seems less urgent in the aftermath of Obama. The anger is directed outward toward Republicans in this polarized moment, and the southern Democratic primaries favored the candidate, Joe Biden, perceived as most likely to bring an end to the Trump presidency. While the South will surely remain distinctive on a number of political points, in this, they resembled the rest of the nation's Democratic electorate.

Kamala Harris Comes Back as a Running Mate

Joe Biden quickly became the anointed candidate after his stunning victory in South Carolina. He had promised to name a female running mate and was actively considering a historically large number of Black, Indigenous, people of color (BIPOC) women for the slot, including Harris, former National Security Advisor Susan Rice, Florida Congressman Val Demings, and Senator Tammy Duckworth. From the start, Harris was seen as a frontrunner. The big strike against her was her attack on Biden in the debates over his record on race. Could the Biden camp trust her and forgive her? Additionally, Harris, unlike some options under consideration, did not have a home state that was a battleground. Some Biden advisors also worried about her staff and her management skills, since her presidential campaign had been notoriously badly run. Still, Biden had said all along that, as a former vice president, he felt the most important thing was a candidate who was "simpatico" with his values and style. In that regard, Harris had what no other potential nominee had, a connection to Biden's beloved son whose death still reverberated in his life (Burns, Martin, and Glueck 2020).

The selection of Harris was intended to increase turnout and support among Black voters. As mentioned, the perception among many Democrats was that the 2020 nominee would have to choose between trying to re-build the Obama coalition or try to boost support among disaffected white working class voters, particularly in the three "blue wall" states of Wisconsin, Michigan, and Pennsylvania, which had gone for Trump in 2016. Biden was obviously selected in part to do the latter, and Harris would balance the ticket and hopefully do the former.

Harris on the campaign trail had a more aggressive style on race than Obama (the only other Black candidate to run in a national general election) had in 2008 (Bierman 2021). This may have been because the times were different, given the rise of Black Lives Matter and the prominence of police brutality in political debate. Or it may have been the difference between running against John McCain and Trump, as Trump directly and divisively raised racial issues, or because Obama had carved out a larger space for racial issues to be openly discussed. But it may have also been a strategic choice, attempting to inspire higher Black turnout in key states, where low black turnout may have doomed Clinton in 2016. Harris called on Black voters to support Biden-Harris to "honor the ancestors" (Ostfeld and Garcia 2020).

Because COVID-19 made traditional campaigning almost impossible for Biden-Harris, the highest profile event for Harris was unquestionably her debate with Vice President Mike Pence. Race featured prominently in that debate, far more than it had in the Biden-Trump debates. Harris attacked Trump for what she called racist policies and for failing to criticize white supremacists such as the Proud Boys and the Charlottesville neo-Nazis. She brought up specific cases of police brutality. By contrast, Pence denied the existence of systemic racism and attacked Biden for suggesting some police agencies had "implicit bias" against Black people, calling the charge "a great insult" to police officers (Ellis 2021).

Ultimately, Biden won a narrow but clear victory over Trump, although it took the United States' creaky decentralized election system many weeks to certify the victory amid false allegations from Trump and others of widespread fraud. Did the historic candidacy of Harris help or hurt the Democratic ticket in the South? Did it work to increase Black turnout in the South and nationally?

On the surface, it seems likely that Harris helped. The three blue wall states of Wisconsin, Michigan, and Pennsylvania flipped to Biden, as did Arizona and one crucial southern state, Georgia. In the South generally, Biden did more than 2 percent better in the popular vote than had Hillary Clinton, and her running mate was a southern governor. Yet when we look at exit polling data, it seems less likely that Harris was crucial, with the exception of the razor thin outcome in Georgia. As shown in Table 7.2, Black support for the Democratic ticket went up 5 percent in Georgia, although the Black percentage of the state electorate had slightly declined. That alone may have been enough to give the state to Biden. In the three blue wall states, Black turnout barely changed, and support levels among Black voters stayed at 92 percent in all three states, an almost eerie level of stability.

The turnout for 2020 was the highest in a hundred years. Evidence for a strong rally to Harris in the national numbers is muted, though. While the Black percentage of the electorate was up by 1 percent over 2016, support for the Democratic ticket dropped by 2 percent among Black voters. Biden lost ground with Black men, whose support for the Democratic ticket dropped to 80 percent, a historically low level. Trump did commit some outreach that might have particularly resonated with some Black men, including an endorsement from L'il Wayne and a partnership with rapper Ice Cube on an

Table 7.2 Biden Vote in Southern and Blue Wall States, and Black Support

State	Biden Vote 2020 (%)	Change from 2016 (%)	Change in Black Vote* (%)	Change in Black % of Electorate
Alabama	36.7	+2	NA	NA
Arkansas	34.8	+1.1	NA	NA
Florida	47.9	+.1	−1	0
Georgia	49.5	+3.9	+5	−1
Louisiana	39.9	+1.4	NA	NA
Mississippi	41.1	+1	NA	NA
North Carolina	48.7	+2.6	+3	+3
South Carolina	43.4	+2.7	−4	+7
Tennessee	37.5	+2.8	NA	NA
Texas	46.5	+3.3	+6	+1
Virginia	54.3	+4.6	+1	−3
Average of all Southern States	43.65	+2.3	+1.66	+ 1.1
Michigan†	50.6	+2.6	0	+1
Pennsylvania†	50	+2.4	0	−3
Wisconsin†	49.6	3.2	0	−1

Notes: * Taken from exit polls. †Switched from Republican to Democrat between 2016 and 2020.

investment plan for Black America dubbed "the Platinum Plan" (Ostfeld and Garcia 2020).

Of course, amid a surge of turnout nationwide across many demographics, caused by increased polarization, the pandemic, or other factors, attributing aggregate statewide outcomes to the vice presidential candidacy of Harris is difficult. In the absence of Harris, perhaps the Black vote would have failed to keep pace with the surge among other voters. We also cannot know if the nomination of a Midwestern moderate White woman, like Michigan Governor Gretchen Whitmer would have helped more or less than Harris. Still, the addition of Harris to the ticket was entirely justified if all she did was give Biden a victory in Georgia. Unlike the Obama victories of 2008 and 2012, the result in 2020 was so close that peeling off just Georgia from the solid GOP South was of intense importance.

The South and National Black Candidates

The epic tale of Black candidates running for national office in the South begins with the quixotic and unsuccessful effort of Chisholm and ends, for now, with the triumphant vice presidential election of Harris. In the forty-eight years separating those two campaigns, Black candidates have become far more frequent, credible, and successful and the southern Black electorate far more energized and important. Still, a paradox remains: all of the Black candidates to run for nationwide office from 1972 to 2020 were from outside the South, with the sole exception of the brief, aborted campaign of Virginia Governor Doug Wilder in 1992, even though the South is the center of Black population in the United States.

The largely unsuccessful efforts by Black candidates in southern statewide elections described in the other chapters of this book is the explanation of the paradox. And this points toward the next step for national Black candidates in the South. Imagine a Kamala Harris or Cory Booker, but this time running for president as a senator from a southern state? The excitement of Black southern voters in voting for one of their own would then include not just race pride but regional preference. The barriers to statewide Black candidates in the South remain formidable, but they seem to be weakening. It seems inevitable that a Black son or daughter of the South, the former home of slavery, Jim Crow, and George Wallace, will one day rise to the presidency.

8

Conclusion

The Future for African American Statewide Candidates in the South

The substantial changes taking place in parts of the South have created an increasingly competitive environment for African American statewide candidates. Focusing on the latest election cycles, our study examined the campaigns of African American nominees in statewide elections in the Growth States of the South. It is in those states that Black statewide candidates have the best chances for breakthrough victories.

All of the cases covered in this volume are of African American Democratic Party nominees, which reflects the reality of the current state of Black politics in the South, and the nation as well. The electoral successes of Senator Tim Scott (R-SC) in 2014 and 2016 suggest that Black statewide candidates in the South are not necessarily limited to running as Democrats, a trend which, if it is repeated in other Southern states, would dramatically alter the partisan and racial politics of the region. There are important qualifiers, though, that make Scott's case different from the elections covered in this volume. Scott initially ran with the advantage of incumbency, having been appointed to the US Senate to fill a vacancy. He ran as a Republican in a heavily red state in non-competitive races, taking nearly two-thirds of the vote each time against weak Democratic opponents. In both elections, both major political party nominees were Black. Moreover, the coalition that elected Scott looks much more like the coalition that elects White Republicans than the backers of Democrats, Black or White. According to the exit poll, in 2016, Scott got 77 percent of the White vote, 7 points better than Donald Trump, while the Black Democrats examined in this volume have struggled to get a third of the White vote. Most of the candidates in this volume got about 90 percent of the Black vote. Scott did no better than 10 percent. The patterns in 2014 are similar, with Scott doing slightly better than White GOP running mates with both Black and White voters.[1] Other than Senator Scott, Black Republican hopes in the South have largely remained unrealized, as all but one of the

African American Statewide Candidates in the New South. Charles S. Bullock, III, Susan A. MacManus, Jeremy D. Mayer, and Mark J. Rozell, Oxford University Press. © Oxford University Press 2022.
DOI: 10.1093/oso/9780197607428.003.0008

region's Black members of the 117th Congress are Democrats. It seems likely that Scott will remain a sui generis case for at least a few more electoral cycles, if not longer.

Key trends and electoral factors help to explain what makes for competitive statewide campaigns for Black Democrats in the contemporary South. We first take up the key trends, drawing from the analysis in our earlier volume on southern political change and applying that to the cases examined in this volume (Bullock et al. 2019).

The Key Trends Driving Southern Political Change

Changing Demographics

The South has had the greatest population growth of any region of the country in the past half century. Economic and social dynamism have driven substantial in-migration from other states and internationally. The southern states leading population growth are Florida, Texas, and Georgia, followed by the Carolinas and Virginia (Bullock 2021).

Population growth has been greatest among racial and ethnic minorities, particularly Hispanics and Asians. In 1970, the South was about three-quarters non-Hispanic White and 20 percent Black; today the region is about 55 percent non-Hispanic White, 20 percent Hispanic, 19 percent Black. Interracial marriages and persons of mixed racial ancestry are increasingly common now in the region where such marriages were illegal as recently as the 1960s. Minority groups will continue to drive future population growth in the South, due not only to in-migration, but also relatively higher birthrates among minority populations, especially Hispanics.

Demographic changes in the region have led to larger numbers of minorities and women being elected to public offices and, increasingly in the Growth States, to competitive two-party politics. The diversity of the population in the region's Growth States, combined with the current tendency of the largest minority groups to vote Democratic, has created an increasingly favorable electoral environment for Black statewide candidates.

Without such profound demographic change in the region, the competitiveness of the African American statewide candidacies featured in this volume never would have been possible. Driven by a surge in minority voting in these contests, along with many progressive and moderate White voters aligning with the Black Democratic nominees, in 2018 Stacey Abrams and Andrew Gillum each came within a whisker of making history in their gubernatorial runs. Raphael Warnock emerged victorious in his January 2021 runoff election due to an unprecedented minority voter surge in Georgia, with substantial progressive and moderate White support. Justin Fairfax's 2017 win for lieutenant governor of Virginia was less a landmark race given that he benefited in part from being down-ticket in a Democratic landslide year in a state that had already become solidly Democratic. The most challenging race involved Jaime Harrison in South Carolina, the Growth State that has shown the least evidence of a Democratic comeback and remains a GOP bastion. Unlike the others covered in this volume, Harrison ran against a long-term incumbent.

Changing Partisanship

The old "Solid Democratic South," that lasted for generations, gave way by the 1990s to 2000s to a nearly solid Republican South (Black and Black 2002). As the Democratic Party nationally embraced increasingly progressive policies beginning in the 1960s, southern Democrats became more alienated from their national party, and by the 1980s Reagan-Bush era, many Southern Democratic voters and officeholders had switched their partisan allegiances to the GOP. What began as a trickle of "Boll Weevil" Democratic congresspersons and other southern elected officials who changed their party identifications, became over time an open floodgate of party switchers (Yoshinaka 2016). Just as many had once believed the old Solid South would always remain a Democratic bastion, observers started looking to the South as the permanent anchor for the national GOP.

As the GOP crested in the South, Democrats began to make important comebacks in the region, first in Virginia. Although the Old Dominion had voted GOP in every presidential race from 1952 to 2004, excepting the 1964 Lyndon B. Johnson landslide, it has now gone Democratic in four consecutive presidential elections. The last Republican elected to the US Senate from Virginia won in 2002. This environment solidly anchored the Justin Fairfax campaign in 2017.

All of the Growth States of the South now are considered two-party competitive, with Virginia leading the Democratic surge and South Carolina still considerably behind. Among the candidacies featured here, Jaime Harrison had the tallest electoral hill to climb in his quest to unseat GOP Senator Lindsey Graham. In addition to the states with Black statewide candidates featured in this volume, North Carolina, where Democrats hold the governorship and three other statewide offices, is very competitive. Texas, where the strong economy serves as a magnet for job seekers, looks to be increasingly competitive for Democrats, with the prospects becoming potentially favorable for Black and other minority statewide candidates.

The Changing Politics of Race and Religion

Race drives much of the political polarization of the South. African Americans are the core constituency of the Democratic Party and White Evangelicals are the most loyal Republicans. Black support for Democrats is overwhelming and is sometimes matched by White Evangelical unity in support of Republicans.

Discussion of religion and politics in the contemporary South has centered generally around the rise of the White Evangelical–led Christian Right movement, a reliable Republican vote, and the role of the Black churches in mobilizing African American Democratic–leaning voters. The rise of the Christian Right played a major role in reconfiguring the southern political landscape (Rozell and Smith 2012; Bullock et al. 2019: 108–127), and the "Solid South," long dominated by a predominantly White Protestant and Democratic Party, became largely Republican, anchored by White Protestants. And yet, as the South has become increasingly diverse and somewhat less distinctive, coalitions of minority groups, including religious minorities, are now the backbone of the Democratic Party. Since the 1980s, White Evangelicals have remained firmly committed to the GOP. Even in presidential elections that favored the Democrats in the popular vote (1992, 1996, 2000, 2008, 2012, 2016, 2020), Republicans' Evangelical base in the South has remained solid.

African American voter mobilization in several of the elections featured here could not overcome the counter-mobilizations of the more numerous White Evangelicals. Now that the White Evangelical vote has become as cohesive as the Black vote, its numbers frequently offset or even exceed Black support for Democrats. Warnock's victory is the outlier. Pastor of Ebenezer Baptist Church in Atlanta, Warnock drew heavily from the state's

Black churches. His opponent, incumbent Kelly Loeffler, notably attacked Warnock as a radical with political ties to a controversial Black pastor, a tack that stoked intensified Black voter mobilization.

There is evidence of a shrinking White Evangelical component of the southern electorate, not merely due to the earlier noted in-migration and relatively high birth rates among minority populations, but also declining church attendance among younger adults. The rise of the so-called religious "nones," or seculars, is accompanied by that group's strong tendency to vote Democratic. The White Evangelical component of the electorate becomes older with each election cycle, portending more political shifting with generational replacement. The Warnock case again is instructive, as he performed especially well among young voters, with his worst showing among senior citizens.

Racial progress in the South has been substantial, although slow until very recently. It is more than half a century since the Voting Rights Act (VRA) wiped away the barriers to registration and voting that had kept Blacks from the voting booth in the South for generations. Only in the past several years did it become possible to write a book such as this one, in which we describe and analyze several highly competitive campaigns by Black statewide candidates in the region and project that this circumstance will soon no longer be unusual. While the demographic and partisan shifts noted earlier set the framework for the new reality for Southern Black statewide candidates, it has been the African American vote that most importantly delivered the results. Today, southern African Americans vote at about the same rate as Whites and in some recent presidential and statewide elections have exceeded White participation (Bullock and Gaddie 2009).

The South has always had a sizable Black population, and more recently other minorities have flocked to the Growth States, so that Texas no longer has a majority-White population, with Georgia and Florida poised to soon reach a similar status. To win, Democrats need a rainbow coalition of support with the mix of colors varying by state. Warnock's runoff victory in January 2021 is telling. In Georgia political circles, the "30–30 rule" describes how a Democrat can win statewide: this formula for success requires that Democrats need Blacks to cast about 30 percent of all votes and the candidate needs to win about 30 percent of the White vote. Warnock came very close, winning 29 percent of the White vote along with Blacks having cast 29 percent of the ballots.[2] Warnock secured 92 percent of the Black vote. But also important was that Warnock won at least 60 percent of the votes of Hispanics and Asians. Having won by 93,000 votes out of nearly 4.5 million cast, each of the minority contributors to his coalition was as critical to the outcome as were college-educated Whites.

The campaigns described and analyzed in this volume took place within a four-year span in dynamic, growing regions of the South that are becoming less White, less Republican, less socially conservative, more racially divisive, and younger. With such trends likely to continue unabated, and then spread to other states in the South, the prospects for Black statewide candidacies in the Growth States appear increasingly favorable.

Key Factors that Affected the Election Outcomes

This volume has focused on the campaigns of five Black statewide candidates who, with the exception of Jamie Harrison, ran competitive campaigns. Two of the candidates won, and two others came within a couple of percentage points of winning. In this next section, the examination of the five candidacies at the heart of our analysis is expanded to include three other 2020 southern Black Senate candidates from Stagnant States in the South: Mike Espy from Mississippi, Marquita Bradshaw from Tennessee, and Adrian Perkins from Louisiana. While none of them came close to winning, it is notable that their inclusion means that African Americans represented the Democratic Party in half of the ten southern states with Senate elections in 2020. Table 8.1 reports the share of the vote received by the Black Democrats and their Republican opponents. For Georgia, the results from the January

Table 8.1 Election Results for 2020 Black Democrat Senate Nominees and Their Republican Opponents

State	Democrat	Vote (%)	Republican	Vote (%)
Georgia	Warnock	51.0	Loeffler	49.0
South Carolina	Harrison	44.2	Graham	54.5
Mississippi	Espy	44.1	Hyde-Smith	54.1
Tennessee	Bradshaw	35.2	Hagerty	62.2
Louisiana	Perkins	19.0	Cassidy	59.3
Louisiana	3 Black candidates	32.8	Cassidy	59.3

Source: Prepared by the author.

runoff are included. Louisiana's jungle primary included two Blacks in addition to Perkins and the last entry in Table 8.1 shows the combined vote for the three African Americans.

It is most notable that African American candidates, excepting Jaime Harrison in South Carolina, ran much better in the Growth States than in the Stagnant States. South Carolina's claim to be a part of the Growth States is the weakest of the six states in that category. It has shown the least degree of Democratic rebirth of those states, apparent in Harrison's showing, a mere 0.1 percent better than Democratic US Senate nominee Mike Espy in Mississippi. Of the other Black nominees in the Growth States, the weakest performance is Stacey Abrams at 48.7 percent. In contrast, all of the African American statewide nominees in the Stagnant States' cycles lost by at least 10 percentage points. Competing in the Growth States does not guarantee a Black candidate success, but it may be a prerequisite, at least for the near future.

Table 8.2 examines the eight Black Democrats in terms of factors that previous research has suggested distinguishing between the successful and unsuccessful. The elements that Sonenshein (1990), Strickland and Whicker (1992), and Frederick and Jeffries (2009) identified as prerequisites to a successful statewide campaign by a Black candidate were cited in Chapter 1. Frederick and Jeffries and Strickland and Whicker compiled lists of essential conditions from case studies of the gubernatorial campaigns of Tom Bradley (D-CA), Carl McCall (D-NY), and Douglas Wilder (D-VA) and the Senate campaigns of Edward Brooke (R-MA), Harvey Gantt (D-NC), and Ron Kirk (D-TX). In Table 8.2, the five campaigns highlighted in this volume along with the three other candidates in Table 8.1 are assessed in light of the criteria identified in the literature as determinative. The literature stressed the importance of high Black turnout and unified party support. Having held an office provides an essential apprenticeship for the candidate. The criteria listed by Frederick and Jeffries also point to the need to compete for an open seat and for the party opposing the Black nominee to be in disarray for the Black to win. To be successful, the candidate must also run as a moderate. The Black candidate must have sufficient funding to be competitive, but it is not necessary to have more funding than the opponent.

The nine categories in Table 8.2 are not particularly helpful in separating winners from losers. Success traditionally is defined only as electoral victory, and yet some of the margins between winning (Warnock), and losing (Abrams, Gillum) were very small.

Table 8.2 Comparison of Black Candidates in Terms of Electability

	Abrams	Gillum	Fairfax	Warnock	Harrison	Espy	Bradshaw	Perkins
Dem Factionalism	No	Yes	Yes	No	No	No	Yes	Yes
GOP Factionalism	Yes	Yes	Yes	Yes	Yes	No	No	No
Open Seat	Yes	Yes	Yes	No*	No	No	Yes	No
Fund Raising	Exceeded opponent	High	Exceeded opponent	Exceeded opponent	Exceeded opponent	Exceeded opponent	Low	Very Low
Moderate	No	No	No	No	No	Yes	No	No
Experience	Legislator	Mayor	No	No	No	Congress	No	Mayor
Endorsement	Extensive	Extensive	Extensive	Extensive	Extensive	Extensive	Modest	Modest
Black Mobilization	High	High	High	Very High	High	Modest	Modest	Moderate
White Mobilization	High	High	High	High	High	High	High	High

*The GOP opponent had been appointed to fill a vacancy but had never run for office.

Source: Prepared by the author.

The degree of Democratic factionalism within each of the political parties doesn't explain very much about who ran a competitive race and who did not. The two winners and two near winners each benefitted from divisions in the GOP ranks. Of the Democrats who performed less well, all but Harrison confronted a unified Republican Party. There seems to be a relationship with running for an open seat, as Abrams and Gillum came close, while Fairfax won an open seat and Warnock faced an incumbent, but not one who had won public support. Of the candidates who lost by 10 points or more, only Bradshaw competed for an open seat.

All of the competitive Black candidates did extremely well in fundraising, and that was clearly necessary for them to run competitive campaigns. Warnock's campaign is second only to that of Jon Ossoff (D-GA) in terms of Senate campaign spending. Harrison was extremely well-funded and set a record for the most funds raised by a Senate candidate in a single quarter. Harrison's haul was so great that his opponent, when appearing on television, bewailed the degree to which he was falling behind in the dollars game. However, despite full coffers, Harrison and Espy did not come close to winning.

Although Democratic candidates in the southern states in the past generally ran to the right of their national and other state regional party counterparts, competing as a moderate clearly was not the formula for success in the races we examined. Warnock and Fairfax ran as progressives and won; Abrams and Gillum did the same and came within whiskers of winning. Abrams had criticized Georgia's 2014 Democratic nominees for governor and senator who lost by two hundred thousand votes for their unsuccessful courtship of conservative Whites rather than using a progressive message to inspire minority turnout. Perhaps taking a cue from Abrams and Gillum, all of the 2020 Senate candidates but Espy ran as progressives, so that the ideological approach does not distinguish success. Espy ran as a moderate in very conservative Mississippi, but that did little to boost his election chances.

Elected or other governmental experience does not explain the electoral competitiveness of the Black statewide candidates. Abrams, Gillum, Perkins, and Espy had previously won elections, but lost. Warnock and Fairfax had never held office, yet won.

The six candidates who fared best had impressive endorsements, both statewide and nationally, including in some cases celebrities. Therefore this variable like several others may be necessary but not sufficient.

Black voter mobilization was impressive in the four most competitive races—perhaps a function of these candidates having embraced progressive agendas of civil rights, racial justice and equity, criminal justice reform, voting rights reform, and healthcare, among other key positions that drove impressive turnouts of minority and also younger voters in the Growth States. Turnout was also high among the more numerous Republican-leaning White voters in these contests. Warnock, though, not only achieved a substantial minority voter mobilization, he held down his losses among White voters just enough to pull through with a victory. Table 8.3 shows how critical that factor was in Warnock's victory and in explaining the near losses of the other featured African American candidates.

The results from the eight campaigns in Table 8.2 allow us to reassess conclusions from the literature. Now, as in the past, to win the Black candidate needs strong African American turnout and it helps to compete against an opposing party in disarray. Competing for an open seat certainly helps the Black candidate, but that alone is insufficient. A major change from the earlier research is that the candidate need not run as a moderate. Today, competing as a progressive seems to spur participation among minorities and young voters. Nor is it essential that the candidate have held office. Finally, success is not conditioned on low turnout among supporters of the other party. In Growth States, it is possible for the mobilized Democratic coalition to outvote the GOP.

Based on a review of their own research and that of others, Frederick and Jeffries (2009) conclude that to win, Black candidates must compete in jurisdictions with "at least a moderate-sized African American population" (691) and they must get a large share of a high Black turnout. It also helps if the candidate runs well with other minorities. Although not explicitly stated by Frederick and Jeffries, statewide winners must also attract a share of the White vote. Although outside the scope of earlier work, in today's world in which rural areas are scarlet and cities and close-in suburbs are blue (Morris 2021) Democratic success requires running up the numbers in urban precincts. These elements are assessed in Table 8.3. The data in this table come from exit polls, and since the Fairfax contest was not subject to an exit poll, he is excluded.

Most useful is to compare Abrams and Warnock since for this comparison we hold the state constant, meaning that the potential electorate is similar, if not identical. From this comparison we see the following:

Table 8.3 Demographic Support for Black Candidates

	Black Vote		Minority Vote		White Vote		White College Vote		Urban		Suburban		Rural
	%	%D	%	%D	%	%D	%	%D	%	%D	%	%D	%D
Warnock	29	92	38	84	24	29	23	39	23	66	62	48	32
Harrison	26	92	34	78	30	27	14	36	14	55	48	42	42
Epsy[+]	30	96	31	93	22	21	9	29	9	63	26	44	42
Bradshaw[+]	14	90	16	81	30	27	15	32	15	67	38	36	25
Perkins[+]	26	44	31	40	23	11	19	19	19	34	36	19	15
Multiple LA Blacks[+]	26	76	31	68	23	18	19	26	19	56	36	30	26
Gillum	13	86	34	69	27	39	43	46	43	56	50	46	29
Abrams	30	92	40	84	21	24	22	39	22	68	62	42	41

%: indicates the share of all votes cast by this group

% D: the share of the votes from the group won by the Democratic nominee. Multiple Black candidates in the Louisiana jungle primary were Derrick Edwards and Antonie Pierce, in addition to Adrian Perkins.

Sources: [+]Results from Fox News Polls. Other results are from the National Pool.

- The share of the vote cast by Blacks is the same, and the share of the vote for the Black candidate is the same.
- The share of the vote from minorities for the candidates is the same, but minorities cast 2 percentage points more of the vote in the Abrams contest.
- *The critical element in terms of voter ethnicity is that even though Whites cast a larger share of the vote in 2021 than 2018, Warnock gets 29 percent compared with Abrams's 24 percent.*
- The advantage that Warnock enjoys with the White vote is due to *White college graduates casting 3 percentage points more of the vote in 2021 than in 2018,* since the share of the vote from this group for the two Black candidates is the same (39 percent).
- The two candidates perform about equally well in urban and suburban Georgia; *Warnock wins because he gets 6 points more of the suburban vote.*

A comparison of the candidates in Table 8.3 shows each attracting roughly comparable shares of the Black vote except in Louisiana where Perkins individually and he and the two other Blacks collectively had the lowest vote share in the table. That Bradshaw had the second poorest finish is due in part to Tennessee's small Black population. The candidacies in Mississippi, Tennessee, and Louisiana suffered from the relatively small share of the vote cast by minorities. Gillum overcame his poorer showing among Blacks and minorities more generally by doing 10 points better among Whites than any of the other candidates, a strong performance rooted in his ability to win over almost half the White college graduates.

The figures on the race of the voters suggest that there are multiple combinations that could elect Blacks statewide. Warnock, like a seasoned brewmaster, had just the right set of ingredients. Had Gillum done as well as Warnock among Blacks and other minorities, he would be governor of Florida today. Abrams would have been in position to veto the controversial elections law passed in Georgia in 2021 if she had been as popular among Whites as Warnock was. Had Espy run as well with better educated Whites as Gillum did, and turned out his state's more numerous Blacks, Mississippi would have a Black senator.

As noted previously, to win in some southern states, Democrats need Blacks to cast about 30 percent of all votes and the candidate needs about 30 percent of the White vote. Warnock, Jon Ossoff, and Joe Biden came very close to those marks in Georgia (Bullock 2021). That was also the formula for Doug Jones's 2017 Alabama win (Bullock and Owen 2021). The 30–30 rule thus may be a reasonably good target in states with sizable Black populations (i.e., Georgia, Alabama, South Carolina, and Louisiana). The larger Black population in Mississippi suggests that a Black candidate could win there with less than 30 percent of the White vote, in conjunction with very strong Black turnout. In Virginia, North Carolina, and Tennessee a Black win will require a larger share of the White vote, since these states have smaller Black populations. Exit poll data do not exist for Fairfax but since his vote total closely approximates that of Governor Ralph Northam, it is likely that similar coalitions elected both of them. The exit poll shows Northam winning 42 percent of the White vote. That is in line with the White support received by other recent winning candidates in Virginia, with Clinton's 35 percent at the low end, while in 2020, Biden and Senator Mark Warner attracted 44 and 45 percent, respectively. This suggests that Fairfax probably attracted about 40 percent of the White vote. Achieving 30–30 would not suffice in two other Growth States. In Florida and Texas, which have relatively small Black populations, Democratic wins by candidates of any race will necessitate a multi-ethnic coalition. Gillum came close with 39 percent of the White vote coupled with 69 percent of the minority vote.

Population growth in the South is largely an urban phenomenon. The three candidates who did best in Table 8.3 competed in the states with the highest percentages of urban voters. Gillum did not get as large a share of the urban vote as did some losers like Bradshaw and Espy, but Florida has a far larger urban population. The three most successful candidates came from the states with the largest suburban populations, while the weakest performing candidates competed in states with far fewer suburbanites. Comparing Gillum and Abrams illustrates that, as with the racial makeup of supporters, there are alternative combinations or urban, suburban, and rural voters that can yield similar overall results.

To summarize, Tables 8.2 and 8.3 suggest that there may be alternative combinations in the electorate or conditions surrounding a candidacy that can elect African Americans or at least bring them to the cusp of victory. *Black victories in statewide elections in the region require, at a minimum, a fully mobilized and cohesive Black electorate coupled with the conversion of moderate Whites* although the percentages of Black voters, other minority voters, and White voters vary depending on the racial composition of the electorate.

The national attention the runoff races in Georgia received may explain why Warnock had more success with White Southern voters than several other recent statewide Black candidates. The presidential election was over, but Georgia had played a crucial part in Joe Biden's victory. And the early success of Biden's presidency, and Republicans' ability to stop his agenda, hinged on the outcome of the Georgia races, which would determine which party controlled the Senate. National political figures visited Georgia and national resources poured in during the runoff election, because it was the only election in the nation at the time. Voters thus responded to national tides and pressures as well as to the specifics of the Georgia race.

The models for statewide elections conducted between 1989 and 2018 indicated that Black candidates paid a penalty. When other variables were controlled, they got about 3.5 percentage points less of the vote than comparable White candidates. This racial penalty seems to be no longer assessed. Both Warnock and Abrams led the Democratic tickets, Gillum ran just 0.8 percentage points behind Nikki Fried, the agriculture commissioner who led the Democratic ticket, and Fairfax trailed Governor Northam by 1.2 percentage points. Mississippi holds elections for its statewide constitutional offices a year before presidential elections, so Espy was the only Democrat competing statewide in 2020. However, his 44.1 percent of the vote compares favorably with the performance of Democrats in 2019. The mean for three White Democratic constitutional candidates was 42.7 percent with only Jim Hood, the candidate for governor who polled 46.8 percent exceeding Espy's 44.1 percent.[3] The only offices elected statewide in Tennessee are governor and senator. Bradshaw's 35.2 percent was far below the 43.9 percent received by Phil Bredesen, the 2018 Democratic candidate for the Senate. Bradshaw did, however, poll a larger share of the vote than any of the Democrats, all White, running for the Senate or governor from 2008 to 2014. Because of Louisiana's jungle first round, it is not possible to compare Perkins's performance with White Democrats in his state.

A sample that included Black candidates for lower profile statewide posts might continue to show a race penalty approximating the size of that estimated in Chapter 1. The evidence we have, however, suggests that the disadvantage confronted by Black statewide candidates for high-profile offices is now, if not eliminated, significantly reduced.

Final Words

The electoral prospects of African American statewide candidates in the South look promising in parts, but not all, of the region. Doug Wilder made history back in 1989 as the nation's first elected Black governor, and he did so in Virginia, the state that has led the rising Democratic Party fortunes in the Growth States of the South. He succeeded by running as a moderate in both of his statewide campaigns, including his 1985 successful run for lieutenant governor. Justin Fairfax successfully ran for lieutenant governor of Virginia three decades later running as a strong progressive, although in 2021 he lost his bid for the Democratic nomination for governor in a campaign that featured three African American candidates.

The four 2018 and 2020 races in Georgia, Florida, and South Carolina tell a somewhat different story; even so, it looks like two of these states—Georgia and Florida—are only a few steps behind the Old Dominion. Stacey Abrams and Andrew Gillum ran strong races in 2018—very near misses, so that just a marginal shift in voter preferences would have produced a different outcome.

Competing as one of twenty candidates in a jungle primary, Warnock led the field but came nowhere near a majority, thus triggering the runoff election. A lot happened between Election Day 2020 and January 5, 2021, and much of it benefited Warnock. In the realm of the unexpected and truly unprecedented events that will never fit into any social scientist's models for explaining election outcomes, the defeated incumbent president, Donald J. Trump, stoked bizarre conspiracy theories of a stolen election, in which the election in Georgia especially, and in other states, had been manipulated. The president repeatedly claimed that the election had been rigged and that Republican voters had their presidential victory stolen from them. The message to GOP voters in Georgia, the one place where voting was continuing, was that their votes did not matter—because Democrats would cheat. It is not possible to determine exactly how much this messaging by the president deterred Georgia Republican voters, but it is hard to discount an impact. Additionally, and most importantly, Georgia had two US Senate runoff elections. The campaigns for these became nationalized, because the outcomes determined control of the legislative chamber and the prospects for a Democratic Administration's policy agenda. Unanswered is whether Warnock could have won had Trump gracefully acknowledged defeat or whether

Warnock would be in the Senate if almost $200 million had not been spent on his behalf.

The 2020 US Senate election outcome in South Carolina perhaps should not have been a surprise. Public opinion polls, though, had consistently projected a close race between Jaime Harrison and Senator Lindsey Graham. Given the findings of this volume, it is clear now that Harrison always faced long odds. He ran against a long-term GOP incumbent in the slowest transitioning of the southern Growth States, with an electorate that still looks more like those of the Stagnant States.

Georgia and Florida appear to be following Virginia in their political transitioning, but South Carolina seems much farther behind. These certainly are reasonable conclusions drawn from very recent election cycles, but not predictions that each of these states will one day look like Virginia politically, or even that Virginia will remain a Democratic stronghold. Indeed, much of what happens going forward depends on how the GOP positions itself in a post-Trump environment. Some GOP candidates in the region in the past, for example, have succeeded in attracting Latino votes, and Senator Tim Scott (SC) certainly showcases the party's ability to win statewide with an African American nominee.

The future electoral prospects of African American statewide nominees in the Growth States indeed are promising as these, at varying paces, begin to move beyond the South that Maxwell and Shields (2019) described as anchored to the GOP by racial resentment, anti-feminism, and religious fundamentalism. The forces that Maxwell and Shields identified still dominate the politics of the Stagnant States but are being eroded in the Growth States as their populations diversify in terms of race through in-migration and generational replacement. As the elections of Raphael Warnock and Jon Ossoff in Georgia indicate, the electorate is edging away from the stultifying influences of the past even as the state's elected Republican leadership remains in the embrace of conservative forces as it enacts laws limiting access to abortion, rejects Obamacare, and explores ways to impede political participation. Progressive Democrats now rule Virginia, as evidenced by its ratification of the Equal Rights Amendment, repeal of its voter ID requirement, and banning of the death penalty.

As further evidence that the dead hand of discrimination has weakened its grip on the Growth States, Black women are playing ever more active roles. Excepting an election as a down-ticket running mate, no Black women have won statewide offices, but they are increasingly seeking those kinds of posts.[4] Each of the last three rounds of elections for Georgia constitutional officers has had at least one Black woman competing as the Democratic Party nominee. In 2014, five of the nine slots were filled by a Black woman. A total of eight Black women have sought these offices compared with only three Black men. North Carolina has seen a Black woman seek the office of lieutenant governor and in South Carolina, Rosalyn Glenn ran for treasurer in 2018. In the Carolinas, Black males have been infrequent nominees for statewide office.

Service in Congress can be a steppingstone for higher office. Florida, Georgia, and Texas each currently have two Black women in their delegations, while North Carolina has one. Of the Stagnant States, only Alabama has sent a Black woman to Congress. Black women hold leadership positions in both chambers of the Georgia and Virginia legislatures and the Tennessee House. In the past, North Carolina's House speaker has been Black. Among major cities, Atlanta currently has its second Black female mayor and the mayors of Charlotte and New Orleans are also Black women. Women officeholders, and especially Vice President Kamala Harris, are likely to serve as role models who encourage other Black women to move beyond voting and organizing and seek office (on women role models, see Owen 2017). The success of those candidacies will depend, in part, on a mobilized electorate such as Stacey Abrams has produced in Georgia.

In the Growth States other than South Carolina, progressive and conservative forces are wrestling for dominance in the electorate even as conservatives hold most of the positions of power. In the Stagnant States, conservatives face few challenges to their dominance.

The results of these statewide elections have important national consequences. If Black candidates remain primarily Democratic and they become even more competitive in the South, national issues such as voting rights and redistricting for Congress will reflect increasingly progressive agendas. If Black governors and US senators emerge from southern elections, they will begin to appear eventually on national tickets. Southern Black candidates for the presidency have been rare, although that is likely to change soon. Importantly, they will have been politically tested in the caldron of southern politics, building the kinds of multi-racial coalitions that increasingly will be key to winning national office in the United States.

Postscript

After the completion of this manuscript, Virginia held its statewide elections on November 2, 2021, just as the book was going to press. The Republican Party swept the three statewide offices, which included the election of former House of Delegates member Winsome Sears as Lieutenant Governor. The Jamaican-born Sears assumes the office in January 2022 as the first woman of color elected statewide in Virginia. Sears thus becomes the second recently elected Black Republican to the office of lieutenant governor. In North Carolina in 2020, both major political parties nominated African American candidates for that office, with the Republican, Mark Robinson, winning a close election.

The 2021 Virginia elections featured multiple Black and other minority statewide candidates, with the GOP putting forth the most diverse ticket in state history. Three African American candidates - the incumbent lieutenant governor, a member of the state Senate, and a former member of the House of Delegates – all ran for the Democratic nomination for governor, ultimately losing to former governor Terry McAuliffe. The Democrats nominated a Latino-Lebanese American candidate for Lieutenant governor, who lost to Sears in the general election. The GOP nominee for Attorney General, a Latino, won his election.

These recent election cycles, along with those featured in this volume, portend a continued growing prominence of African American and other minority candidates for statewide offices in the South.

Notes

Preface

1. The Growth States are Florida, Georgia, North Carolina, South Carolina, Texas, and Virginia. The Stagnant States are Alabama, Arkansas, Louisiana, Mississippi, Oklahoma, and Tennessee.

Chapter 1

1. See for example, *Busbee v. Smith* (1982) in which the District Court of the District of Columbia held up the redistricting of Atlanta's Fifth Congressional District until the state redrew the district so that its population was 65.02 percent Black. Also see *United Jewish Organizations of Williamsburgh v. Carey*, 430 U.S. 144 (1977).
2. Not all states elect members of their appellate tribunals in statewide contests. Judges are chosen by the legislature in South Carolina and Virginia, while in Louisiana and Mississippi justices on the Supreme Court are elected from districts. Florida uses a Missouri Plan with the justices initially appointed by the governor and subsequently running in a referendum that asks voters whether they should continue to serve. Not all southern states elect their appellate judges statewide. In South Carolina and Virginia, the legislature chooses judges. In Louisiana and Mississippi members of the Supreme Court are chosen from districts.
3. Tim Scott represented the First District of South Carolina (2011–2013) prior to his appointment to the Senate. Allen West represented the Twenty-Second District of Florida for one term. Hurd announced in 2019 that he would not seek reelection in 2020. Byron Donalds was elected from Florida in 2020.
4. South Carolina reports participation for Whites and non-Whites with no additional breakouts.
5. The Stagnant States are Alabama, Arkansas, Louisiana, Mississippi, and Tennessee. For discussion of the differences in southern Growth versus Stagnant States see chapters 1 and 2 in Bullock et al. (2019).
6. A minor figure in the mob of 2020 Democratic candidates, Wayne Messam, is the first Black mayor of Miramar, Florida.
7. Hiram Revels and Blanche Bruce represented Mississippi in the Senate during Reconstruction but were selected by the state legislature and not through popular vote, which was instituted by Seventeenth Amendment beginning in 1914.

8. We thank Michael Bitzer, Scott Buchanan, Angie Maxwell, Dick Murray, and Chuck Prysby for help in identifying Black candidates in their states. In addition, Bullock's research assistant Mitchell Redd and secretary Bridget Pilcher did yeoman service in identifying the race of candidates in Alabama, Florida, Mississippi, South Carolina, and Texas.

9. Although outside the scope of the statistical analysis in this chapter, the ranks of Black nominees continued to swell in 2019 and 2020, with Blacks nominated for four constitutional offices in Mississippi in 2019, and 2020 seeing the nomination of five Black Senate candidates.

10. South Carolina provides data for Whites and non-Whites. Georgia uses a greater number of categories: White, Black, Hispanic, Asian, and American Indian.

11. The Deep South states (Alabama, Georgia, Louisiana, Mississippi, and South Carolina) have higher concentrations of African Americans than the rest of the South, with at least a quarter of the population in each of the five states being Black.

Chapter 2

1. Exit polls do not provide a precise indication of how blue-collar voters' preferences changed, but some idea of the shift can be obtained by comparing results of the 2000 and 2004 Senate elections. In 2000 the Democratic nominee Zell Miller attracted 69 percent of voters whose family income was $15,000–$30,000 and 62 percent of those in the $30,000–$50,000 category. Four years later, Denise Majette, representing the Democratic Party, won 62 percent and 44 percent of the vote in those two categories, respectively. The exit poll for 2002 was so flawed it has never been released.

2. Georgia has had a lieutenant governor only since 1947.

3. Cagle (2016).

4. In 2019 the Randolph County Board of Elections voted unanimously to close three majority-White precincts that had a total of 515 registrants. The three accounted for just a tenth of the county's Black registrants. As it had in 2018, the county justified its decision on budgetary grounds. The facilities in the precincts slated for closure lacked bathrooms, access for the handicapped, sufficient parking, and air conditioning. The poor county, which ran a $2 million deficit in 2018, has a total budget of $6 million. It claims not to have the funds necessary to make needed improvements on the facilities (Niesse 2019). A civil rights group opposed the closures.

5. According to the post-election audits conducted by the secretary of state's office, the electorate in the GOP primary was 51.3 percent male; the GOP runoff electorate was 51.6 percent male.

6. In a special session, just prior to the 2016 general election, North Carolina's legislature passed legislation that required transgendered individuals to use the restrooms that accorded with their birth status. This state law overturned a Charlotte ordinance. In response to the state action, North Carolina lost sporting events, concerts, and jobs.

7. In 2019 the legislature passed and Kemp signed a bill to increase teacher pay by $3,000. The governor explained that this was a down payment on his pledged $5,000 increase. A few local school boards announced, much to the chagrin of their teachers, that they would not receive the full $3,000 as the board would use some of the additional state funding for other purposes.

8. The state reported twenty-one thousand provisional ballots; the higher figure was used by the Abrams team.

9. The percent Black figures for Georgia come from post-election audits conducted by the secretary of state. This is feasible since when registering to vote in Georgia one indicates race or ethnicity. Most states do not gather this type of information so that for most states and nationally, estimates of racial composition rely on those of the Census Bureau, which conducts post-elections surveys or exit polls.

10. A bivariate model was estimated as Abrams's vote = .122 + .896 percent Black. The standard error for the percent Black coefficient = .033 and the model explains 82.7 percent of the variance.

11. Dan O'Connor provided the figures on the Abrams vote in Congressional Districts six and seven.

12. Republicans got control of the Senate in 2003 when four Democrats changed parties. Two years later the GOP won a majority in the House after a federal court replaced the Democratic districting plan found to be unconstitutional in *Larios v. Cox*.

13. Georgia's now-replaced touchscreen voting machines did not generate a paper ballot or receipt showing voter choices.

14. Exceptions exist to protect the health of the mother and in cases of rape or incest. However, invocation of the rape or incest exceptions requires that the woman have filed a police report.

Chapter 3

1. Citation dates refer to 2018 unless otherwise noted.

2. Pew Research Center (Dimock 2019) defines these generations as: Gen X, born 1965–1980; Millennials, born 1981–1996; and Gen Z, born after 1996.

3. Democrat Sean Shaw lost to Republican Ashley Moody by 6 percent.

4. Democrat Andrew Gillum lost to Republican Ron DeSantis by 0.4 percent (DeSantis 49.6 percent; Gillum 49.2 percent; the remainder was split among minor-party and third-party candidates).

5. Much of this discussion is from MacManus (2015) and MacManus (2017).

6. Meek lost the race for the Senate seat to Republican Marco Rubio.

7. These figures are from author's analysis of Florida Division of Elections voter extract data.

8. Gillum was elected to the Tallahassee City Commission in 2003—the youngest person ever to be elected to that position. In 2014, he was elected mayor.

9. Florida Chapter, American Association of Political Consultants conference, Fort Lauderdale, February 27, 2019; the author moderated the panel of pollsters.

10. Graham won Pinellas County (St. Petersburg area).

11. Gillum, who spent $6.5 million in the primary, defeated three opponents who each spent more than $100 million in their campaigns. Gillum, the only candidate who was not a millionaire, received $650,000 in last-minute contributions from donors such as Tom Steyer and George Soros (Austin 2018).

12. These figures are from author's analysis of Florida Division of Elections voter extract data.

13. Smith, Adam C. 2018. "Fueled by Trump, Ron DeSantis Easily Beats Adam Putnam in GOP Race for Governor." *Tampa Bay Times*, August 28.

14. According to the campaign, 66 percent of likely primary voters watched Fox News Network anywhere from every day to a few times a week (Martin 2018), and 52 percent saw themselves as more Trump supporters than GOP supporters. Their polling also showed that 37 percent of GOP voters watched Fox daily; 47 percent of those identifying as Trump Republicans (Caputo 2018b).

15. This figure includes loans, candidates giving to themselves, public matching funds, and money from their political committees (Fineout 2018).

16. Diversity was important to DeSantis. His initial list of nine running mates included three Spanish speakers, four people of color, and four women (Caputo 2018a).

17. Gillum (and other Florida Democrats) had signed a pledge to support the group's manifesto: "I will fight for a Florida that divests from prisons, detention centers, guns, and police and invest in the basic needs and safety of our people, especially its children" (Farrington 2018).

18. Gillum was on a trip to New York City with a lobbyist friend and undercover FBI agents who posed as developers interested in creating businesses in Tallahassee (Schmitz 2018).

19. These included high-profile newspapers in big metropolitan areas: *Miami Herald, Tampa Bay Times, Orlando Sentinel, Palm Beach Post,* and *Sun Sentinel.*

20. Schweers. 2018b. *Tallahassee Democrat,* November 9.

21. The head of the Miami-Dade Young Republicans pointed out that "in Florida most immigrants are not impacted by border policies." More than 60 percent of Florida's Hispanic voters are Puerto Ricans, Americans by birth, and Cuban Americans, who have had immigration privileges since the 1960s (Sopo 2018).

Chapter 4

1. In Virginia separate elections are held for the offices of governor and lieutenant governor.

2. Fairfax also has said that he may take legal action against his accusers and possibly seek damages for defamation. One of his accusers has requested that she and Fairfax appear before a bipartisan committee of the Virginia General Assembly to state their cases. Neither accuser has filed criminal charges, and in one case the statute of limitations already has expired.

3. In 1982 Pickett was the presumed Democratic nominee for US Senate, but upon announcing his candidacy he paid tribute to the Byrd political organization that had perpetuated years of segregation in the state. An enraged state senator Doug Wilder announced he would run as an independent if Pickett were the Democratic nominee, and thus siphon off enough votes to guarantee victory to the Republican nominee Paul Tribble. Pickett, realizing he could not win a three-way race, withdrew his candidacy.

4. The heat of political campaigns often produces intensive conflicts and angry words of this nature. Years later in his memoir, Wilder expressed admiration for Sabato's scholarship and understanding of the African American vote in the state (Wilder 2018: 197).

5. Republican Party of Virginia state nominating convention, Roanoke Convention Center, Roanoke, Virginia, June 11, 1988 (attended by author as observer).

6. Press conference attended by author as observer, Roanoke, Virginia, June 12, 1988.

7. The nation's only previous Black governor had been appointed to the office. Lieutenant Governor P. B. S. Pinchback of Louisiana, a Republican, held the office of governor for about four weeks while the elected governor underwent an impeachment trial.

8. A study of the 1989 Virginia exit polls published in *Public Opinion Quarterly* concluded that a major reason for the discrepancy was that the polling firm had used face-to-face interviews conducted in person—a circumstance that made it more likely that voters who did not want to be seen as racially motivated in their opposition to Wilder simply lied to the polling firm workers. Many respondents had thus chosen to give what they thought was the "socially desirable" answer (Traugott and Price 1992).

9. Another explanation, highly controversial and impossible to prove, emerged from a scholarly article that contrasted the outcomes of the Wilder race for governor of Virginia in 1989 and Democratic Party nominee Harvey Gantt's unsuccessful run for US Senator in North Carolina in 1990. The authors concluded that Black candidates are likely to be more successful in statewide races when they "look white," a reference to Wilder having light black skin. They maintained that Gannt had a much darker skin hue than Wilder, thus appeared "more black," and therefore faced a tougher election quest than the Virginian did the previous year (Strickland and Whicker 1992).

10. Virginia US Senate candidates' debate at Hampton-Sydney College, Farmville, Virginia, September 6, 1994 (attended by author as an observer).

11. Between Wilder's gubernatorial win and Fairfax's lieutenant gubernatorial victory in 2017 there were two African American statewide party nominees: Donald McEachin in 2001 as the Democratic nominee for attorney general and Rev. E. W. Jackson as the GOP nominee for lieutenant governor in 2013. With ethics charges swirling around his campaign, McEachin lost to his GOP opponent by 20 percentage points, despite a Democratic sweep that year of the other statewide offices. Jackson was a political novice with a long history of controversial and at times inflammatory rhetoric, and he lost by a wide margin. Under these circumstances it is difficult to attribute to race any likely role in their defeats.

12. *The Daily Show with John Stewart* ran a more than six-minute-long segment "Punanny State—Virginia's Transvaginal Ultrasound Bill" on February 21, 2012, that became the talk of Virginia political circles with some state leaders lamenting that the bill had made Virginia a national laughingstock, http://www.cc.com/video-clips/83xa8q/the-daily-show-with-jon-stewart-punanny-state---virginia-s-transvaginal-ultrasound-bill (last accessed, April 11, 2020).

13. Jackson pointed out that he won the Virginia Democratic Party presidential primary in 1988, but of course that was a very different voter turnout—a small minority of eligible voters within one political party—than that faced by Wilder a year later.

Chapter 6

1. The final polls by the two GOP candidates showed them in a dead heat.
2. An experienced campaign consultant has calculated that the amount spent promoting Loeffler's candidacy in the jungle primary may have totaled $56 million.
3. After the storming of the Capitol, Loeffler reneged on her promise and did not object to Georgia's electoral votes being counted.
4. Trump's message so overwhelmed the state Republican Party's promotion of absentee voting that Mike Pence was booed when he urged an audience to vote absentee (Bluestein 2020c).
5. In the early voting, African Americans constituted 31 percent during the runoff compared with 28 percent in November. This may be the basis for claims that the Black share of the electorate increased to 31 percent in the runoff. Getting a precise read on the ethnic makeup of Georgia's electorate has become more difficult as increasing numbers of registrants either fail to indicate their ethnicity or check "Other."
6. The most reliable source on the share of votes from Blacks has been the post-election audit done by the secretary of state. A problem is that growing numbers of registrants are not indicating their ethnicity, by checking "Other," and even greater numbers are skipping this question. Consequently, the official figures on Black registration and turnout are undercounts.

Chapter 7

1. LBJ ended his presidency far more liberal on domestic policy than when he appeared on the national scene in 1957–1964. When elected in 1960 to the vice presidency, he was still more moderate than JFK by most measures, but became strongly associated with dramatic new social programs from 1965 on.
2. In 1972 Washington, DC, delegate Walter Fauntroy entered his name as a candidate for president in the DC primary. As he ran in no other states, raised almost no money, and never contested in a southern primary, he is omitted from this paper.

3. Memorable, and deeply personal, since Jackson was shaped by the refusal of his wealthy biological father to acknowledge the relationship with his impecunious mother that produced Jackson.

4. In 1984, Wisconsin Democrats held both a primary and a caucus. Jackson results were 15 percent and 10 percent, so these were averaged.

5. In the intervening years, two Black politicians ran for president. In 1992, Doug Wilder, governor of Virginia, entered the Democratic race. Had the Wilder race continued, it would have been the first and until then, only case of a Black southern politician running for president. However, Wilder was never a factor and left the race early. Illinois Senator Carol Moseley Braun, who ran for president in 2004, withdrew before the Iowa caucuses after a disappointing showing in the semi-official DC primary that year. In the same year, Black minister and political gadfly Al Sharpton also ran for president. However, as Sharpton never really seriously contested any primary, and seemed to mostly use the campaign as a way to spend vast sums on his personal needs and to gain attention for his second life as a TV star, it is perhaps better to think of Sharpton's race as a template for what Donald Trump may have initially been intending in his own race for president: a publicity stunt. The fact that both men were managed by Roger Stone during their initial campaign is indeed suggestive of this (Slackman 2004).

6. For 2008, the Michigan results are omitted, because the primaries in Michigan were not fully contested due to dispute about the rules. Also, Texas held both primaries and precinct conventions in the same three-day period with popular voting reported, so they were averaged. More than most years, 2008 featured a number of contests in which subsequent conventions or quasi-caucuses seemed to affect the allocation of delegates. However, we are assuming both campaigns contested the primaries and that in states with both, primaries are the best measure of popular support rather than conventions happening weeks or months later.

7. Data for vote totals for all years came from Wikipedia pages on the Democratic Primaries. Data on population levels for 1980 are from the US Census. For 2008, the census estimates are taken from the Kaiser Family Foundation website (Kaiser Family Foundation n.d.).

8. Some would argue Gore did in fact win Florida if all the votes had been counted and had thousands of Black voters not been purged from the rolls illegally for out of state felonies.

9. There is probably less tension on this question for a Black woman than there is for a Black male politician.

Chapter 8

1. The 2014 exit polls show the following for Scott, Lindsay Graham—who was seeking reelection to a full term while Scott sought the remainder of the term from which Jim DeMint had resigned—and Nikki Haley who was up for reelection as governor.

	Support from	
	White (%)	Black (%)
Tim Scott	82	10
Lindsay Graham	74	6
Nikki Haley	76	6

2. The exit poll reported that Blacks cast 29 percent of the vote. The post-election audit by Georgia's secretary of state reported their share at 28.1 percent; however, 6.9 percent of the voters had not indicated their race when they registered to vote. Some share of those for whom race is unknown were Black. Media accounts in the immediate aftermath of the election put the Black vote share at 31 percent, which was the proportion of the early vote (absentee and early in-person) cast by African Americans. White Republicans dominated the Election Day voting.

3. The Democratic slate in 2019 had three Whites and four Blacks. The mean for the four Black statewide candidates was 40.3 percent, which was 2.4 points below the mean for the three Whites. But if the vote for Jim Hood, who, as attorney general, had been the only Democrat elected statewide for years is excluded, the average for the two remaining Whites is almost identical to that for the Blacks, being 40.7 percent.

4. Jennifer Carroll was elected Florida's lieutenant governor in 2010 as a ticket-mate of gubernatorial victor Rick Scott.

References

Abramowitz, Alan I., and Jeffrey A. Segal. 1992. *Senate Elections*. Ann Arbor, MI: University of Michigan Press.

Adimpact. 2020. "Spotlight: Media Spending in the GA Senate Special." December 4.

Akin, Stephanie, and Bridget Bowman. 2021. "3 Takeaways from the Georgia Runoffs." *Roll Call*. January 7.

Allen, Nick. 2020. "The Trump Dilemma: President Casts Long Shadow over Race to Clinch the Senate." *The Telegraph*. December 5.

Anderson, Carol. 2018. "Brian Kemp's Lead in Georgia Needs an Asterisk." *Atlantic*. November 7.

Anderson, Zac. 2018. "Trump's Backing Gives DeSantis Lead over Well-Financed Putnam." *Florida Times-Union*. July 30.

Astor, Maggie, Shane Goldmacher, and Trip Gabriel. 2020. "Jaime Harrison Raises $57 Million as Democratic Cash Floods Senate Races." *New York Times*. October 11. https://www.nytimes.com/2020/10/11/us/politics/jaime-harrison-lindsey-graham-south-carolina.html.

Atkinson, Frank. 1988. *The Dynamic Dominion: Realignment and the Rise of the Virginia Republican Party since 1945*. Fairfax, VA: George Mason University Press.

Atkinson, Frank. 2006. *Virginia in the Vanguard: Political Leadership in the 400-Year Old Cradle of Democracy*. Lanham, MD: Rowman & Littlefield.

Austin, Sharon. 2018. "Could Andrew Gillum Be the Next Governor of Florida?" *The Conversation*. August 31. https://theconversation.com/could-andrew-gillum-be-the-next-governor-of-florida-102451.

Axelrod, Tal. 2020. "Jaime Harrison Seeks to Convince Democrats He Can Take Down Lindsey Graham." *The Hill*. July 4. https://thehill.com/homenews/campaign/505709-jaime-harrison-seeks-to-convince-democrats-he-can-take-down-lindsey-graham.

Ball, Molly. 2018. "Coming for Georgia." *Time*. August 6.

Baker, Donald P. 1989. *Wilder: Hold Fast to Dreams*. Cabin John, MD: Seven Locks Press.

Barlow, Katie. 2020. "Kelly Loeffler and the GOP's War on Internal Aggression." *Insider*. December 17.

Barrow, Bill. 2018. "Inside Stacey Abrams's Strategy to Mobilize Georgia Voters." *US News*. October 12.

Bean, Riley, and Nick Reagan. 2020. "S.C.'s First Senate Debate Highlights Differences Between Graham and Harrison." *Live 5 News (WCSC)*. https://www.live5news.com/2020/10/04/scs-first-senate-debate-highlights-differences-between-graham-harrison/.

Bennett, George. 2018. "Police Union Backs DeSantis Over Gillum in Florida Governor Race." *Palm Beach Post*. October 3.

Bierman, Noah. 2021. "For Black pioneers Harris and Obama, Different Times Mean Different Approaches on Race." *Los Angeles Times*. January 24.

Bitzer, Michael. 2019. Personal communication.

Blinder, Alan, and Richard Fausset. 2018. "Stacey Abrams Ends Fight for Georgia Governor with Harsh Words for Her Rival." *New York Times*. November 16.

Black, Earl, and Merle Black. 1989. *Politics and Society in the South*. Cambridge, MA: Harvard University Press.

Black, Earl, and Merle Black. 2002. *The Rise of Southern Republicans*. Cambridge, MA: Belknap Press of Harvard University Press.

Blakemore, Erin. 2017. "The Battle Over Confederate Heritage Month." *JSTOR DAILY*. April 14. https://daily.jstor.org/the-battle-over-confederate-heritage-month/.

Bluestein, Greg. 2017. "What Worries Democrats? Themselves." *Atlanta Journal-Constitution*. August 27.

Bluestein, Greg. 2018a. "Abrams Takes High Road for Now vs. Kemp." *Atlanta Journal-Constitution*. August 7.

Bluestein, Greg. 2018b. "Culture Wars Shape GOP Race for Governor." *Atlanta Journal-Constitution*. July 10.

Bluestein, Greg. 2018c. "Dem in Governor Race Has Big Debt." *Atlanta Journal-Constitution*. March 15.

Bluestein, Greg. 2018d. "Evans Vows to 'Finish the Job' with HOPE Scholarship in First TV Ad." *Atlanta Journal-Constitution*. April 6.

Bluestein, Greg. 2018e. "Georgia GOP Race Hurtles toward a Close Finish." *Atlanta Journal-Constitution*. July 13.

Bluestein, Greg. 2018f. "How Race for Governor Came Down to the Wire." *Atlanta Journal-Constitution*. December 2.

Bluestein, Greg. 2018g. "Kemp Lead Shrinks; Abrams to Sue." *Atlanta Journal-Constitution*. November 12.

Bluestein, Greg. 2018h. "Kemp Moderates His Message." *Atlanta Journal-Constitution*. September 27.

Bluestein, Greg. 2018i. "Law and Order Is a Central Focus of Kemp's Pitch to Conservatives." *Atlanta Journal-Constitution*. May 5.

Bluestein, Greg. 2018j. "Political Debate Shifting to Suburbs." *Atlanta Journal-Constitution*. November 11.

Bluestein, Greg. 2018k. "Poll of GOP Voters Shows Cagle with Strong Lead in the Governor's Race." *Atlanta Journal-Constitution*. April 27.

Bluestein, Greg. 2018l. "Trump Gives Support to Kemp." *Atlanta Journal-Constitution*. July 19.

Bluestein, Greg. 2018m. "Social Issues Still Key for Some Voters." *Atlanta Journal-Constitution*. October 10.

Bluestein, Greg. 2020a. "Losing Moderate Image, Loeffler Turns Hard Right." *Atlanta Journal-Constitution*. December 23.

Bluestein, Greg. 2020b. "Ralston Slams Loeffler in North Georgia: Warnock Aims for Outright Win." *Atlanta Journal-Constitution*. October 21.

Bluestein, Greg. 2020c. "Republican Candidates Pushing Mail-in Votes." *Atlanta Journal-Constitution*. December 3.

Bluestein, Greg. 2020d. "Trump 'Ashamed' to Have Endorsed Kemp." *Atlanta Journal-Constitution*. November 30.

Bluestein, Greg. 2020e. "Wild Race for Senate Is Just the Beginning." *Atlanta Journal-Constitution*. February 2.

Bluestein, Greg. 2021. "Contentious, Expensive Races Near Finish Line." *Atlanta Journal-Constitution*. January 3.

Bluestein, Greg, and Bria Felicien. 2018. "Abrams Brings Star: Kemp Draws Contrast." *Atlanta Journal-Constitution*. October 5.

Bluestein, Greg, and Tamar Hallerman. 2020. "In Runoffs, Ground Game Calls for Bringing A-Game." *Atlanta Journal-Constitution*. December 20.

Bluestein, Greg, and Rodney Ho. 2018. "Ga. Leaders Facing Revolt by Film Stars." *Atlanta Journal-Constitution*. November 19.

Bluestein, Greg, and Daniel Malloy. 2015. "Voting Initiative Faces Fresh Scrutiny." *Atlanta Journal-Constitution*. April 12.

Bluestein, Greg, Tia Mitchell, and Mark Niesse. 2018. "Pressure for Final Results Builds." *Atlanta Journal-Constitution*. November 13.

Bluestein, Greg, and Patricia Murphy. 2020. "National Spotlight Will Be Intense with Control of Senate at Stake." *Atlanta Journal-Constitution*. November 9.

Bluestein, Greg, and James Salzer. 2018. "Governor's Race Already Costliest Ever." *Atlanta Journal-Constitution*. July 11.

Bort, Ryan. 2018. "Despite Trump's Wishful Thinking, Andrew Gillum Won the Florida Debate." *Rolling Stone*. October 22.

Bostock, Bill. 2021. "As Rioters Stormed the Capitol, Trump Was Reportedly Telling People He Was Glad Perdue and Loeffler Lost Their Georgia Senate Seats, Calling Them Not Loyal Enough." *Business Insider*. January 7.

Bousquet, Steve, and Emily L. Mahoney. 2018. "Shakeup: Ron DeSantis Hires Susie Wiles to Take Over Floundering Campaign." *Tampa Bay Times*. September 26.

Brater, Jonathan, and Rebecca Ayala. 2018. "What's the Matter with Georgia?" Brennan Center for Justice. October 12.

Brown, Kevin. 2020. "Ad Infinitum: Spending Nears $500 Million in Georgia's Senate Runoffs." *Ad Age*. December 22.

Brown, Kirk. 2020. "SC is 'So Red it is Sunburned,' but Jaime Harrison Might Have Chance v. Lindsey Graham. *Greenville News*. October 20. https://www.greenvilleonline.com/story/news/local/2020/10/02/lindsey-graham-and-jaime-harrison-close-fight-u-s-senate-seat/3569597001/.

Buchanan, Scott E. 2018. "South Carolina: The GOP's Continued Dominance." In *The New Politics of the Old South*, 45–66, edited by Charles S. Bullock III and Mark J. Rozell. Lanham, MD: Rowman & Littlefield.

Buckner, Candace. 2021. 'WNBA Players' Actions Helped Elect Warnock." *Atlanta Journal-Constitution*. January 8.

Bullock, Charles S., III. 1984. "Racial Crossover Voting and the Election of Black Public Officials." *Journal of Politics* 46, no. 1: 238–251.

Bullock, Charles S., III, and Loch K. Johnson. 1992. *Runoff Elections in the United States*. Chapel Hill, NC: University of North Carolina Press.

Bullock, Charles S., III. 2010. *Redistricting: The Most Political Activity in America*. Lanham, MD: Rowman and Littlefield.

Bullock, Charles S., III. 2018a. "Georgia." In *The New Politics of the Old South*, 6th ed., edited by Charles S. Bullock III and Mark J. Rozell, 67–90. Lanham, MD: Rowman and Littlefield.

Bullock, Charles S., III. 2018b. "The History of Redistricting in Georgia." *Georgia Law Review* 52, no. 4: 1057–1104.

Bullock, Charles S., III. 2021. "Growth Versus Stagnation and a New Alignment." In *The New Politics of the Old South: An Introduction to Southern Politics*, 7th ed., 17–38, edited by Charles S. Bullock III and Mark J. Rozell. Lanham, MD: Rowman & Littlefield.

Bullock, Charles S. III, Scott E. Buchanan and Ronald Keith Gaddie. 2015. *The Three Governors' Controversy: Skullduggery, Machinations and the Decline of Progressive Politics in the Peach State.* Athens: University of Georgia Press.

Bullock, Charles S., III, and Richard E. Dunn. 1999. "The Demise of Racial Districting and the Future of Black Representation." *Emory Law Journal* 48, no. 4: 1209–1253.

Bullock, Charles S., III, and Ronald Keith Gaddie. 2006-7. "Voting Rights Progress in Georgia." *New York University Journal of Legislation and Public Policy* 10, no. 1: 1–49.

Bullock, Charles S., III, and Ronald Keith Gaddie. 2009. *The Triumph of Voting Rights in the House.* Norman, OK: University of Oklahoma Press.

Bullock, Charles S., III, Susan A. MacManus, Jeremy D. Mayer, and Mark J. Rozell. 2019. *The South and the Transformation of U.S. Politics.* New York: Oxford University Press.

Bullock, Charles S., III, and Karen L. Owen. 2018. "Some Things Money Can't Buy: The 2017 Runoff in Georgia's Sixth Congressional District." Paper presented at the Citadel Symposium on Southern Politics, Charleston, SC, March 1–2.

Bullock, Charles S., III, and Mark J. Rozell, eds., 2018. *The New Politics of the Old South: An Introduction to Southern Politics.* 6th ed. Lanham, MD: Rowman & Littlefield.

Bullock, Charles S., III, and Mark J. Rozell, eds., 2012. *The Oxford Handbook of Southern Politics.* New York: Oxford University Press.

Bump, Philip. 2018. "4.4 Million 2012 Obama Voters Stayed Home in 2016—More Than a Third of Them Black." *Washington Post.* March 12.

Burns, Alexander. 2018. "Trump Weighs in on Georgia Governor's Race." *New York Times.* July 19.

Burns, Alexander, Jonathan Martin, and Katie Glueck. 2020. "How Biden Chose Harris: A Search That Forged New Stars, Friends and Rivalries." *New York Times.* August 13. https://www.nytimes.com/2020/08/13/us/politics/biden-har ris.html.

Byrd, Caitlin. 2019. "Sen. Tim Scott Says His 2022 SC Reelection Bid Will Be His Last Political Race." *The Post and Courier* (Columbia, SC). August 9. https://www.postand courier.com/politics/sen-tim-scott-says-his-2022-sc-reelection-bid-will-be-his-last-political-race/article_0ef94de6-bab4-11e9-a59c-9bbb31fbdf41.html.

Cadelago, Christopher. 2019. "The Rude Awakening Creeping Up on Kamala Harris." *Politico.* April 23.

Cain, Andrew. 2017. "Wilder Endorses Fairfax for LG, Says Candidate 'Has Not Been Dealt a Good Hand.'" *Richmond Times Dispatch.* November 2. https://www.richmond. com/news/virginia/government-politics/wilder-endorses-fairfax-for-lg-says-candid ate-has-not-been/article_8ee1d7ec-793b-5529-95fd-9749b45a1552.html.

Capehart, Jonathan. 2020. "A New Ad Makes the Case Against Lindsey Graham with Graham Doing All the Talking." *Washington Post.* May 22. https://www.washingtonp ost.com/opinions/2020/05/22/new-ad-makes-case-against-lindsey-graham-with-gra ham-doing-all-talking/.

Call, James. 2018a. "Bernie Sanders Endorses Gillum To Be Florida Governor." *Tallahassee Democrat.* August 1.

Call, James. 2018b. "Mayor Andrew Gillum Launches Statewide Bus Tour in Final Push for Democratic Nomination." *Tallahassee Democrat.* August 20.

Call, James. 2018c. "Four Factors That Dragged Andrew Gillum Down in Florida Governor's Race." *Tallahassee Democrat.* November 7.

Call, James. 2018d. "Ron DeSantis Slams Mayor Andrew Gillum about Hamilton Tickets, FBI Probe." *Tallahassee Democrat.* October 24.

Center for Responsive Politics. 2020. "South Carolina Senate 2020 Race, Geography." OpenSecrets.org. https://www.opensecrets.org/races/geography?cycle=2020&id=SCS2&spec=N.

CDC. 2018. "National Vital Statistics Report." Vol. 67, No. 1. https://www.cdc.gov/nchs/data/nvsr/nvsr67/nvsr67_01.pdf.

Chira, Susan. 2018. "In Georgia, No Door Goes Un-Knocked." *New York Times.* November 6.

Chira, Susan. 2019. "After Her Narrow Loss, Abrams Takes Stock and Regroups." *New York Times.* March 6.

Caputo, Marc. 2018a. "DeSantis Has List of 9 Running Mates, Considers Pre-Primary Pick." *Politico.* August 10.

Caputo, Marc. 2018c. "How Ron DeSantis Won the Fox News Primary." *Politico.* August 29.

Caputo, Marc. 2018d. "New Racial Controversy Batters DeSantis." *Politico.* September 20.

Caputo, Marc, and Nancy Cook. 2018. "Trump Asserts Dominance over Florida GOP with Rally for DeSantis." *Politico.* July 31.

Ceballos, Ana. 2018a. "DeSantis Gets Money in Race for Governor fFrom Previous Putnam Political Donors." *Naples Daily News.* August 7.

Ceballos, Ana. 2018b. "Ron DeSantis and Andrew Gillum Clash during Florida Governor Debate on CNN." *USA TODAY Network-Florida.* October 21.

Ceballos, Ana. 2018c. "With Millions in TV ads, Top Spenders Are Not Top Performers in Florida's Governor Race." *Naples Daily News.* August 10.

Ceballos, Ana, and Janie Haseman. 2018. "Andrew Gillum Wins Florida Primary with Big Margins in Four Counties with Most Black Voters." *Naples Daily News.* August 29.

Clyburn, Jim. 2020. "Clyburn: Defund the Police 'Hurt' Jaime Harrison in South Carolina Senate Race." Interviewed on *Meet the Press.* November 8. https://www.nbcnews.com/meet-the-press/video/clyburn-defund-the-police-hurt-jaime-harrison-in-south-carolina-senate-race-95543877890.

"CNN Tonight." 2019. Transcript. *CNN.com.* February 11.

Coates, Ta-Nehisi. 2007. "Is Obama Black Enough?" *Time.* February 1.

Coates, Ta-Nehisi. 2015. "It Was No Compliment to Call Bill Clinton 'The First Black President.'" *Atlantic.* August 27.

Collins, Eliza. 2018. "Florida Gubernatorial Candidate Poised to Make History, and Other Takeaways from Tuesday's Elections." *USA Today.* August 29.

Contorno, Steve. 2018a. "Adam Putnam Was on a Path to Governor's Mansion. Then Trump and DeSantis Happened." *Tampa Bay Times.* August 29.

Corasaniti, Nick. 2020. "Ad Spending Soars in Georgia Races with Stakes Far beyond State." *New York Times.* December 21.

Cotterrell, Bill. 2018. "Running Mate Choices Were Interesting, Maybe Important." *Tallahassee Democrat.* September 9.

Craig, Tim. 2007. "In Va. House, 'Profound Regret' on Slavery." *Washington Post.* February 3. http://www.washingtonpost.com/wp-dyn/content/article/2007/02/02/AR2007020201203.html.

Daugherty, Alex, Caitlin Ostroff, and Martin Vassolo. 2018. "Post-Hurricane Maria Puerto Ricans Won't Swing Florida's Election." *Tampa Bay Times.* October 30.

Davis, Rebecca Shriver. 2017. *Justice Leah Ward Sears.* Athens: University of Georgia Press.

DeFede, Jim. 2018. "A Frustrated Ron DeSantis Dogged by Questions of Race." *CBS News 4 Miami.* September 20.

Denery, Jim. 2018. "Kemp Blamed for GOP's Suburb Woes." *Atlanta Journal-Constitution.* November 18.

Derby, Kevin. 2018. "Jeanette Nunez Reaches Out to Hispanic Voters for Ron DeSantis." *Floridadaily.com.* October 24.

Desiderio, Andrew. 2020. "How Jaime Harrison Thinks He Can Knock Off Lindsey Graham." *Politico.* October 21. https://www.politico.com/news/2020/10/21/jaime-harrison-south-carolina-trump-430371.

Dimock, Michael. 2019. "Defining Generations: Where Millennials End and Generation Z Begins." Pew Research Center Fact-Tank. January 17.

Dixon, Chris. 2019. "Challenger Takes on S.C. Senate Race with Rags-to-Prominence Story, Record Fundraising." *Washington Post.* December 7. https://www.washingtonpost.com/politics/challenger-takes-on-sc-senate-race-with-rags-to-prominence-story-record-fundraising/2019/12/07/1e0cd80e-17a5-11ea-8406-df3c54b3253e_story.html.

Dixon, Matt. 2018a. "Gillum Not Listed as 'Subject' in FBI Affidavit, but Political Damage May Already Be Done." *Politico.* February 6.

Dixon, Matt. 2018b. "Levine Hears Boos at Democratic Gubernatorial Debate Featuring Nasty Exchanges." *Politico.* June 9.

Donato, Christopher, and Sonnet Swire. 2018. "Florida Democrat Andrew Gillum Targeted by Second Racist Robo Call." *ABC News.* October 24.

Dumenco, Simon. 2018. "Still-Undecided Florida Races Saw a Last Minute Ad Spending Surge." *Ad Age.* November 12.

Dumenco, Simon. 2021. "Inside the $700 Million Ad Battle for the U.S. Senate." *Ad Age.* January 5.

Dunkelberger, Lloyd. 2018. "Putnam, DeSantis Show Contrast in Strategy." *Sunshine State News.* June 30.

Editorial Board. "Endorsements for Va.'s Democratic Primaries." 2013. *Washington Post.* May 19. https://www.washingtonpost.com/opinions/endorsements-for-vas-democratic-primary/2013/05/19/b2091d2a-bf3b-11e2-97d4-a479289a31f9_story.html?utm_term=.dc05c6cf8fb6.

Ellis, Nicquel Terry. 2018a. "Georgia Governor's Race: Claims of a Hack, Voter Suppression, Racist Robocall." *USA Today.* November 5.

Ellis, Nicquel Terry. 2018b. "Will Georgia Voting Controversies Discourage Voters from Turning Out?" *USA Today.* November 2.

Ellis, Terry Nicquel. 2021. "Pence Denies Systemic Racism, Harris Decries Trump Administration 'Pattern' of Racism in Historic Debate." *USA Today.* October 8. https://www.usatoday.com/story/news/nation/2020/10/07/pence-haris-spar-over-systemic-racism-breonna-taylor-vp-debate/5919398002/.

Ember, Sydney. 2020. "With Senate at Stake in Georgia, Progressives Focus on 'Bigger Picture.'" *New York Times.* December 2.

Estep, Tyler, and Amanda C. Coyne. 2018. "Black Caucus Suspects Voter Suppression." *Atlanta Journal-Constitution.* October 19.

Fandos, Nicholas, and David Enrich. 2020. "Senate Appointee Got Lucrative Parting Gift from a Public Company." *New York Times.* May 7.

Farhi, Paul. 2020. "'Help Me!' Lindsey Graham Begs Fox News Viewers in Unusual Plea for Campaign Cash." *Washington Post.* September 25. https://www.washingtonpost.com/lifestyle/media/lindsey-graham-help-me-money-contributions-fox/2020/09/25/ea2d6d14-ff57-11ea-8d05-9beaaa91c71f_story.html.

Farrington, Brendan. 2018a. "Ron DeSantis, Andrew Gillum Fight over Trump and More in Florida Debate on CNN." *Associated Press.* October 21.

Farrington, Brendan. 2018b. "Civil Rights Groups in Center of Florida Governor's Race." *Associated Press.* October 30.

Fauntroy, Michael K. 2012. "Enforcing Section 5 of the Voting Rights Act." In *The Oxford Handbook of Southern Politics,* 450–469, edited by Charles S. Bullock III and Mark J. Rozell. New York, NY: Oxford University Press.

Fausset, Richard. 2018a. "In Georgia Race, Progressive or Pragmatist? Maybe Both." *New York Times.* August 20.

Fausset, Richard. 2018b. "Proposal to Close 7 of 9 Polling Places in Rural County Hits Nerve in Georgia." *Atlanta Journal-Constitution.* August 24.

Fausset, Richard. 2018c. "Supporters of Candidate Who Lost Georgia Race Take the State to Court." *New York Times.* November 28.

Fausset, Richard. 2020a. "From High Society to the Right of Attila." *New York Times.* October 6.

Fausset, Richard. 2020b. "South Carolina Is Changing. Is It Enough to Put Jaime Harrison in the Senate?" *New York Times.* October 13. https://www.nytimes.com/2020/10/13/us/politics/jaime-harrison-south-carolina.html.

Fausset, Richard, Jonathan Martin, and Stephanie Saul. 2021. "For Democrats, Victory amid Tumult." *New York Times.* January 7.

Fineout, Gary. 2018. "Good Morning." Twitter. August 25.

Fiske, Warren. 2007. "Kaine Endorses Obama at Richmond Fundraiser." *Virginian-Pilot.* February 18.

FiveThirtyEight. 2020. "Latest Polls: South Carolina." November 2, 2020. https://projects.fivethirtyeight.com/polls/south-carolina/.

Florida Division of Elections. 2018. "Campaign Finance Information." https://dos.myflorida.com/elections/candidates-committees/campaign-finance/.

Folley, Aris. 2018. "Top Trump Official: Florida Governor's Race Is 'So Cotton-Pickin' Important.'" *Hill.* November 3.

Follow the Money. 2018. "Election Overview: Florida 2018 Elections." https://www.followthemoney.org/tools/election-overview?s=FL&y=2018.

Fowler, Stephen. 2019. "Kemp, Abrams's 'Fair Fight' Group Bring in Large Q2 Fundraising Numbers." *Georgia Public Broadcasting.* July 10.

Frederick, Kristofer A., and Judson L. Jeffries. 2009. "A Study of African American Candidates for High-Profile Statewide Office." *Journal of Black Studies* 39 (May): 665–688.

Freeman, Jo. 2005. "Shirley Chisholm's 1972 Campaign." https://www.jofreeman.com/polhistory/chisholm.htm.

Cagle, Casey. 2016. *Education Unleashed.* Macon, GA: Mercer University Press.

Gallagher, Julie. 2007. "Waging "The Good Fight": The Political Career of Shirley Chisholm, 1953–1982." *The Journal of African American History* 92, no. 3: 392–416. http://www.jstor.org.mutex.gmu.edu/stable/20064206.

Galloway, Jim. 2018. "Apartment Dwellers Prove a True Force in Northern Arc." *Atlanta Journal-Constitution.* December 9.

Garrett, Heath. 2021. "GOP Aims to Restrict Voting as Loeffler Launches Voter Registration Group." Political Rewind. *Georgia Public Broadcasting.* February 22.

Geggis, Anne. 2018. "Milano Brings Star Power to Gillum Rally." *South Florida Sun Sentinel.* September 30.

Gibson, Campbell, and Kay Jung. 2002. "Historical Census Statistics on Population Totals by Race, 1790 to 1990, and By Hispanic Origin, 1970 to 1990, For The United States, Regions, Divisions, and States." https://web.archive.org/web/20141224151538/http://www.census.gov/population/www/documentation/twps0056/twps0056.html.

Goldberg, Michelle. 2018. "We Can Replace Them." *New York Times*. October 30.

Goldmacher, Shane. 2020. "Now Airing in Florida: Ads for 4 Candidates for Senate in Georgia." *New York Times*. December 24.

Goldmacher, Shane. 2021. "A Puppy So Cute He Helped Tug Georgians Left." *New York Times*. January 25.

Goodyear, Dana. 2019. "Kamala Harris Makes Her Case." *New Yorker*. July 22. https://www.newyorker.com/magazine/2019/07/22/kamala-harris-makes-her-case.

Greenblatt, Alan. 2018. "In Florida's GOP Primary for Governor, It's Establishment vs. Trump." *Governing*. August.

Grofman, Bernard, and Lisa Handley. 1989. "Minority Population and Black and Hispanic Congressional Electoral Success in the 1970s and 1980s." *American Politics Quarterly* 17, no. 1: 436–445.

Grose, Christian R. 2007. "Cues, Endorsements and Heresthetic in a High-profile Election: Racial Polarization in Durham, North Carolina." *PS: Political Science and Politics* 40, no. 2: 325–332.

Grose, Christian R. 2011. *Congress in Black and White*. New York: Cambridge University Press.

Grunwald, Michael. 2019. "Is Cory Booker for Real?" *Politico*. February 1. https://www.politico.com/magazine/story/2019/02/01/cory-booker-president-2020-profile-newark-projects-224539/.

Grunwald, Michael, and Marc Caputo. 2018. "The Democrats' Hispanic Problem." *Politico Magazine*. December 4.

Haines, Matt. 2020. "Georgia Republicans Debate Whether to Vote in Runoff Elections." *Voice of America*. December 20.

Hallerman, Tamar. 2019. "Dems Seek Records on Ga. Voting Results." *Atlanta Journal-Constitution*. March 7.

Harrison, Jaime. 2019a. "Jaime Harrison Tells Rachel Maddow: 'I'm Running for the U.S. Senate." *The Rachel Maddow Show*. YouTube Video. May 28. https://www.youtube.com/watch?v=AeomuXkOAqk.

Harrison, Jaime. 2019b. "Character." YouTube Video. May 29. https://www.youtube.com/watch?v=qGL5dclzjHo.

Harrison, Jaime. 2020a. "Lindsay Graham Has Changed." Facebook Video. August 25. https://www.facebook.com/JaimeHarrisonSC/videos/lindsey-graham-has-changed/2514107178882841/.

Harrison, Jaime. 2020b. "Character Counts." YouTube Video. September 28. https://www.youtube.com/watch?v=IHcDJU052oA.

Harrison, Jaime. 2020c. "Right." YouTube video. September 28. https://www.youtube.com/watch?v=uSXXdudE3KA.

Harrison, Jaime. 2020d. Tweet from @HarrisonJaime. October 14, 11:00 a.m. Twitter. https://twitter.com/harrisonjaime/status/1316393477081632769.

Hart, Ariel. 2018. "Medicaid Expansion Question Fuels Georgia Governor's Race." *Atlanta Journal-Constitution*. September 5.

Hatter, Lynn. 2018. "Polling Accuracy Once Again at Issue Following Gillum Primary Win." *WFSU.org*. August 30.

Hearn, Josephine. 2008. "Black Caucus Divided Over Obama." *Politico*. January 17.

Heinemann, Ronald L. 1996. *Harry Byrd of Virginia*. Charlottesville: University Press of Virginia.

Herndon, Astead W. 2020. "For Black Women, a Long Fight to Change How Georgia Voted." *New York Times*. December 4.

Herndon, Astead, and Nick Corasaniti. 2020. "Republicans on Attack in Costly Georgia Runoffs." *New York Times*. November 24.

Herndon, Astead W., Shane Goldmacher, and Jonathan Martin. 2019. "Kamala Harris Says She's Still 'in This Fight,' but out of the 2020 Race." *New York Times*. December 3.

Highton, Benjamin. 2004. "White Voters and African American Candidates for Congress." *Political Behavior* 26, no. 1: 1–25.

Hollis, Henri. 2020a. "Loeffler Accuses Warnock of Anti-Israel Extremism." *Atlanta Journal-Constitution*. December 28.

Hollis, Henri. 2020b. "Warnock Accuses Loeffler of 'Dumping Stock.'" *Atlanta Journal-Constitution*. December 9.

Hood, M. V. III. 2021. "AJC Pre-Legislative Survey." School of Public and International Affairs, University of Georgia.

Hunter, Tera W. 2011. "The Forgotten Legacy of Shirley Chisholm: Race versus Gender in the 2008 Democratic Primaries." In *Obama, Clinton, Palin: Making History in Election 2008*, edited by Gidlow Liette, 66–85. Urbana; Chicago; Springfield: University of Illinois Press. http://www.jstor.org.mutex.gmu.edu/sta ble/10.5406/j.ctt2tt9t8.9.

Hurt, Emma. 2020. "In U.S. Senate Race, Georgia Republicans Are Divided, Can They Reunite in a Presumed Runoff?" *WABE*. October 19.

Isenstadt, Alex, and Melanie Zanona. 2019. "Georgia Governor Set to Buck Trump on Senate Appointment." *Politico*. December 1.

Jamison, Peter, and Scott Clement. 2019. "Virginians Are Split on Governor's Fate amid Blackface Scandal, Poll Shows." *Washington Post*. February 9. https://www.washing tonpost.com/local/virginia-politics/virginians-split-on-governors-fate-amid-blackf ace-scandal-poll-shows/2019/02/09/93002e84-2bc1-11e9-b011-d8500644dc98_story. html?utm_term=.36b98069794f.

Jarvie, Jenny. 2018a. "In Georgia's Gubernatorial Race, Stacey Abrams Has a Real Chance to Make History." *Los Angeles Times*. November 1.

Jarvie, Jenny. 2018b. "Not over Yet? Georgia's Brian Kemp Declares Victory but Stacey Abrams Holds Out for Final Count." *Los Angeles Times*. November 7.

Jeffries, Judson. 1997. *Doug Wilder and the Politics of Race*. PhD dissertation, University of Southern California.

Jeffries, Judson L. 1999. "U.S. Senator Edward W. Brooke and Governor L. Douglas Wilder Tell Political Scientists How Blacks Can Win High-Profile Statewide Office." *PS: Political Science and Politics* 32 (September): 583–587.

Johnson, Eliana. 2021. "Inside the GOP's Week from Hell." *Politico Playbook*. January 10.

Johnson, Tharon. 2021. "Is Georgia Now a 'Blue State?'" Political Breakfast Podcast. *WABE*. January 6.

Jones, Sarah. 2019. "Andrew Gillum's Next Campaign: Registering Voters in Florida." *Intelligencer*. March. 20.

Joyce, Fay. 1984. "Jackson Tells Alabama It "Will Never be the Same." *New York Times*. February 10. https://www.nytimes.com/1984/02/10/us/jackson-tells-alabama-it-will-never-be-the-same.html.

Judd, Alan. 2018b. "Kemp Turned Security Flaws against Democrats." *Atlanta Journal-Constitution.* December 16.

Kaiser Family Foundation. n.d. "Population Distribution by Race/Ethnicity." https://www.kff.org/other/state-indicator/distribution-by-raceethnicity/?currentTimeframe=11&sortModel=%7B%22colId%22:%22Location%22,%22sort%22:%22asc%22%7D.

Kam, Dara. 2018. "Gwen Graham Is Still Optimistic Despite Losing Florida Democratic Primary." *Orlando Weekly.* December 17.

Kam, Dara, and Lloyd Dunkelberger. 2018. "Gillum and DeSantis Brawl in Fiery Final Debate of Florida Governor's Race." *News Service of Florida.* October 24.

Key, V. O., Jr. 1949. *Southern Politics in State and Nation.* New York: Knopf.

Keith, Tamara. 2020. "Democrats Raised More Than $46 Million Following RBG's Death." *NPR.* September 19. https://www.npr.org/sections/death-of-ruth-bader-ginsburg/2020/09/19/914764789/democrats-raised-more-than-30-million-following-rbgs-death.

Kilgore, Ed. 2018a. "Will Andrew Gillum's Christian Running Mate Help Him Win Evangelicals." *Intelligencer. New York Magazine.* September 11.

Kilgore, Ed. 2018b. "2018 Midterms Offered More Proof That Split-Ticket Voting Is a Thing of the Past." *New York Magazine.* November 18. https://nymag.com/intelligencer/2018/11/2018-midterms-split-ticket-voting.html.

Kinnard, Meg. 2019. "Democratic Official Gets Party Backing for Graham Challenge." *Associated Press.* May 30. https://apnews.com/article/3666f33429834481b04f4d4dd850e53b.

King, James D. 1999. "Running on Their Own: The Electoral Success (and Failure) of Appointed U.S. Senators." *American Politics Quarterly* 27 (October): 434–449.

Klas, Mary Ellen. 2018. Twitter. August 28.

Koh, Elizabeth. 2018. "Andrew Gillum Names Chris King as His Running Mate on Florida's Democratic Ticket." *Miami Herald.* September 6.

Korte, Gregory. 2020. "'Crooks' Versus 'Socialists': Ads Frame Georgia's Bitter Runoffs." *Bloomberg.* December 31.

Kousser, J. Morgan. 1974. *The Shaping of Southern Politics: Suffrage Restriction and the Establishment of the One-Party South, 1880–1910.* New Haven, CT: Yale University Press.

Krogstad, Jens Manuel, and Mark Hugo Lopez. 2017. "Black Voter Turnout Fell in 2016, Even as a Record Number of Americans Cast Ballots." Pew Research Center. March 12.

LeBlanc, Paul. 2020. "Lindsey Graham Campaign Ad Features Image of Opponent with Digitally Altered Darker Skin Tone." *CNN.* July 29. https://www.cnn.com/2020/07/28/politics/lindsey-graham-jaime-harrison-skin-tone-ad/index.html.

Legum, Judd, and Tesnim Zekeria. 2020. "Before Her Scorched-Earth Attacks, Loeffler Shared a Pupil with Warnock and Praised His Church." *Popular Information.* December 2.

Lemongello, Steven. 2018. "Andrew Gillum Releases First TV Ad, 'What's Impossible?'" *Orlando Sentinel.* July 25.

Lemongello, Steven, and Gray Rohrer. 2018. "How Andrew Gillum Won His Primary—and How Democrats Think He Can Win in November." *Orlando Sentinel.* August 29.

Lovegrove, Jamey. 2019. "To Stick out from 2020 Pack, Cory Booker Goes Beyond SC's Big Cities Early." *Post Courier.* March 2. https://www.postandcourier.com/politics/to-stick-out-from-pack-cory-booker-goes-beyond-sc/article_9dc4cad8-3d09-11e9-a356-9fc7cf9fdb68.html.

Lovegrove, Jamie. 2020a. "Lindsey Graham to Face 3 Little-Known GOP Primary Challengers for 2020 Reelection." *The Post and Courier* (Columbia, SC). March 30. https://www.postandcourier.com/politics/lindsey-graham-to-face-3-little-known-gop-primary-challengers-for-2020-reelection/article_145864ec-72a2-11ea-a784-77b2597d49c8.html.

Lovegrove, Jamie. 2020b. "Harrison Depends on Rare Party Ticket-Splitting Voters to Upset Graham in SC Senate Race." *The Post and Courier* (Columbia, SC). July 5. https://www.postandcourier.com/politics/harrison-depends-on-rare-party-ticket-splitting-voters-to-upset-graham-in-sc-senate-race/article_2fbc2600-bc63-11ea-bce1-e7d2d18d134a.html.

Lovegrove, Jamie. 2020c. "SC Senate Policy Stakes: Graham, Harrison Agree on Climate Change, Differ on Approach." *The Post and Courier* (Columbia, SC). August 16. https://www.postandcourier.com/politics/sc-senate-policy-stakes-graham-harrison-agree-on-climate-change-differ-on-approach/article_7344eac6-ddb3-11ea-ba08-57325748cc34.html.

Lovegrove, Jamie. 2020d. "Harrison Elevates Third-Party Candidate in Bid to Pull GOP SC Senate Votes from Graham." *The Post and Courier* (Columbia, SC). October 19. https://www.postandcourier.com/columbia/politics/harrison-elevates-third-party-candidate-in-bid-to-pull-gop-sc-senate-votes-from-graham/article_f742abd4-1237-11eb-90e4-071b9c755abc.html.

Lovegrove, Jamie. 2020e. "Obama Tapes New Ad for Harrison While Haley, Scott Tout Graham in SC Senate Race." *The Post and Courier* (Columbia, SC). October 20. https://www.postandcourier.com/columbia/politics/obama-tapes-new-ad-for-harrison-while-haley-scott-tout-graham-in-sc-senate-race/article_4ed06034-12de-11eb-be6c-f368dfcddf6d.html (accessed January 19, 2021).

Lozado, Carlos. 2017. "Before Michelle, Barack Obama Asked Another Woman to Marry Him. Then Politics Got in the Way." *Washington Post*. May 2.

MacManus, Susan A. 2017. *Florida's Minority Trailblazers: The Men and Women Who Changed the Face of Florida Government.* Gainesville: University of Florida Press.

MacManus, Susan A., and Amy N. Benner. 2020. "Winning at the Margins: Party Micro-Targeting Strategies in Swing State Florida 2020." Paper presented at the Citadel Symposium on Southern Politics, Charleston, SC, March 5–6.

Mahoney, Emily L. 2018a. "Is Trump's Firing Up the Florida Republican Base Enough For DeSantis to Win?" *Tampa Bay Times*. August 1.

Mahoney, Emily L. 2018b. "'Trump Is the 'Closer in Chief' as Republican Candidates Rally Together in Pensacola." *Tampa Bay Times*. November 3.

Man, Anthony. 2018a. "Donald Trump's Pick for Florida Governor Has So Much Momentum He May Be Unstoppable." *South Florida Sun Sentinel*. July 27.

Man, Anthony. 2018b. "Election Ad Pitch to Young Voters: 'Our Chance to Finally Elect Florida's First Black Governor.'" *South Florida Sun Sentinel*. October 20.

Man, Anthony, and Skyler Swisher. 2018. "3 Big reasons behind Andrew Gillum's Upset Victory in Democratic Primary." *South Florida Sun Sentinel*. August 29.

Marchant, Bristow. 2019. "U.S. Sen. Kamala Harris Racks up Early SC Endorsements for 2020 Run." *The State*. March 28. https://www.thestate.com/news/politics-government/article228526869.html#storylink=cpy.

Martin, Jonathan. 2013. "Graham Faces Down Primary Challenge." *Politico*. May 19. https://www.politico.com/story/2013/05/lindsey-graham-2014-primary-challenge-091108.

Martin, Jonathan. 2020. "Lindsey Graham Leads Jaime Harrison in South Carolina Race, Polls Show." *New York Times*. October 15. https://www.nytimes.com/2020/10/15/us/politics/south-carolina-polls.html.

Maraniss, David. 1996. *First in His Class: A Biography of Bill Clinton*. New York: Simon and Schuster.

Martin, Jonathan, and Alexander Burns. 2020. "In Senate Runoffs, Hopefuls Speak Plainly on Race." *New York Times*. October 27.

Mayer, Jeremy D. 2002. *Running on Race: Racial Politics in Presidential Campaigns 1960–2000*. New York: Random House.

Mayer, Jeremy D. 2013. "Reading Coates, Thinking Obama." *American Interest* 11 (November–December): 91–97.

Maxwell, Angie, and Todd Shields. 2019. *The Long Southern Strategy: How Chasing White Voters in the South Changed American Politics*. New York: Oxford University Press.

Mazzei, Patricia, and Jonathan Martin. 2019. "Stung by Florida Midterm Losses, Democrats See a Swing State Drifting Away." *New York Times*. January 13.

Mazzei, Patricia, and Lisa Lerer. 2018. "Andrew Gillum and Ron DeSantis Trade Attacks over Corruption and Racism in Florida Debate." *New York Times*. October 24.

Mazzei, Patricia, and Frances Robles. 2018. "Andrew Gillum Concedes to Ron DeSantis in Florida Governor's Race." *New York Times*. November 6.

McAuliffe, Danny. 2018. "An Energized Andrew Gillum Circles Campaign Back to Tallahassee." *FloridaPolitics.com*. August 28.

McElhannon, Joel. 2018. Interview with the Author. November 26.

Melton, R.H. 1989. "Wilder's Embrace of Jackson Stays a Long Arm's length Away." *Washington Post*. September 30. https://www.washingtonpost.com/archive/local/1989/09/30/wilders-embrace-of-jackson-stays-a-long-arms-length-away/f2c77dbe-391e-4ae9-804f-f7c5735356bf/?utm_term=.08b4457f11d6.

Morin, Rebecca. 2020. "Lindsey Graham in Debate Forum: Black People Can Go Anywhere in SC Politics, If They're 'Not Liberal.'" *USA Today*. October 10. https://www.usatoday.com/story/news/politics/2020/10/10/lindsey-graham-black-people-can-go-anywhere-sc-if-conservative/5954115002/.

Morris, Irwin L. 2021. *Movers and Stayers: The Partisan Transformation of Twenty-First Century Southern Politics*. New York: Oxford University Press.

Murphy, Patricia. 2018. "What Stacey Abrams Will Tell Us about America Tonight." *Roll Call*. November 6.

Murphy, Patricia. 2020a. "Ad Blitz Leaves Voters with Nowhere to Hide." *Atlanta Journal-Constitution*. December 24.

Murphy, Patricia. 2020b. "Warnock, Loeffler Trade Sharp Attacks." *Atlanta Journal-Constitution*. December 7.

Muse, Benjamin. 1969. *Virginia's Massive Resistance*. Gloucester, MA: Peter Smith.

"Muskie Summary." 1971. Nixon Papers, Nixon Presidential Library.

Morning Edition. 2019. "Sen. Kamala Harris on Reparations." *NPR*. March 14. https://www.npr.org/2019/03/14/703299534/sen-kamala-harris-on-reparations.

Newkirk, Margaret, and Anousha Sakoui. 2019. "Abortion Ban Rattles America's Top Film State." *Bloomberg News*. June 8.

Newkirk, Margaret, Michael Sassso, and Jonathan Levin. 2018. "Democrats Discover New Path to Beating Trump in Deep South." *Bloomberg News*. November 12.

News Service of Florida. 2018 "Democratic Candidates for Governor Square Off in First Debate." *Orlando Sentinel*. April 18.

Niesse, Mark. 2000. "State Investigators: No Evidence to Back Kemp's Voter Registration Hacking Claim." *Atlanta Journal-Constitution*. March 4.

Niesse, Mark. 2018a. "Voter Registration Battle Sets Stage." *Atlanta Journal-Constitution*. August 19.

Niesse, Mark. 2018b. "Why Did Some Voting Machines Sit Unused?" *Atlanta Journal-Constitution*. November 8.

Niesse, Mark. 2019. "Precinct Closures Moving Forward after Earlier Defeat." *Atlanta Journal-Constitution*. July 12.

Niesse, Mark, and Tyler Estep. 2018. "What You Need to Know about Georgia's 53,000 Pending Voters." *Atlanta Journal-Constitution*. October 15.

Niesse, Mark. 2020a. "Authenticity of Absentee Ballots Confirmed in Audit." *Atlanta Journal-Constitution*. December 30.

Niesse, Mark, and Jennifer Peebles. 2021. "Lower GOP Turnout Helped Flip Senate." *Atlanta Journal-Constitution*. February 3.

Nilson, Ella. 2020. "9 Questions about the Georgia Senate Runoffs You Were too Embarrassed to Ask." *Vox*. November 30.

Nirappil, Fenit. 2017. "Black Democrat Omitted from Some Democratic Campaign Flyers in Virginia." *Washington Post*. October 19. https://www.washingtonpost.com/local/virginia-politics/reeks-of-subtle-racism-tensions-after-black-candidate-left-off-fliers-in-virginia/2017/10/18/de74c47a-b425-11e7-a908-a3470754bbb9_story.html?utm_term=.7edf9f02bb67.

Nirappil, Fenit. 2018. "Justin Fairfax Would Become Virginia' 2nd Black Governor if Northam Resigns." *Washington Post*. February 2. https://www.washingtonpost.com/local/virginia-politics/justin-fairfax-would-become-virginias-2nd-black-governor-if-northam-resigns/2019/02/02/a632c054-266a-11e9-90cd-dedb0c92dc17_story.html.

O'Connor, Dan. 2019. Personal Communication. February 22.

Ogles, Jacob. 2018. "Andrew Gillum Continues Editorial Board Dominance with Miami Herald Endorsement." *Florida Politics*. October 21.

Ostfeld, Mara, and Michelle Garcia. 2020. "Black Men Shift Slightly towards Trump in Record Numbers, Polls Show." *NBC News*. November 4.

Owen, Karen L. 2017. *Women Officeholders and the Role Models Who Pioneered the Way*. Lanham, MD: Lexington Books.

Parker, Frank R. 1990. *Black Votes Count: Political Empowerment in Mississippi after 1965*. Chapel Hill: University of North Carolina Press.

Papantonis, Nicholas. 2020. "Harrison Says He's For I-73, Broadband, against Police Defunding in 1-on-1 Interview." *ABC 15 News* (WPDE). https://wpde.com/news/local/harrison-says-hes-for-i-73-broadband-against-police-defunding-in-1-on-1-interview.

Patrick, Deval. 2011. *A Reason to Believe*. New York: Broadway Books.

Payne, Melanie. 2018. "Rich Donors Give DeSantis Slight Lead in Fundraising for Florida Governor's Race." *Naples Daily News*. October 25.

Pluralist. 2019. "Kamala Harris Asked Why She Married a White Man: It Just 'Happened.'" February 12. https://pluralist.com/kamala-harris-married-a-White-man-it-just-happened/.

Prabhu, Maya. 2018a. "Evans Touts Her Rise from Poverty. *Atlanta Journal-Constitution*. May 4.

Prabhu, Maya. 2018b. "Spotlight Helps to Fuel Abrams's Bid." *Atlanta Journal-Constitution*. May 3.

Pew Research Center. 2020. "Large Shares of Voters Plan to Vote a Straight Party Ticket for President, Senate and House." October 21. https://www.pewresearch.org/politics/2020/10/21/large-shares-of-voters-plan-to-vote-a-straight-party-ticket-for-presid ent-senate-and-house/.

Perry, Mitch. 2018. "The Political Battle for Florida's Latino Vote." *Florida Phoenix*. October 3.

Pisani, Madelaine. 2018. "Gillum Launches Final TV Ad." *National Journal*. November 6.

Politico Pro Staff. 2018. "Trump-Backed DeSantis Wins Florida GOP Gubernatorial Primary." *Politico*. August 28, 8:13 PM EDT.

Powers, Scott. 2018. "Jeff Greene Ad Mauls Gwen Graham on Megamall, Environment." *FloridaPolitics.com*. August 3.

Raju, Manu, Ale Rogers, and Ali Zaslav. 2020. "Republicans on the Run in Georgia with Two Senate Seats within Democratic Reach." *CNN*. October 30.

Redmon, Jeremy. 2020. "Warnock Alleges Loeffler 'Purchased' Her Seat." *Atlanta Journal-Constitution*. December 31.

Reeves, Keith. 1997. *Voting Hopes or Fears? White Voters, Black Candidates and Racial Politics in America*. New York: Oxford University Press.

Rodrigo, Chris Mills. 2019. "Booker Slams Conversation about Reparations: More Than 'Just a Box to Check' on a Presidential List." *Hill*. March 27. https://theh ill.com/homenews/campaign/436189-booker-slams-conversation-about-reparati ons-more-than-just-a-box-to-check.

Rohrer, Gray. 2018. "Florida Governor's Race: Where Ron DeSantis, Adam Putnam Stand, Differ." *Orlando Sentinel*. August 14.

Roth, Zachary. 2016. "Black Turnout Down in North Carolina after Cuts to Early Voting." *NBC News*. November 7. https://www.nbcnews.com/storyline/2016-election-day/Black-turnout-down-north-carolina-after-cuts-early-voting-n679051.

Roulette, Joey. 2018. "While Visiting Orlando, Ron DeSantis and Donald Trump Jr. Rip 'Toast of Tallahassee' Adam Putnam." *Orlando Weekly*. July 18.

Rozell, Mark J., and Mark Caleb Smith. 2012. "The Christian Right and the Transformation of Southern Politics." In *The Oxford Handbook of Southern Politics*, edited by Charles S. Bullock III and Mark J. Rozell, 133–152. New York: Oxford University Press.

Rozell, Mark J., and Clyde Wilcox. 1996. *Second Coming: The New Christian Right in Virginia Politics*. Baltimore, MD: The Johns Hopkins University Press.

Ruiz, Rebecca R. 2020. "Graham and Harrison Battle Over the 'New South,' in Their Final Appeals." *New York Times*. November 2. https://www.nytimes.com/2020/11/02/us/lind sey-graham-jaime-harrison-south-carolina.html.

Sabato, Larry J. 1977. *The Democratic Party of Virginia: Tantamount to Election no Longer*. Charlottesville: University Press of Virginia.

Sabato, Larry J. 1990a. "Virginia Governor's Race, 1989: Part 2: The General Election." *University of Virginia Newsletter* 66, no. 6 (January).

Sabato, Larry J. 1990b. "Virginia Governor's Race, 1989: Part 3: The General Election Issues." *University of Virginia Newsletter* 66, no. 6 (February).

Sakuma, Amanda. 2016. "Trump Did Better with Blacks, Hispanics than Romney in '12: Exit Polls." *NBC News*. November 9. https://www.nbcnews.com/storyline/2016-election-day/trump-did-better-Blacks-hispanics-romney-12-exit-polls-n681386.

Salzer, James. 2018a. "Capitol Crowd that Backed Cagle Now Donate to Kemp." *Atlanta Journal-Constitution*. July 30.

Salzer, James. 2018b. "Dark Money Flooding Ga. Campaigns." *Atlanta Journal-Constitution*. July 23.

Salzer, James. 2018c. "Out-of-State Money Fuels Georgia Races." *Atlanta Journal-Constitution*. September 12.

Salzer, James. 2019. "Abrams's Voting Rights Group Raised $3.9M in Past 6 Month." *Atlanta Journal-Constitution*. July 7.

Salzer, James, and Greg Bluestein. 2018. "Ga. Capitol Crowd Supporting Cagle." *Atlanta Journal-Constitution*. February 18.

Sarlin, Benjy. 2018. "DeSantis Wins Florida Governor's Race, Defeating Progressive Andrew Gillum." *NBC News*. November 6.

Saul, Stephanie, and Maggie Astor. 2020. "Deval Patrick, Latecomer to the 2020 Race, Drops Out." *New York Times*. February 12. https://www.nytimes.com/2020/02/12/us/politics/deval-patrick-drops-out.html.

Saul, Stephanie, Patricia Mazzei, and Jonathan Martin. 2018. "Ron DeSantis Reboots in Close Florida Governor's Race, after Early Stumble." *New York Times*. October 4.

Scanlan, Quinn. 2020. "Trump, Pence to Campaign in Georgia as Senate Runoff Turnout Concerns Grow among GOP." *ABC News*. December 4.

Schale, Steve. 2018. "So, About Tuesday Night . . ." Steveschale.squarespace.com/blog. November 19.

Schexnider, Alvin J. 1990. "The Politics of Pragmatism: An Analysis of the 1989 Gubernatorial Election in Virginia. (Symposium: Black Electoral Success in 1989)." *PS: Political Science & Politic* 23, no. 2 (June): 154–156.

Schmitz, Ali. 2018. "Andrew Gillum, Ron DeSantis Spar in Final Florida Governor Debate." *Treasure Coast Newspapers*. October 24.

Schneider, Avie. 2021. "DNC Chairman Jaime Harrison Wants to Build the 'Next Generation' of Democratic Talent." *NPR*. January 22. https://www.npr.org/2021/01/22/959573611/dnc-chairman-jaime-harrison-wants-to-build-the-next-generation-of-democratic-tal.

Schouten, Fredreka. 2018. "How Upstart Groups Helped Andrew Gillum's Quest to Become Florida's First Black Governor." *USA Today*. August 30.

Schweers, Jeffrey. 2018a. "Historic Florida Governor Election Mired in Name-Calling, Racist Accusations." *Tallahassee Democrat*. November 6.

Schweers, Jeffrey. 2018b. "Election 2018 Overtime: Andrew Gillum Pulls Back Concession as Ron DeSantis Calls for Unity." *Tallahassee Democrat*. November 10.

Shane, Scott, and Sheera Frenkel. 2018. "Russian 2016 Influence Operation Targeted African-Americans on Social Media." *New York Times*. December 17. https://www.nytimes.com/2018/12/17us/politics/russia-2016-influence-campaign.html.

Silver, Nate. 2008. "Appointed Senators Rarely Win Re-Election." *FiveThirtyEight*. December 11.

Slackman, Michael. 2004. "Sharpton's Bid Aided by an Unlikely Source." *New York Times*. January 25.

Smiley, David. 2018a. "DeSantis Plays the Role of DC Champ, Tallahassee Outsider in Gov Campaign Launch." *Miami Herald*. January 29.

Smiley, David. 2018b. "DeSantis Rips CNN for Releasing 'Misleading Poll' ahead of First Debate with Gillum." *Miami Herald*. October 21.

Smiley, David. 2018c. "Gwen Graham Targeted in Final Debate of Florida's Democratic Primary for Governor." *Miami Herald*. August 2.

Smiley, David. 2018d. "Florida Democrats Confident at Halfway Point as Andrew Gllum Rides High in the Polls," *Tampa Bay Times*. September 30.

Smith, Adam C. 2018. "Ron DeSantis Announces Endorsements from 36 Puerto Rican Electeds." *Tampa Bay Times*. October 20.

Smith, David, and Daniel Strauss. 2020. "Cory Booker Drops Out of 2020 Race and Promises to 'Carry this Fight Forward.'" *The Guardian*. January 13. https://www.theg uardian.com/us-news/2020/jan/13/cory-booker-drops-out-2020-presidential-race-democrats.

"So Sweet and Clear." 2021. *Economist*. January 9.

Sollenberg, Roger. 2021. "Kelly Loeffler's New Facebook Ad Darkens Skin of Raphael Warnock, Her Black Opponent." *Salon*. January 5.

Sonenshein, Raphael J. 1990. "Can Black Candidates Win Statewide Elections?" *Political Science Quarterly* 105, no. 2: 219–241.

Sopo, Giancarlo. 2018. "Why Florida Remains the Democrats' Gordian Knot." *National Review*. December 18.

South Carolina Revenue and Fiscal Affairs Office. n.d.a "Population Estimates by Non-Hispanic Race & Ethnicity—2019." https://rfa.sc.gov/data-research/population-demographics/census-state-data-center/population-estimates-non-hispanic-race.

South Carolina Revenue and Fiscal Affairs Office. n.d.b "Urban and Rural Population." https://rfa.sc.gov/data-research/population-demographics/census-state-data-center/urban-and-rural-population.

South Carolina State Election Commission. n.d. "Fact Sheets: Straight Party Voting History (2006–2020)." https://www.scvotes.gov/fact-sheets.

Stevens, Matt. 2019. "When Kamala Harris and Joe Biden Clashed on Busing and Segregation." *New York Times*. July 31. https://www.nytimes.com/2019/07/31/us/polit ics/kamala-harris-biden-busing.html.

Stout, Christopher T. 2015. *Bringing Race Back In: Black Politicians, Deracialization, and Voting Behavior in the Age of Obama*. Charlottesville: University of Virginia Press.

Strickland, Ruth Ann, and Marcia Lynn Whicker. 1992. "Comparing the Wilder and Gantt Campaigns: A Model for Black Candidate Success in Statewide Elections." *PS: Political Science and Politics* 25 (June): 204–2012.

Suggs, Ernie. 2018. "'Black Belt' Is Key to Abrams's Strategy." *Atlanta Journal-Constitution*. September 30.

Suggs, Ernie. 2020a. "Black Organizations Work to Help Boost Democrats." *Atlanta Journal-Constitution*. November 11.

Suggs, Ernie. 2020b. "Parties Courting Latinos with Differing Strategies." *Atlanta Journal-Constitution*. December 30.

Spencer, Terry, and Brendan Farrington. 2018. "DeSantis, Gillum Exchange Insults in Final Florida Debate." *U.S. News & World Report*. October 25.

Strickland, Ruth Ann, and Marcia Lynn Whicker. 1992. "Comparing the Wilder and Gantt Campaigns: A Model for Black Statewide Success in Statewide Elections." *Political Science & Politics* 25, no. 2 (June): 204–212.

Tarrant, Bill. 2018. "U.S. Courts Rule against Georgia on Voter Suppression Cases." Reuters. November 2.

Taylor, Jessica. 2018. "Progressive Upset Means a Sanders vs. Trump Battle for Florida Governor." *NPR*. August 28.

Taylor, Jessica. 2020. "South Carolina Senate Moves to Toss Up." October 7. https://cookpo litical.com/analysis/senate/south-carolina-senate/south-carolina-senate-moves-toss.

Tensley, Brandon. 2020. "Jaime Harrison Says There's One Battle He's Already Won." *CNN*. October 3. https://www.cnn.com/2020/10/03/politics/jaime-harrison-black-vot ers-south-carolina/index.html.

Terkildsen, Nayda. 1993. "When White Voters Evaluate Black Candidates: The Processing Implications of Candidate Skin Color, Prejudice and Self-Monitoring." *American Journal of Political Science* 37: 1032–1053.

Thrush, Glenn, and Jeremy W. Peters. 2018. "Vitriol over Vote-Stealing Charges Sets a Troubling Tone for 2020." *New York Times*. November 19.

Toobin, Jeffrey. 2018. "Deval Patrick's Presidential Prospects." *New Yorker*. November 12.

Traugott, Michael, and Vincent Price. 1992. "A Review: Exit Polls in the 1989 Virginia Gubernatorial Race: Where Did They Go Wrong?" *Public Opinion Quarterly* 56, no. 2 (July): 245–253.

Voss, D. Stephen, and David Lublin. 2001. "Black Incumbents, White Districts: An Appraisal of the 1996 Congressional Elections." *American Political Research* 29: 141–182.

Washington Post, 2013. "Endorsement's for Va.'s Democratic Primaries." May 2013.

Waters, TaMaryn. 2018. "In One of Biggest Concerts of the Year, Diddy, DJ Khaled 'Bring It Home' for Andrew Gillum." *Tallahassee Democrat*. November 6.

Wieder, Ben. 2018. "Stacey Abrams, Andrew Gillum Draw Cash from Same Bank of National Donors." *McClatchy Washington Bureau*. November 1.

Wilder, L. Douglas. 2018. *Son of Virginia: A Life in America's Political Arena*. Lanham, MD: Lyons Press.

Williams, Ross. 2020. "Warnock Preachings Reverberate in Bid to Leap from Pulpit to Senate." *Georgia Recorder*. December 20.

Wilson, Kirby. 2018. "4 Key Moments From Saturday's Democratic Gubernatorial Debate." *Tampa Bay Times*. June 9.

Wilson, Patrick. 2017. "How Outsider Justin Fairfax Broke Through the Democratic Party in Bid for Lieutenant Governor." *Richmond Times Dispatch*. March 18. https:// www.richmond.com/news/virginia/government-politics/how-outsider-justin-fair fax-broke-through-the-democratic-party-in/article_672c7f1d-718b-53e2-890c-0f266 eb61aec.html.

WIS News 10. 2020. "Vulgar, Offensive Tweets Surface from Two of Jaime Harrison's Campaign Staffers." September 18. https://www.wistv.com/2020/09/18/vulgar-offens ive-tweets-surface-two-jaime-harrisons-campaign-staffers/.

Wise, Lindsay. 2020. "Graham Debates Harrison Over 'Good Old Days of Segregation' Comment." *Wall Street Journal*. October 14. https://www.wsj.com/livecoverage/amy-coney-barrett-supreme-court-confirmation-hearing-day-three/card/2i9AMkjSP1xz0 u7y8mW6.

Yancey, Dwayne. 1988. *When Hell Froze Over*. Dallas, TX: Taylor Publishing.

Yokley, Eli. 2020. "Graham Is Weak with GOP Voters. Strategists Think Another Supreme Court Fight Will Help." *Morning Consult*. September 22. https://morningconsult.com/ 2020/09/22/majority-makers-south-carolina-senate-harrison-graham/.

Yoshinaka, Antoine. 2016. *Crossing the Aisle—Party Switching by U.S. Legislators in the Postwar Era*. New York: Cambridge University Press.

Young, Anna, and Bristow Marchant. 2019. "'Six More Years': VP Pence Touts Graham at Senator's Re-Election Launch in Myrtle Beach." *Myrtle Beach Online*. March 30. https:// www.myrtlebeachonline.com/news/local/article228635614.html.

Zeleny, Jeff. 2008. "Black Leader Changes Endorsement to Obama." *New York Times*. February 28.

Index

For the benefit of digital users, indexed terms that span two pages (e.g., 52–53) may, on occasion, appear on only one of those pages.

Tables and figures are indicated by *t* and *f* following the page number